STUDY GUIDE

Prepare

Teresa M
Mount Royal University

CONTEMPORARY LINGUISTIC ANALYSIS
An Introduction

Eighth Edition

Edited by
William O'Grady
University of Hawaii

John Archibald
University of Victoria

Toronto

For Chris and his girls, especially J., M., and D.

T.M.

ISBN: 9780134086613

Senior Acquisitions Editor: Matthew Christian
Program Manager: Madhu Ranadive
Developmental Editor: Patti Sayle
Project Manager: Jessica Mifsud
Production Services: Cenveo® Publisher Services

PEARSON

CONTENTS

PREFACE

This study guide is intended to accompany the eighth edition of *Contemporary Linguistic Analysis: An Introduction*. It began as a series of worksheets distributed to students in class and gradually expanded to include brief explanations of course content and additional practice exercises. This material was eventually linked together with reminders and review sheets. As the study guide evolved, it became more generic and all-encompassing. As a result, the study guide is of potential use to any instructor of introductory linguistics using *Contemporary Linguistic Analysis: An Introduction*.

The study guide contains a preview of major concepts followed by chapters on the core components of theoretical linguistics: phonetics, phonology, morphology, syntax, and semantics. The study guide focuses on these aspects of theoretical linguistics, since these are areas of introductory linguistics in which students typically require a great deal of practice to better understand the methods of analysis used within each of these branches of linguistics. The study guide also allows students practice using these methods of analysis in other branches of linguistics, including language classification, historical linguistics, language acquisition, neurolinguistics, psycholinguistics, sociolinguistics, and writing systems.

Each chapter in the study guide begins with a list of the main topics found in that chapter. Each of these topics is expanded on within a section of the chapter. Each section of the chapter contains brief explanations of important concepts, questions for students about these concepts, and numerous exercises. Each chapter is closely linked to the text through references to tables, figures, examples, and diagrams of linguistic structure (e.g., syllable, word, and sentence representations). Each chapter also includes general questions aimed at getting students to actively think about the concepts presented in the text. This feature is designed to complement the text's ability to engage students with the material. All chapters include reminders of important concepts and conclude with a review checklist that students can use to prepare for exams. Students who wish to work and study independently will find an answer key to this study guide on the Companion Website at **www.pearsoncanada.ca/ogrady** (access code protected).

I gratefully acknowledge Anna Moro's extensive contributions to the material found in Chapters 9, 12, 14, and 15 of the study guide. Without her, these chapters would not have the depth that they do. I also acknowledge contributions made by Carrie Dyck, Elaine Sorensen, Leone Sveinson, Joyce Hildebrand, and Lorna Rowsell to Chapters 1 through 6 and Chapter 8. I would like to thank all the reviewers for their comments, especially Carrie Dyck and William O'Grady for their invaluable suggestions and advice, which have improved the overall quality of the study guide. Thanks also go to Elizabeth Ritter for using an earlier version of the study guide with her students and providing valuable feedback, and to John Archibald for his continued support. Finally, I extend my gratitude in memoriam to Michael Dobrovolsky for his inspiration and for encouraging me as an undergraduate to pursue linguistics.

Teresa Merrells

CHAPTER 1. LANGUAGE: A PREVIEW

The following are some of the important concepts found in this chapter. Make sure you are familiar with them.

1. Specialization for Language
2. Creativity of Language
3. Linguistic Competence
4. Grammar

SPECIALIZATION FOR LANGUAGE

Humans are specialized for language. The characteristics below illustrate some of the aspects of our special capacity for language.

1. Speech Organs

Our lungs, vocal cords, tongue, teeth, lips, and nasal passages are used both for survival (e.g., breathing and eating) and for producing the sounds of our language.

2. Speech Perception

We are also equipped for speech perception, and we have this ability at birth. Studies have shown that newborns are able to perceive subtle differences between sounds, even sounds they have never heard before.

3. The Human Mind

Our minds form words, build sentences, and interpret meanings in ways not found in other species.

This specialization for language sets us apart from all other creatures!

CREATIVITY OF LANGUAGE

Human language is creative. That is, language does not provide us with a set of pre-packaged messages. Rather, it allows us to produce and understand new words and sentences whenever needed. However, there are limitations on both the form and the interpretation of new words and sentences. Linguists attempt to identify, understand, and explain these limitations.

Exercise!   Think about the limitations on the creativity of language while answering the following questions.

1. Put a checkmark beside those words that are possible English words.

   a. tlim _____

   b. stuken _____

   c. tseg _____

   d. fomp _____

   e. plog _____

   f. skpit _____

   g. ngan _____

   h. breb _____

   Think! Why are some of the above not possible English words? (HINT: Look at the combination of sounds found at the beginning of the words.)

2. Put a checkmark beside those words that are possible English words.

   a. speakless _____

   b. beautifulness _____

   c. unrug _____

   d. reglorify _____

   e. horseable _____

   f. weedic _____

   Think! Why are some of the above not possible English words? (HINT: Think about the prefix or suffix and its contribution to the meaning of the word.)

3. Put a checkmark beside those sentences that are possible English sentences.

   a. The building was tossed yesterday away.   _____

   b. The building is swept every morning.   _____

   c. Every child should obey parents his.   _____

   d. Somebody left their gloves in the theatre.   _____

   e. George surprised Mary with a party.   _____

   f. Joe surprised the stone.   _____

   Think! Why are some of the above not possible English sentences?

4. Now try this!

    a. Arrange the words "bird," "worm," "catches," "early," "every," and "a" into an English sentence.

    b. Think of other arrangements of the same words that result in different sentences from the one you just put together.

    c. How could you arrange the words so that the sentence you create is not an acceptable English sentence?

So. . . Even though the above exercises contain new words and sentences, not all of these are acceptable. You use your knowledge of the rules of English to decide which are okay and which are not!

LINGUISTIC COMPETENCE

Linguistic competence can be defined as subconscious knowledge that enables the native speakers of a language to produce and understand an unlimited number of both familiar and novel utterances. The native speakers of a language are those who acquired it as children in a home rather than in a classroom.

Linguists divide the subconscious knowledge that the native speakers of a language share into the following fields of study:

1. Phonetics: the study of the articulation and perception of speech sounds

2. Phonology: the study of how speech sounds pattern in language

3. Morphology: the study of word structure and word formation

4. Syntax: the study of sentence structure

5. Semantics: the study of the interpretation of words and sentences

This subconscious knowledge allows the speakers of a language to produce an infinite number of sentences, many of which they have never uttered or heard before. We don't memorize language: we create it.

Now. . . Go back to the exercise on creativity. For each data set, determine which aspect of your linguistic competence allows you to decide which are possible English words and sentences.

GRAMMAR

Grammar, to a linguist, refers to all the elements of our linguistic competence: phonetics, phonology, morphology, syntax, and semantics. In very general terms, grammar can be defined as the mental system of knowledge needed to form and interpret the sounds, words, and sentences of our language. The study of grammar is central to understanding language and to what it means to know a language. This is because

- all languages have sounds, words, and sentences that allow for the expression of any thought (generality),
- all grammars share common principles and tendencies called universals (universality),
- all grammars are equal (parity), and
- all grammars change over time (mutability).

However, our grammatical knowledge is unconscious (inaccessibility): we can decide what sounds right and what does not, even though we may not be sure why this is so.

Remember. . . Every language has rules that the native speakers of that language know and follow. One way to think of these is as the socially acceptable rules for language use. The following examples illustrate a prescriptive view of grammar. As you read through the examples, ask yourself if this type of rule captures the knowledge you have that allows you to use English every day in a variety of social settings.

1.   Which is correct: "Between you and I" or "Between you and me"?

"Between you and I" is **WRONG.**	You might say, "Many believe that there's an enormous rivalry between you and I." That may sound correct, but the pronoun *I* is wrong here.
"Between you and me" is **RIGHT.**	*Between* is a preposition, and prepositions are followed by objects. *I* is a subject or nominative pronoun. Objective pronouns that follow a preposition are *me, you, him, her, us,* and *them.*

2. Which is correct: "She is older than me" or "She is older than I"?

"She is older than me" is **WRONG.**	The word *than* is a conjunction. It joins two sentences, words, or phrases. There are two sentences here: (1) "She is older" and (2) "I am."
"She is older than I" is **RIGHT.**	In a comparison joined by *than* or *as*, you need to complete the sentence. You wouldn't say "She is older than me am," so it must be "She is older than I."

3. Which is correct: "Who do I ask" or "Whom do I ask"?

"Who do I ask?" is **WRONG.**	*Who* is generally appropriate whenever you use *he*, *she*, or *they*, and *whom* acts as a substitute for *him*, *her*, or *them*.
"Whom do I ask?" is **RIGHT.**	You would not say "I ask he," so the correct wording is "Whom do I ask?" (It sounds formal—which is why the incorrect "Who do I ask?" is usually used in informal speech.)

4. Which is correct: "The list of upgrades are the same" or "The list of upgrades is the same"?

"The list of upgrades are the same" is **WRONG.**	The subject of a sentence must agree with the verb with respect to person (first, second, or third) and number (singular or plural).
"The list of upgrades is the same" is **RIGHT.**	The subject of this sentence is *list*, which is third-person singular. The verb *be* therefore must be in the third person, singular (present tense) form *is* and not *are*, which is plural.

While such rules are useful in helping people learn a foreign language, they do not capture the linguistic competence of native speakers. Linguists are interested in objectively describing this unconscious knowledge.

Spot the Difference! Each of the following aspects of linguistic competence contains two statements. See if you can identify which statement is prescriptivist (P) and which is descriptivist (D).

1. Sounds

_____P_____ The English words *Mary, merry, marry* should be pronounced differently because they are spelled differently.

_____D_____ English contains over 20 different consonant sounds.

Think! How many different vowel sounds are found in English?

Do all languages have the same consonant and/or vowel sounds? Think of a language that has different vowel or consonant sounds from English.

2. Words

_____ *P* The use of *thunk* and not *thought* as the past tense of the verb *think* is an example of how change is causing the English language to deteriorate.

_____ *P* Many nouns in English are formed by adding the suffix *-ment* to words (e.g., achievement, government, judgment).

Think! Why would no English speaker construct the word *chairment*?

3. Sentences

_____ *P* There are at least two ways in English to make a sentence refer to the future.

_____ *P* The auxiliary *will* should be used with the third-person singular (i.e., *he, she, it*), whereas *shall* should be used for all other persons (e.g., "He will go, but we shall stay").

Think! How can you change the sentence *The horses eat hay* to refer to the future? Think about how other languages make statements that refer to future time.

4. Meaning

_____ *P* The word *cool* should only be used to refer to temperature.

_____ *P* Many words in a language often have opposite meanings (e.g., hot/cold, light/dark).

Think! How can the meaning of a sentence different from the meaning of the words that it is composed of?

QUICK REMINDER!

Linguistics is the study of the structure of human language, and linguists attempt to describe and explain, in an objective and non-judgmental fashion, the internalized and unconscious knowledge that the native speakers of a language share and that allows them to both speak and understand their language. While the primary focus of this guide is on Canadian English, many of the principles and theories discussed apply to all other languages as well.

REVIEW EXERCISE

Each of the statements below illustrates a concept found in Chapter 1. For each statement, determine which concept is being illustrated. Write the number of the concept beside the appropriate statement. The first is done for you.

Concepts:
1. Linguistic Competence
2. Prescriptive Rule
3. Descriptive Statement
4. Universal (i.e., something common to all languages)

Statements:

a. __4__   All languages have a way of expressing negatives.

b. _____   Speakers of Canadian English know that one way to make questions is to move an auxiliary verb to the position before the subject noun phrase.

c. _____   Many nouns in English are formed by adding -ness to an adjective: for example, sadness, silliness, and happiness.

d. _____   Brung should never be used as the past tense of bring.

e. _____   Every language has a set of vowels and consonants.

f. _____   Speakers of any language are capable of producing an unlimited number of novel sentences.

g. _____   In English, there is theoretically no limit to the number of adjectives that can occur before a noun.

h. _____   In the sentence "My friend is smarter than me," me is incorrect because it is an object pronoun and this comparative construction requires the subject pronoun I.

i. _____   In English, the plural is formed by adding either [-s], [-z] or [-əz] to the end of nouns.

j. _____   Every language has a way of forming questions.

k. _____   Speakers of Canadian English know that the different vowel sounds in the words bat, bet, but, and bit are crucial to their meanings.

REVIEW! REVIEW! Make sure you understand the terms listed below.

- creativity
- descriptive
- generality
- grammar
- the human mind
- inaccessibility
- linguistic competence
- mutability
- native speaker
- parity

- prescriptive
- speech organs
- speech perception
- universality

QUESTIONS? PROBLEMS? DIFFICULTIES?

_____

_____

_____

_____

_____

_____

_____

_____

_____

_____

_____

_____

_____

CHAPTER 2. PHONETICS:
THE SOUNDS OF LANGUAGE

Phonetics is the study of the articulation and perception of speech sounds. Important topics and concepts found in this section include the following:

1. International Phonetic Alphabet
2. Segments
3. Sound producing system
4. Consonant articulation
5. Vowel articulation
6. Phonetic transcription
7. Suprasegmentals
8. Processes

PHONETIC TRANSCRIPTION

The speech sounds of language are transcribed using the symbols found in the International Phonetic Alphabet (IPA). Here are some things to keep in mind when using the IPA:

- Each IPA symbol represents one and only one speech sound.
- Each speech sound found in language corresponds to one and only one IPA symbol.
- Since symbols represent sounds, the same symbols can be used in whatever language that sound occurs in. See table 2.1 on p. 15 of the text for some examples of how the symbol [ð] can be used to represent the same sound in different languages.

⇒ The focus in this chapter is on learning the sounds of English and their corresponding IPA symbols. For examples of some sounds not found in English and their IPA symbols, see tables 2.28 and 2.29 on p. 51.

⇒ It is important to remember that IPA symbols represent sounds and not how that sound is spelled in a particular language. To indicate this difference, symbols are enclosed in [ ] brackets. Don't forget to use them!

SEGMENTS

Words typically consist of a number of segments (individual speech sounds). Doing phonetic transcription involves determining what these segments are, along with their corresponding phonetic symbols. In doing transcription, it can be useful, as a starting point, to determine the number of segments in a word. But don't be fooled by spelling! Each of the following boxes illustrates a reason why we can't rely on spelling to determine the number of speech sounds in an English word.

9

Some letters or combinations of letters have more than one speech sound associated with them. In each of the example sets below, determine if the underlined letter (or letters) is pronounced the same way for all the words presented.

⇒ 'o'   as in   h<u>o</u>t   ech<u>o</u>   w<u>o</u>man

⇒ 'c'   as in   <u>c</u>areful   <u>c</u>entury

⇒ 'ou'   as in   sh<u>ou</u>ld   t<u>ou</u>gh   s<u>ou</u>nd

Sometimes one speech sound can be represented using different letters or combinations of letters. In each of the example sets below, determine if the underlined letters have the same or different speech sounds.

⇒ thr<u>ough</u>   cl<u>ue</u>   sh<u>oe</u>   t<u>oo</u>

⇒ r<u>ea</u>l   s<u>ee</u>   sorr<u>y</u>   Sh<u>ei</u>la

⇒ str<u>aw</u>   t<u>a</u>lk   f<u>ough</u>t   l<u>o</u>st

Many words in English contain double letters. Double letters do not necessarily mean that there are two speech sounds. Say each of the words below and determine if you pronounce the double letter twice.

str<u>ee</u>t   b<u>oo</u>k   mi<u>tt</u>en   ki<u>ll</u>er

Finally, many words in English contain silent letters. These are letters that we do not pronounce and that therefore do not correspond to a speech sound. Say each of the words below and determine if you pronounce all of the letters.

knife   leave   psychology   thumb

The above points also illustrate some of the reasons for using IPA rather than conventional spelling for doing phonetic transcription. In IPA, unlike in spelling, each symbol corresponds to only one sound and always the same sound. The lesson is . . . when you are doing phonetic transcription, you need to forget about spelling!

Practice! Practice! To get ready for transcription, try the following exercises.

1. Determine the number of speech sounds in each of the following words.

a. thing ___3 th___

d. phosphate ___6___

b. comb ___3___

e. scene ___3___

c. psychic ___5___

f. fright ___4___

2. Say each of the following words. Which letter(s) correspond to the first sound in each word?

a. Thomas _____

d. knee _____

b. unemployed _____

e. choice _____

c. committee _____

f. ease _____

3. Say each of the following words. Which letter(s) correspond to the last sound in each word?

a. laugh _____

d. lamb _____

b. sang _____

e. use _____

c. bow _____

f. choice _____

SOUND-PRODUCING SYSTEM

Human language contains a finite number of speech sounds, or phones. The system that produces these sounds includes the following.

⇒ **Lungs.** The lungs provide the moving air necessary for speech.

⇒ **Larynx.** The larynx contains the vocal folds (or cords) that provide the source of the sound. See figure 2.2 on p. 18 of the text for a representation of the larynx. The vocal folds can be positioned in different ways. The space between the vocal folds is called the glottis. The different positions of the vocal folds are called glottal states. There are four glottal states that you should be familiar with; see figure 2.3 on p. 19 for a representation of each of these states.

- Voiceless
- Voiced
- Whisper
- Murmur

⇒ **Pharynx.** This is the tube of the throat between the larynx and the oral cavity.

⇒ **Oral cavity.** This is the mouth.

⇒ **Nasal cavity.** This is also known as the nasal passages. The velum controls airflow through the nasal passages. Raising the velum cuts off airflow through the nasal passages. Lowering the velum allows air to flow through the nasal passages.

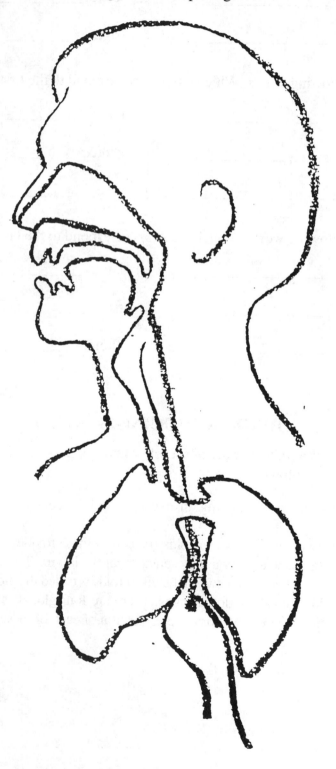

The pharynx, oral cavity, and nasal cavity act as filters that modify the sound in various ways. Together they constitute the vocal tract.

Try This! Label the different elements of the sound-producing system on the diagram on the previous page. You can also label the trachea (windpipe) and the velum. If you're having difficulty, refer to figure 2.1 on p. 17 of the text.

SOUND CLASSES

Sounds can be divided into three major classes: consonants, vowels, and glides. Each class of sounds shares some phonetic properties. The defining characteristics of each class are given below.

⇒ **Consonants.** Consonants are sounds that can be either voiced or voiceless and that are made with a narrow or complete obstruction in the vocal tract. This is an articulatory characteristic of consonant sounds.

⇒ **Vowels.** Vowels are sounds that are typically voiced and that are made with little obstruction in the vocal tract. Vowels tend to be more sonorous than consonants. As a result, we perceive vowels as louder and longer lasting. This is an acoustic characteristic of vowels. Vowels are also classified as syllabic sounds, meaning that they can form the nucleus of a syllable.

⇒ **Glides.** Glides are sounds that have characteristics of both consonants and vowels. They are sometimes called semivowels or semiconsonants. Glides are like vowels in their articulation, but they are like consonants in that they never form the nucleus of a syllable.

Exercise! Each of the following words has one or more letters underlined. The underlined letters correspond to one sound. Identify this sound as a consonant, vowel, or glide. The first is done for you.

1. rottweiler _____consonant_____

2. through _____

3. lovely _____

4. year _____

5. myth _____

6. whistle_____

7. suffer_____

8. judge_____

REMINDER!

Some types of consonants can also be syllabic (i.e., function as the nucleus of a syllable). For this reason, you should think of sounds not just as being consonants, vowels, or glides, but also as being syllabic or non-syllabic elements. This will be useful in doing phonetic transcription and also when doing phonology (Chapter 3).

CONSONANT ARTICULATION

Consonants are sounds that are made with obstruction in the vocal tract. Consonants do not normally form the nucleus of a syllable (that is, they are not usually syllabic) and can be voiced or voiceless. The following pages contain information about consonants that you should become very familiar with.

Articulatory Description

All sounds, regardless of whether they are consonants, vowels, or glides, are described in terms of how they are articulated. This information is contained in the sound's articulatory description. Consonants and vowels are described differently. There are three parameters necessary to describe consonant (and glide) articulations.

1. Glottal state
2. Place of articulation
3. Manner of articulation

⇒ Glottal state refers to whether a sound is voiced or voiceless.

⇒ Place of articulation refers to where in the vocal tract an obstruction occurs. Places of articulation are found

- at the lips (labial)
- within the oral cavity (dental, alveolar, alveopalatal, palatal, velar, uvular)
- in the pharynx (pharyngeal)
- at the glottis (glottal)

See figure 2.5 on p. 23 of the text for diagrams of places of articulation at the lips (labial) and at some points within the oral cavity (alveolar, interdental, palatal, and velar).

Try This! Each place of articulation has an articulatory term used to describe sounds made at that particular spot in the vocal tract. For example, sounds made with the lips are called labial sounds. Give the articulatory term describing sounds made at each of the following places of articulation.

a. lips and teeth   _____

b. hard palate   _____

c. uvula   _____

d. alveolar ridge   _____

Now. . . Label all places of articulation on the diagram below. For each place of articulation, give the corresponding articulatory term. You can also label the different parts of the tongue (tip, blade, body, back, and root). If you are having difficulty, refer to figure 2.4 on p. 22 of the text.

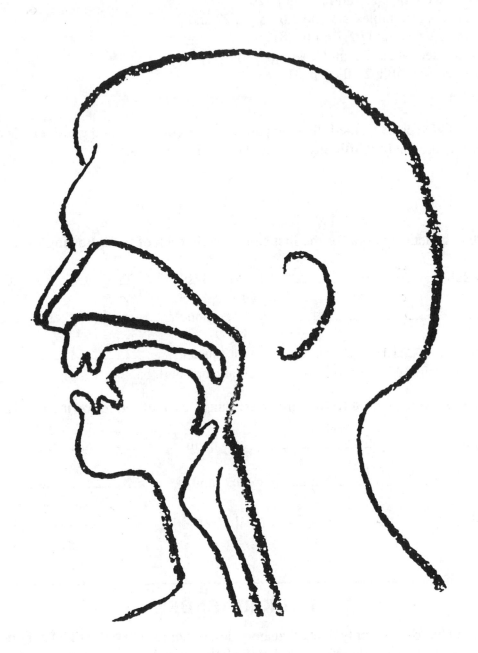

⇒ Manner of articulation refers to the different types of sounds resulting from different positions of the lips, tongue, velum, and glottis. Manners of articulation include

- Stops (see tables 2.3 and 2.4 on p. 26)
- Fricatives (see tables 2.5 and 2.6 on pp. 27 and 28)
- Affricates (see table 2.7 on p. 28)
- Nasals (see tables 2.3 and 2.4 on p. 26)
- Liquids (see table 2.10 on p. 31)
- Glides

Now. . . Fill in the chart on the following page with the consonant and glide sounds of Canadian English. If you are having difficulty, refer to table 2.12 on p. 33.

Now Try This!

1. Give the phonetic symbol for the first consonant in each of the following words.

   a. through θ d. whistle w

   b. shave $\int$ e. phone f

   c. knee n f. queen k^w

2. Give the phonetic symbol for the last consonant in each of the following words.

   a. laugh f d. myth δ

   b. sang η e. lamb m

   c. choice s f. box s

QUICK REMINDER!

Every sound has one and only one articulatory description. And every articulatory description corresponds to one and only one symbol in the International Phonetic Alphabet (IPA).

CANADIAN ENGLISH CONSONANT CHART

		Bilabial	Labiodental	Interdental	Alveolar	Alveopalatal/Palatal	Velar	Glottal
PLACE OF ARTICULATION	**GLOTTAL STATE**							
Stop	voiceless							
	voiced							
Fricative	voiceless							
	voiced							
Affricate	voiceless							
	voiced							
Nasal	voiced							
Liquid a. lateral	voiced							
b. retroflex	voiced							
Glide	voiced							

MANNER OF ARTICULATION

Some more about . . .

Voiceless Stop Articulations

⇒ **Aspiration.** Sometimes when the voiceless stops [p, t, k] are pronounced, they are produced with a small puff of air. This puff of air is called aspiration and is represented as [ʰ]. Aspiration is caused by a delay in voicing. See figures 2.6, 2.7, and 2.8 on pp. 29 and 30 for some diagrams outlining when and why aspiration does and does not occur in English.

Try This! Say the words in the boxes below. Pay close attention to the first sound, and see if you can feel when aspiration does and does not occur. You can feel this extra release of air by putting your hand close to your mouth as you produce the words.

Voiceless Aspirated Stops		Voiceless Unaspirated Stops	
[pʰ]	pit punk	[p]	spit spunk
[tʰ]	take tab	[t]	stake stab
[kʰ]	kill car	[k]	skill scar

⇒ **Unreleased Stops.** Sometimes when the voiceless stops [p, t, k] are pronounced, they are not released. That is, the articulation ends with either the lips closed or the tongue on the place of articulation. The symbol for this articulation is a raised [˺].

Try This! Say the words in the boxes below. For the words in the first column, pay close attention to the first sound and see if you can feel your lips opening or your tongue moving away from the place of articulation. For the words in the second column, pay close attention to the final sound and see if your lips remain closed or if your tongue remains at the place of articulation.

Voiceless Aspirated Stops		Voiceless Unreleased Stops	
[pʰ]	pit punk	[p˺]	cap leap
[tʰ]	take tab	[t˺]	pot most
[kʰ]	kill car	[k˺]	back sack

Fricative and Affricate Articulations

⇒ **Strident/Sibilant.** Some fricatives and affricates are noisier than others. Say the words in the box below. See if you can hear which fricatives and affricates are noisier. The noisier fricatives and affricates are considered to be strident (sibilant). The quieter fricatives and affricates are considered non-strident. This is an acoustic criterion used in describing fricatives and affricates.

Non-strident Fricatives		Strident Fricatives & Affricates	
[f] and [v]	fit vat	[s] and [z]	sip zen
[θ] and [ð]	thick though	[ʃ] and [ʒ]	ship pleasure
		[ʧ] and [ʤ]	cherub gem

Now. . . Go back to the Canadian English consonant chart on p. 17 and put a box around the group of fricatives and affricates considered to be strident. If you are having difficulty, see table 2.8 on p. 28 of the textbook.

Liquid and Nasal Articulations

⇒ *l* **and** *r* **Articulations** *l*. Since [l] is normally voiced, *lateral* usually means voiced lateral. However, [l] can also be voiceless, in which case it is represented using [l̥]. Say the words in the table below and see if you can hear the difference between the voiced and voiceless laterals.

Voiced Lateral		Voiceless Lateral	
[l]	lip love lullaby lamp	[l̥]	please play clean clever

⇒ *r*. Like [l], [r] (or [ɹ]) is normally voiced. *Retroflex* therefore usually means voiced retroflex. Also like [l], [r] can be voiceless, in which case it is represented using [r̥]. English also has a flap sound, which is another type of sound commonly identified with *r*. A flap is made when the tip of the tongue strikes the alveolar ridge as it passes by. [ɾ] represents a flap. Say the words in the following table and see if you can hear the difference between the voiced and voiceless [r], and the flap.

Voiced Retroflex		Voiceless Retroflex		Flap	
[ɹ]	ride right car	[ɹ̥]	pray train crayon	[ɾ]	bitter butter

⇒ **Alveolar and Velarized *l*.** Not every lateral [l] is pronounced in the same way. Say the words in the table below. Pay close attention to where your tongue is when you articulate the [l] sound. See if you can feel if your tongue is more toward the front or back of your mouth. The [l] in the first group is considered to have an alveolar articulation, while the [l] in the second group is considered to be velarized. The alveolar [l] is often called "clear l" and the velarized [l] "dark l".

Alveolar *l* (clear)		Velarized *l* (dark)	
[l]	lip love lullaby	[ɫ]	swallow guilt silk

⇒ **Syllabic and Non-syllabic.** Liquid and nasal articulations can be either syllabic or non-syllabic. Remember that a syllabic sound (e.g., a vowel) forms the nucleus of a syllable. It is only when a liquid or nasal forms the nucleus of a syllable that it is considered to be syllabic. If the liquid or nasal does not form the nucleus of a syllable, it is considered to be non-syllabic. Say the words in the table below and see if you can hear when the liquid or nasal is syllabic and when it is non-syllabic. See table 2.11 on p. 32 for some more examples of English syllabic and non-syllabic liquids and nasals.

	Some syllabic sounds	Some non-syllabic sounds
Liquids	twinkle father	lawn rain
Nasals	glutton winsome	hamburger master

Exercise!

1. Say the following words. Put a checkmark beside those words containing aspirated voiceless stops.

   1. scratch _____   4. pending _____

   2. talk _____   5. stripe _____

   3. segments _____   6. careful _____

2. Say the following words. Put a checkmark beside those words containing a syllabic liquid or nasal.

   a. laugh _____   e. kitten _____

   b. bottom _____   f. bushel _____

   c. mad _____   g. rugby _____

   d. suffer _____   h. note _____

3. Say the following words. Put a checkmark beside those words containing a velarized (dark) [l].

   a. malign _____   d. pull _____

   b. silly _____   e. lamb _____

   c. allow _____   f. meal _____

VOWEL ARTICULATION

Vowels are sounds that are sonorant, are articulated with little obstruction in the vocal tract, and are syllabic (can form the nucleus of a syllable). Vowels are also usually voiced.

Articulatory Description

Four parameters are necessary to describe vowel articulations.

1. Height   3. Tenseness
2. Backness   4. Roundness

⇒ Different vowel sounds are made by varying the position of the body of the tongue. High, mid, and low (height), and front and back (backness) are used to describe tongue placement.

⇒ Tenseness refers to the amount of constriction in the vocal tract muscles when the sound is articulated. Vowels made with greater constriction are described as tense. Vowels made with less constriction are described as lax. Tense vowels tend to be longer than lax vowels.

⇒ Roundness refers to whether the lips are rounded. Vowels with the lips rounded are described as rounded; vowels without lip rounding are described as unrounded.

Simple Vowels and Diphthongs

⇒ Simple vowels are vowels whose quality does not change during their articulation, while diphthongs are vowels that exhibit a change in quality within a single syllable. This change in quality is the result of the tongue moving away from a vowel articulation to a glide articulation. Say the words in the table below and see if you can hear the change in quality during a diphthong articulation.

Some simple vowels	Some diphthongs
sit	boy
lost	now
cup	cry
met	pray
bat	sew

⇒ Diphthongs can be classified as either major or minor. The major diphthongs are those whose quality change is easy to hear. The quality change in the minor diphthongs is harder to hear. Say the words containing diphthongs in the above table again, and see if you can tell which are the major diphthongs and which the minor diphthongs.

See table 2.13 on p. 35 of the text for some examples of simple vowels, and major and minor diphthongs, in Canadian English.

Some other vowels . . .

⇒ [a] is found in Canadian English as a single vowel only before [r] in words such as *car*.

⇒ [ɔ] is found in Canadian English only before [r] in words such as *more*.

Now. . . Fill in the chart on the following page with the phonetic symbols corresponding to both the simple vowels and diphthongs found in Canadian English. Circle all tense vowels. Use the lines outside the vowel chart to add a sample word for each vowel. This can help you to remember the sound a particular symbol represents. See figure 2.11 on p. 37 if you are having difficulty.

Practice!   Give the phonetic symbol for the vowel sound in each of the following English words.

a. stool_____   d. pot _____

b. sight_____   e. sit _____

c. meet_____   f. put _____

QUICK REMINDER!

For every articulatory description, you need to be able to provide the corresponding phonetic symbol:

   e.g., voiceless bilabial stop   →   [p]

For every phonetic symbol, you need to be able to provide the corresponding articulatory description:

   e.g., [p]   →   voiceless bilabial stop

You need to be able to do this for both consonants and vowels!

CANADIAN ENGLISH VOWEL CHART

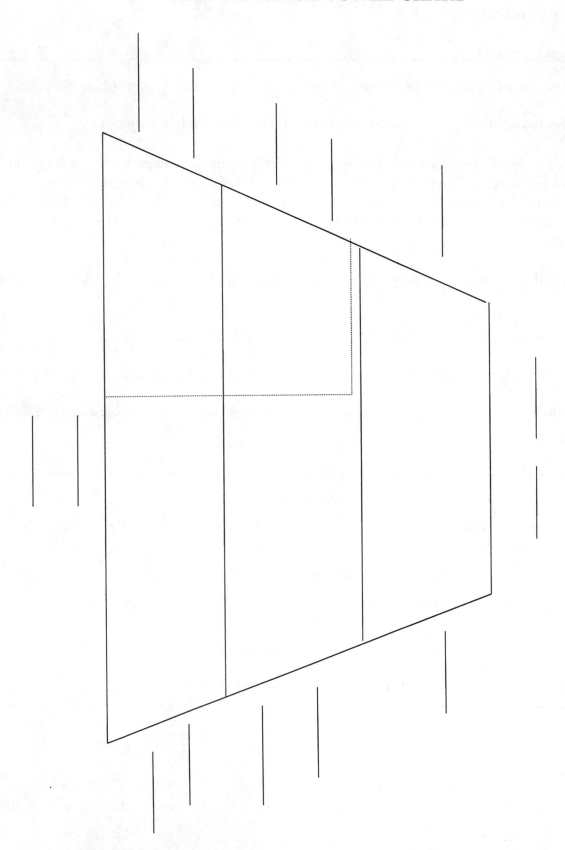

FACIAL DIAGRAMS FOR CONSONANTS

There are four important parts to either completing or deciphering facial diagrams for consonants.

Glottal State. Voiced sounds are shown by two wavy lines where the larynx would be. Voiceless sounds are represented by two lines shaped like an ellipse.

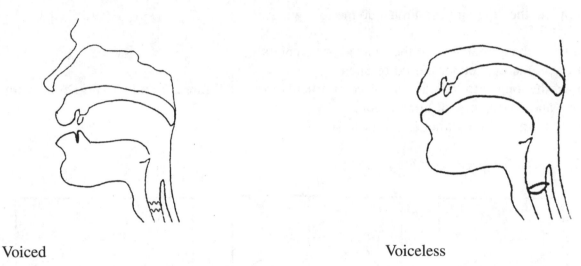

Voiced   Voiceless

Place of Articulation. The narrowest point in the airstream passage is the place of articulation.

Manner of Articulation. If no air escapes past a given articulator (i.e., in a stop), then the articulator must touch the place of articulation. If the air does escape (i.e., in a fricative), then there is a space between the articulator and the place of articulation. If the sound is an affricate, then the diagram is shown with the articulator touching the place of articulation and an arrow indicating the direction in which the articulator moves.

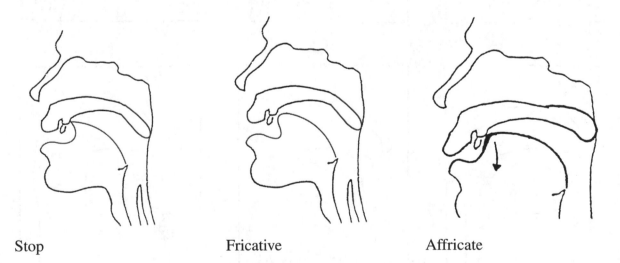

Stop   Fricative   Affricate

Nasal Passage. For oral sounds, the nasal passage is closed (the velum is raised), while for nasal sounds the nasal passage is open (the velum is lowered).

Complete the following diagrams so that each of the sounds listed below is depicted.

1. [s]   3. [ʧ]   5. [g]
2. [p]   4. [n]   6. [ð]

To complete the diagrams, you must do the following:

- Draw in the glottal state: either voiced or voiceless.
- Draw in the lips: either closed or open.
- Draw the tongue to indicate the place of articulation (see figure 2.5 on p. 23 for some examples) and the manner of articulation.
- Draw in the velum: either raised or lowered.

The first sound has been done for you.

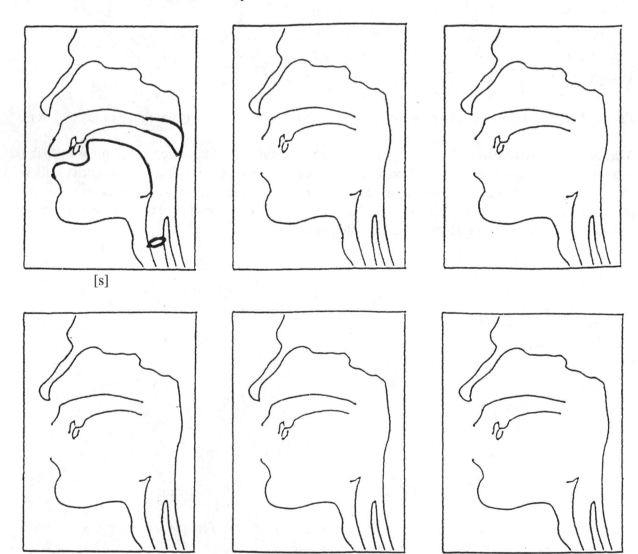

[s]

For each drawing presented below, there is only one sound that could be produced by the vocal tract position. You are to figure out which consonant sound is represented and write the phonetic symbol for that sound between square brackets below the drawing.

Make sure that you pay attention to voicing, place and manner of articulation, and the position of the velum.

The first drawing has been labelled for you.

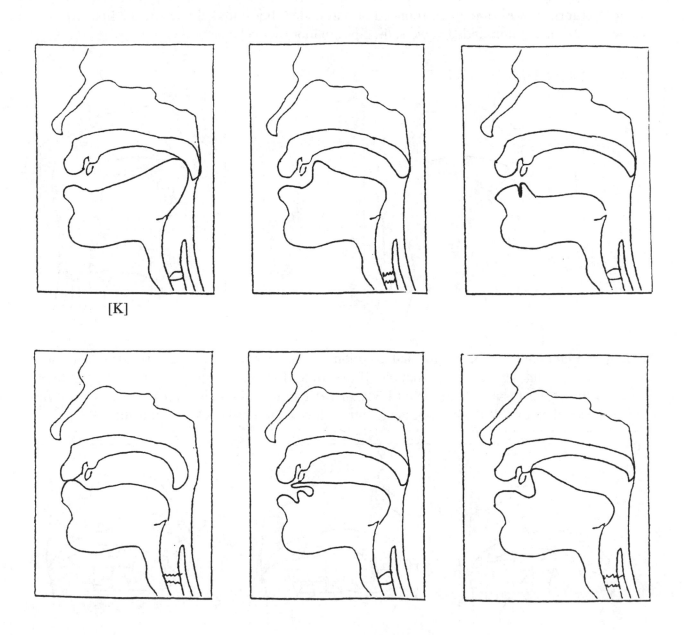

[K]

FACIAL DIAGRAMS FOR VOWELS

There are four important parts to either completing or deciphering facial diagrams for vowels.

Glottal State.   Vowels are always voiced. As on facial diagrams for consonants, voicing is shown by two wavy lines where the larynx would be.

Nasal Passage.   For oral vowels, the nasal passage is closed (the velum is raised), while for nasal vowels, the nasal passage is open (the velum is lowered).

Lip Position.   Vowels are either rounded or unrounded. For rounded vowels, the lips are closer together, while for unrounded vowels, the lips are more spread apart.

Unrounded:
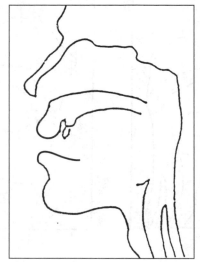

Rounded:
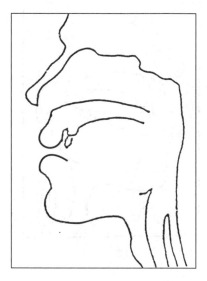

Tongue Placement.   The height and position of the tongue determine the particular vowel articulation being depicted. For example, if the front of the tongue is high in the mouth, then a high front vowel results. If the main body of the tongue is neither high nor low, then a mid central vowel results. If the back of the tongue is low, then a low back vowel results.

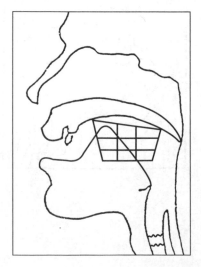
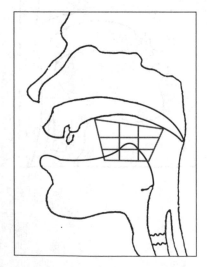
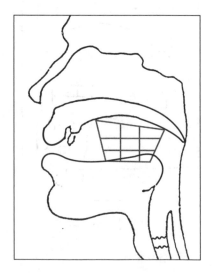

Complete the following diagrams so that each of the sounds listed below are depicted.

1. [æ]   2. [ʌ]   3. [ĩ]

To complete the diagrams, you must do the following:

*   Draw in the glottal state.
*   Draw in the velum: either raised or lowered.
*   Draw in the lips: either rounded or unrounded.
*   Draw the appropriate portion of the tongue to the appropriate height.

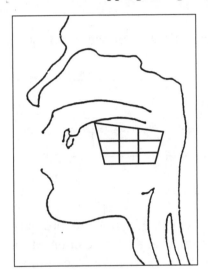
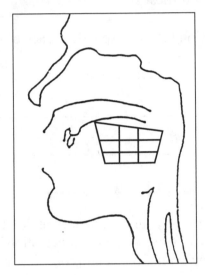
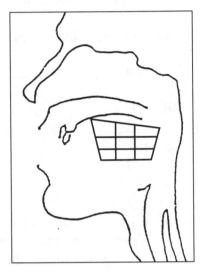

For each drawing presented below, determine which vowel sound is represented and write the phonetic symbol for that sound between the brackets below the drawing.

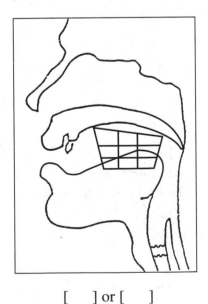
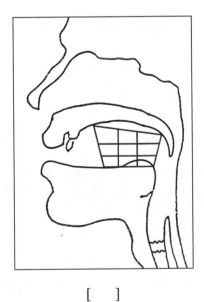
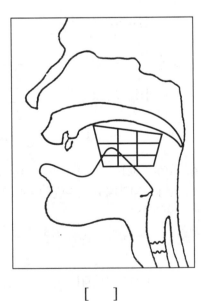

[   ] or [   ]   [   ]   [   ]

PRACTICE WITH SOUNDS

1. Give the phonetic symbol for each of the following articulatory descriptions.

    a. [   ]   voiceless glottal stop

    b. [   ]   high front unrounded tense vowel

    c. [   ]   voiced bilabial nasal

    d. [   ]   voiceless interdental fricative

2. Give the articulatory description that corresponds to each of the following phonetic symbols.

    a. [æ]   _____

    b. [f]   _____

    c. [j]   _____

    d. [ʌ]   _____

3. Each of the following groups of sounds contains at least one shared phonetic property (e.g., glottal state, place of articulation, manner of articulation, tongue height, lip position, etc.). For each group of sounds, give some phonetic properties that the sounds have in common. Include as many as possible.

    a. [b, d, g]   _____

    b. [ʃ, ʧ, ʒ]   _____

    c. [j, r, n]   _____

    d. [ɑ, o, ʊ]   _____

    e. [æ, ɪ, ɛ]   _____

4. For each of the following groups of sounds, circle the sound that does not belong and state a phonetic property that the remaining sounds share. There may be more than one possible answer!

    a. [f ð v z]   _____

    b. [d t n g]   _____

    c. [ɑ o ɪ u]   _____

TRANSCRIPTION HINTS

Each of the boxes below contains some examples of sounds that often cause difficulty when first learning to do transcription. For more examples of transcribed words containing Canadian English vowel and consonant symbols, see tables 2.16 and 2.17 on pp. 39 and 40.

SYLLABIC CONSONANTS

r	[r] for the 'r' sound in 'real', 'right', etc. [ər], [r̩], or [ɚ] for the syllabic 'r' sound in 'butter', 'bird', 'purr', etc. [ɾ] for the 't' sound in words like 'butter', 'writer', 'putter', 'potter', etc.
l	[l] for the 'l' sound in 'light', 'pill', 'please', etc. [əl] or [l̩] for the syllabic 'l' in 'bottle', 'puddle', 'poodle', etc.
m	[m̩] for the syllabic 'm' in 'bottom', 'winsome', etc. [m] for any other 'm' sound
n	[n̩] for the syllabic 'n' in 'button', 'hidden', etc. [n] for any other 'n' sound

DIPHTHONGS

Diphthongs are transcribed as vowel-glide sequences. Remember that diphthongs are a single speech sound. Remember as well that diphthongs are described in terms of the vowel, not the glide.

- Use [a], not [ɑ], for the major diphthongs (i.e., [aj], [aw], not [ɑj], [ɑw]). The symbols [a] and [ɑ] do not represent the same vowel sound.
- The mid tense vowels [e] and [o] are considered to be minor diphthongs and are transcribed as [ej] and [ow].
- The high tense vowels [i] and [u] are sometimes also considered to be minor diphthongs. You may be required to transcribe these as [ij] and [uw].

VOWELS BEFORE [r]

[r] is a very powerful sound, making it difficult to hear the preceding vowel sound. The following examples may help.

[bir]	beer	[bɔr]	boar	[bejr]	bear
[bar]	bar	[bur]	boor	[bər], [br̩], or [bɚ]	burr

SCHWA AND WEDGE

Schwa [ə]	Wedge [ʌ]

– used for unstressed vowels
   e.g., [əbawt] 'about'
– found before [r]
   e.g., [bərd] 'bird'
– used in the words 'the' and 'a'
	– used when there is some degree of
	   stress on the vowel
	     e.g., [sʌpər] 'supper'
	– not found before [r]

ASPIRATION

p, t, k	use [pʰ, tʰ, kʰ] for any 'p', 't', 'k' sound that occurs at the beginning of a syllable followed by a vowel that receives some degree of stress. e.g., [pʰæt] 'pat', [tʰɑt] 'taught', [kʰejk] 'cake' [əpʰír] 'appear', [ətʰǽk] 'attack'
	use [p, t, k] for any other 'p', 't', 'k' sound. e.g., [splæt] 'splat', [stown] 'stone', [skejt] 'skate'

You may also be required to transcribe the following:

⇒ Unreleased voiceless stops. Use the symbol [˺].

⇒ Velarized *l*. Use the symbol [ɬ].

TRANSCRIPTION EXERCISES

A Start! Transcribe the following words as you would say them in normal everyday speech. Remember to include brackets and remember to forget spelling. Watch out for syllabic consonants!

1. craft
2. rich
3. thought

4. sigh
5. tape
6. had [hæd]

7. health
8. vague
9. exit [ɛksɪt] [ɛgsɪt]

10. luge
11. rooster
12. sugar [ʊgər]

13. frog
14. instead
15. unit [ʌnɪt] [jʊnɪt]

16. paddle
17. bottom
18. question

19. angel
20. church

Vowel Practice!

1. key [kij]   2. cheese   3. bone

4. due [djuv]   5. ate   6. east

7. loaf [lowf]   8. wheeze   9. mainsheet

10. made [mejd]   11. through   12. throw

More Vowels! This time watch out for vowels before *r* sounds.

1. cheer [tʃiir]   2. there   3. chair

4. car [kar]   5. star [star]   6. score

7. sir [sər]   8. her [hər]   9. floor

10. oar [or]   11. horse [howrs] 12. course

13. heart [hart]   14. hard [hard]   15. harm

16. sharp [sarp]   17. shirt   18. thwart

Practice with Diphthongs. Transcribe the following words as you would say them in normal everyday speech. Watch out for those diphthongs!

1. voice [vojs]   2. trial [trajl]   3. bicycle

4. hour [awr]   5. oily [ojli]   6. goat [gowt]

7. eyes ajz   8. prize [prajz]   9. embroider

10. sailing sejliŋ   11. crow [krow]   12. cried krajd

13. prowl prowl   14. counter [kawntər] 15. lazy [lejzi]

16. knifed nifd   17. down d   18. daze [dejz]

Remember . . . Transcription takes a lot of practice!

æbsulut

Practice with Schwa and Wedge.
In this one, pay close attention to the schwa and wedge sounds. You might want to determine which vowel gets primary stress to help you out.

1. sludge
2. thunder
3. hung
4. quality
5. behave
6. oven
7. luck
8. separate
9. stuff
10. nation
11. announce
12. understand

One More Try!
This one has everything in it. Again, transcribe the word as you would say it in normal everyday speech. Watch out . . . they get harder!

1. days
2. agitate
3. gnome
4. Xerox
5. roast
6. pinstripe
7. guess
8. theatrical
9. masculine
10. yellow
11. bargain
12. precious
13. science
14. machine
15. formula
16. motorcycle
17. surrounded
18. comedy
19. extinguish
20. costume
21. graduate
22. implement
23. ponder
24. irrigate
25. isolate
26. timetable
27. unforgivable
28. frighten
29. lemonade
30. called

Reverse Transcription.
Give the correctly spelled English word for each of the following transcriptions.

1. [liʒər] *leisure*
2. [ʃaj] *sigh*
3. [pʰajp] *pipe*
4. [æks] *axe*
5. [swit] *sweet*
6. [safənd] *softened*
7. [wərði] *worthy*
8. [tʰub] *tube*
9. [fowni] *phony*
10. [wʌns] *once*
11. [tʃojs] *choice*
12. [stætʃuw] *statue*
13. [ʃejd] *shade*
14. [mɛnʃən] *mention*
15. [skwejr] *square*

SUPRASEGMENTALS

Suprasegmentals refer to inherent properties that are part of all sounds regardless of their place or manner of articulation. The three main suprasegmentals are pitch, length, and stress. Pitch is further divided into tone and intonation.

Pitch

⇒ Tone languages are languages in which pitch movement is used to signal differences in meaning. Mandarin Chinese is a good example. Tone languages may use register and/or contour tones. A register tone is a level pitch, while a contour tone is a moving pitch. See figure 2.14 on p. 42 for some examples of register and contour tones in Mandarin. Figures 2.12 and 2.15 on pp. 41 and 42 give some examples from other tone languages.

⇒ Intonation is pitch movement that is not related to differences in word meaning. For example, in English, rising pitch is often used to signal a question (an incomplete utterance), and falling intonation a statement (a complete utterance). See figures 2.16 to 2.19 on p. 43 of the text for some examples of different intonations and their representation.

Length

⇒ Long vowels and consonants are sounds whose articulation simply takes longer relative to other vowels and consonants. Length is indicated with [ː]. See table 2.19 on p. 44 for some examples of short and long vowels in Yapese and table 2.20 on p. 45 for some examples of short and long consonants in Italian.

Stress

⇒ Stress is associated with vowels. Stressed vowels are perceived as more prominent than other vowels. The most prominent vowel receives primary stress. Primary stress is usually indicated with [′]. In English, stressed vowels tend to be higher in pitch, louder, and longer than unstressed vowels. See table 2.21 on p. 45 for some examples of differing stress placement in English.

Exercise! Mark primary stress on each of the following words.

1. scorned
2. discovery
3. explosion
4. genius
5. macaroni
6. duplicate
7. dictate
8. occupied
9. informative
10. idolize

Now . . . Go back and transcribe each word.

PROCESSES

Processes describe articulatory adjustments that occur during speech. Processes typically function to make words easier to articulate. Processes also occur to make speech easier to perceive. The boxes below define and illustrate the different articulatory processes found in language.

ASSIMILATION

Assimilation involves sounds changing to become more like nearby sounds. While there are many different kinds of assimilation, in general, assimilation can be divided into three main types:

1. Voicing Assimilation:
    – A sound takes on the same voicing as a nearby sound.
    – Includes   voicing
                         devoicing

2. Assimilation for Place of Articulation:
    – A sound takes on the same place of articulation as a nearby sound.
    – Includes   palatalization
                         homorganic nasal assimilation . . . and more!

3. Assimilation for Manner of Articulation:
    – A sound takes on the same manner of articulation as a nearby sound.
    – Includes   nasalization
                         flapping . . . and more!

In addition. . . Some types of assimilation, such as nasalization, can be either regressive or progressive. In regressive assimilation, a segment takes on some characteristic of the following segment. That is, a sound is influenced by what comes after it. In progressive assimilation, a segment takes on some characteristic of the preceding segment. That is, a sound is influenced by what comes before it. See tables 2.22 and 2.24 on pp. 47 and 48 of the text for examples of progressive assimilation, and table 2.23 on p. 48 for examples of regressive assimilation.

DISSIMILATION

A sound changes to become less like a nearby sound so that the resulting sequence of sounds is easier to pronounce: e.g., fifths: [fɪfθs] → [fɪfts].

DELETION

The process of deletion simply removes a sound from a phonetic context. Deletion frequently occurs in rapid speech: e.g., fifths: [fɪfθs] → [fɪfs]. See table 2.25 on p. 49 for some examples of schwa deletion in English.

EPENTHESIS

The process of epenthesis adds a segment to a phonetic context. Epenthesis is common in casual speech: e.g., warmth: [warmθ] → [warmpθ]. See tables 2.26 and 2.27 on p. 50 for more examples of this process.

METATHESIS

Metathesis is a process that changes the order of segments: e.g., prescribe → perscribe. Metathesis is common in the speech of young children: e.g., animal → aminal.

VOWEL REDUCTION

In vowel reduction, vowels move to a more central position when they are in unstressed syllables. That is, a vowel is pronounced as a full vowel when in a stressed syllable, and as a schwa when in an unstressed syllable.

Identifying Processes. . . To identify processes, you need to look for differences between the starting and ending pronunciations.

⇒ If a sound is missing, **deletion** has occurred.
⇒ If a sound has been added, **epenthesis** has occurred.
⇒ If the order of sounds has changed, **metathesis** has occurred.
⇒ If a sound has changed, you need to determine if either **assimilation** or **dissimilation** has occurred. To do this, take the following steps:
   • Determine the phonetic property that has changed (voice, place, or manner of articulation).
   • Compare this phonetic property with the phonetic properties of the nearby sounds.
   • If the changed phonetic property matches a phonetic property of a nearby sound, then **assimilation** has occurred. The phonetic property that matches will tell you the specific type of assimilation that has occurred.
   • If the phonetic properties do not match, then **dissimilation** has occurred.

Remember. . . For assimilation, you also need to be able to identify when processes such as nasalization or place of articulation assimilation are regressive and when they are progressive. To determine this, you need to look at whether the influencing sound comes before (progressive) or after (regressive) the sound that is undergoing the change.

An example. . .

prince: [prɪns]   →   [prĩnts]

⇒ [t] occurs in the ending pronunciation but not the starting; therefore, epenthesis has occurred.

⇒ [ɪ] has changed to [ĩ]. Remember that [˜] indicates a nasalized sound. The vowel, therefore, has changed from an oral to a nasal sound, and since the following sound is a nasal, assimilation—in particular nasalization—has occurred. The influencing sound is the following nasal, meaning that the nasalization is regressive.

The change in the pronunciation of the word 'prince' from [prɪns] to [prĩnts] involves two processes: epenthesis and regressive nasalization.

Try These! Identify the process(es) at work in each of the following:

1. ask: [æsk]   →   [æks]   _____

2. winter: [wɪntər]   →   [wĩnər]   _____

3. clear: [kl̥ir]   →   [kəlir]   _____

4. puddle: [pʰʌdəl]   →   [pʰʌɾəl]   _____

5. sixths: [sɪksθs]   →   [sɪksts]   _____

6. wash: [wɑʃ]   →   [wɑrʃ]   _____

7. sandwich: [sændwɪʧ]   →   [sæ̃mwɪʧ]   _____

REVIEW! REVIEW! Make sure you know the following:

- the different parts of the sound-producing system, including the vocal tract
- the difference between voiced and voiceless sounds
- the difference between nasal and oral sounds
- the characteristics of consonants, glides, and vowels
- the places and manners of articulation for consonant sounds
- the different tongue placements required to describe vowels
- the difference between tense and lax, and rounded and unrounded vowels
- the symbols and articulatory descriptions for English consonants
- the strident fricatives and affricates
- the symbols and articulatory descriptions for English vowels
- when and why aspiration occurs
- how to complete and decipher facial diagrams
- how to identify processes
- the suprasegmentals of tone, intonation, length, and stress
- transcription, transcription, transcription!

QUESTIONS? PROBLEMS? DIFFICULTIES?

_____

_____

_____

_____

_____

_____

_____

_____

_____

_____

_____

CHAPTER 3. PHONOLOGY: CONTRASTS AND PATTERNS

Phonology is the study of how languages organize speech sounds into a system of contrasts and patterns. Important terms, concepts, and topics of discussion within this chapter include the following:

1. Phonemes and allophones
2. Minimal pairs and near minimal pairs
3. Complementary distribution
4. Cross-linguistic variation
5. Phonology problems
6. Rules and generalizations
7. Phonetic and phonemic representations
8. Syllables
9. Features
10. Derivations and rule ordering

Since we will be dealing with many languages besides English, you will come across some phonetic symbols that have not been discussed. Articulatory descriptions will be provided for any unfamiliar sounds.

PHONEMES AND ALLOPHONES

As discussed in Chapter 2, a segment is an individual speech sound. Each IPA symbol represents a segment. Segments within a language are organized into phonemes and their allophones.

⇒ **Phonemes (/ /).** Phonemes represent the contrastive sounds (or segments) of a language. Sounds are said to contrast when their presence alone is responsible for words having different meanings. For example, [l] and [r] contrast in English as shown by the words *lamp* and *ramp*. Native speakers' phonological knowledge includes knowledge of which sounds are contrastive in their language. Phonemes are used to capture this knowledge.

⇒ **Allophones ([ ]).** Allophones are the sound(s) assigned to a phoneme. Part of native speaker knowledge is knowledge of which allophones belong to the same phoneme, and which belong to different phonemes. Allophones assigned to the same phoneme do not contrast with each other; they are the predictable phonetic variants of the phoneme.

FINDING PHONEMES

Determining which sounds contrast is a first step in phonological analysis.

⇒ **Minimal Pairs.** A minimal pair is defined as two phonetic forms that have different meanings and that differ by one sound that is in the same environment in both forms. *Environment* refers to the phonetic context in which the sound is found. A minimal pair means that sounds contrast.

    e.g., English: [pæt] 'pat' and [bæt] 'bat'

⇒ **Near Minimal Pairs.** A near minimal pair is defined as two phonetic forms that contain differences other than the one involving the key contrast; the extra differences must not involve sounds right next to the contrasting sounds. Like a minimal pair, these forms have different meanings, and like a minimal pair, a near minimal pair means that sounds contrast. ḅ

    e.g., Hindi: [bara] 'large' and [ḅari] 'heavy'

Sounds that contrast are said to be **allophones belonging to separate phonemes**. Sounds belonging to separate phonemes can be represented as follows.

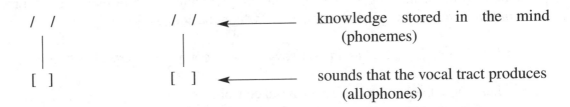

/ /	/ / ⟵	knowledge stored in the mind (phonemes)
[ ]	[ ] ⟵	sounds that the vocal tract produces (allophones)

Think. . . Which sounds contrast in the English and Hindi examples above? Put together a representation of the contrastive sounds in each example.

Try This!. . . Can the sounds [m] and [n] both occur in each of the following environments? What English words result from using [m] and [n] in the same environment? Are these words minimal pairs? If so, what does this tell us about how [m] and [n] pattern in English?

    [____ajt]   [____it]   [pʰæ____]

See table 3.1 on p. 58 of the text for some consonantal contrasts in English, and table 3.2 on p. 59 of the text for examples of vowel contrasts in English.

Exercise! State whether each of the following pairs of words is a minimal pair, a near minimal pair, or neither. Make sure you pay attention to the meanings provided.

1. [ʧogʊr] 'necklace' and [ʧogʊl] 'bracelet' _____

2. [pækt] 'towel' and [sægt] 'roof' _____

3. [telʌm] 'book' and [tɛlʌm] 'book' _____

4. [kətɑge] 'letter' and [kətɑge] 'fork' _____

5. [supt] 'bulb' and [depts] 'sugar' _____

6. [nozər] 'frog' and [hoʒəlʊp] 'valley' _____

7. [fɪθæk] 'rain' and [fɪðæk] 'window' _____

COMPLEMENTARY DISTRIBUTION

Not all sounds found in a language contrast with each other. Some sounds are in complementary distribution. Two sounds are in complementary distribution when they never occur in the same phonetic environment. That is, they are found in predictable environments. Remember, the term *environment* refers to the phonetic context in which the sounds occur.

In English, for example, oral and nasal vowels are in complementary distribution.

> i.e., Nasal vowels occur before nasal consonants.
> Oral vowels occur before oral consonants, after nasal consonants, and in several other types of environments.

Sounds that are in complementary distribution are **allophones belonging to the same phoneme.** Allophones belonging to the same phoneme can be represented as follows.

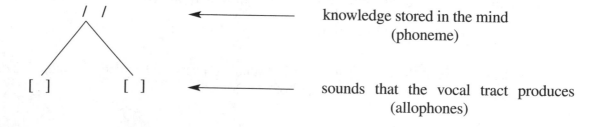

/ / ⟵—————— knowledge stored in the mind (phoneme)

[ ]   [ ] ⟵—————— sounds that the vocal tract produces (allophones)

One allophone is used to represent the phoneme. This is typically the allophone that occurs in the greatest number of phonetic environments and is referred to as "elsewhere."

The distribution of English nasal and oral vowels becomes the following:

Nasal vowels occur before nasal consonants.
Oral vowels occur elsewhere.

Now. . . Using the above information, put together a representation for English [i] and [ĩ]. Which is the elsewhere allophone? Which is the non-elsewhere allophone?

Exercise! The following exercises are designed to help you understand the predictable nature of complementary distribution.

1. In English, [p] has (at least) three allophones:
    [p] – unaspirated
    [pʰ] – aspirated
    [p̚] – unreleased

    The following list gives examples of words containing each allophone.

[p]	[pʰ]	[p̚]
spook	pig	collapse
spirit	police	apt
operate	appear	flipped
happening	repair	ape
		cop
		clap

Using the data in the above chart, determine which allophone occurs in each of the following environments:

– at the beginning of a word (word initially)   _____

– before a stressed vowel   _____

– before a consonant   _____

– at the end of a word (word finally)   _____

– after [s]   _____

– after a stressed vowel   _____

Now. . . Can [p], [pʰ], and [p̚] all occur in each of the following environments? Think about whether the words that result from using each of these sounds in the same environment have different meanings. Then, determine which sound can occur in each of the following environments. Make sure you pay attention to which vowel is stressed.

[hɪ _____ i] [_____ ɑt] [kɛ _____ t]

2. English [l] has (at least) three allophones:

[l] – alveolar (clear) l
[ɫ] – velarized (dark) l
[ḷ] – syllabic l

The following list gives examples of words containing each allophone.

[l]	[ɫ]	[ḷ]
lip	swallow	paddle
love	silly	obstacle
allow	salt	twinkle
malign	ilk	bushel
slip	pull	hurdle

Using the data in the above chart, determine which allophone occurs in each of the following environments:

– at the end of a word after a consonant _____

– at the end of a word after a vowel _____

– after a stressed vowel _____

– before a stressed vowel _____

– after [s] _____

– at the beginning of a word (word initially) _____

Now. . . Can [l], [ɫ], and [ḷ] all occur in each of the following environments? Think about whether the words that result from using each of these sounds in the same environment have different meanings. Then, determine which sound can occur in each of the following environments. Again, be sure and pay attention to which vowel is stressed.

[s_____ ajd]   [mi ____]   [hæs _____]

Remember. . . The environments in the above exercises are not to be taken as a complete list of environments to look for when doing phonological analysis. They are only examples of some possible environments, many of which pertain only to these exercises.

FINDING COMPLEMENTARY DISTRIBUTION

For each data set below, find the complementary distribution and put together a representation of the phoneme. Remember: The allophone that occurs in the greater number of environments is chosen as elsewhere and is used to represent the phoneme. All data is given in phonetic transcription.

1. The following data is from Oneida. Examine the sounds [s] and [z].

[s]		[z]	
[lashet]	"let him count"	[kawenezuze?]	"long words"
[la?sluni]	"white men"	[khaiize]	"I'm taking it along"
[loteswatu]	"he's been playing"	[lazel]	"let him drag it"
[skahnehtat]	"one pine tree"	[tahazehte?]	"he dropped it"
[thiskate]	"a different one"	[tuzahatiteni]	"they changed it"
[sninuhe]	"you buy"	[wezake]	"she saw you"
[wahsnestake?]	"you ate corn"		

2. The following data is also from Oneida. Examine the sounds [s] and [ʃ].

[s]		[ʃ]	
[lashet]	"let him count"	[ʃjatuhe?]	"you write"
[la?sluni]	"white men"	[tehʃja?k]	"let you break"
[loteswatu]	"he's been playing"	[ja?teʃjatekhahʃjahte?]	"they would suddenly
[skahnehtat]	"one pine tree"		separate again"
[thiskate]	"a different one"		
[sninuhe]	"you buy"		
[wahsnestake?]	"you ate corn"		

3. The following data is from Japanese. Examine the sounds [t], [tʃ], and [ts].

Note: The symbol [ts] is a single segment representing a voiceless alveolar affricate.

[tatami]	"mat"	[tsukue]	"desk"
[tegami]	"letter"	[ato]	"later"
[tʃitʃi]	"father"	[tsutsumu]	"to wrap"
[ʃita]	"under"	[kata]	"person"
[matsu]	"to wait"	[tatemono]	"building"
[natsu]	"summer"	[te]	"hand"
[tʃizu]	"map"	[utʃi]	"house"
[koto]	"fact"	[otoko]	"male"
[tomodatʃi]	"friend"	[tetsudau]	"to help"
[totemo]	"very"		

VARIATION

There is a great deal of cross-linguistic variation in which sounds contrast and which do not.

⇒ **Differences in phonemes across languages.** Whether segments contrast or not is determined on a language-by-language basis. Sounds that are contrastive in one language may not be contrastive in another. Consider the following examples.

Language	Segments	Phonetic Forms
Khmer	[kʰ] [k]	[kʰat] 'to polish' and [kat] 'to cut'
Turkish	[ɛ] [æ]	[bɛn] 'I' and [bæn] 'I'
Japanese	[i] [iː]	[tori] 'bird' and [toriː] 'shrine gate'

See tables 3.5 and 3.7 on p. 61 of the text for examples of more minimal pairs in Japanese and Khmer.

Think. . . Do the sounds [kʰ] and [k] contrast in Khmer? What about in English? Do the sounds [ɛ] and [æ] contrast in Turkish? Think of an English minimal pair containing [ɛ] and [æ]. Do the sounds [i] and [iː] contrast in Japanese? Do they contrast in English? Remember that [ː] indicates a long sound.

⇒ **Differences in allophones across languages.** The patterning of allophones can also vary from language to language. For example, both English and Scots Gaelic have nasal vowels; however, the distribution is different in the two languages. In English, nasal vowels only occur before nasal consonants, while in Scots Gaelic, nasal vowels occur on both sides of a nasal consonant. In both languages, oral vowels occur elsewhere.

See tables 3.8 and 3.9 on p. 63 of the text for some examples of nasal vowels in English and Scots Gaelic.

Think. . . How would the representation of nasal vowels be different for Scots Gaelic than for English? Think of a language in which nasal and oral vowels are separate phonemes (i.e., they contrast).

SOLVING PHONOLOGY PROBLEMS

The basic goal in solving a phonology problem is to determine if the sounds being examined are separate phonemes or if they are allophones of the same phoneme.

PHONEME means ...   1. The way in which sounds are stored in the mind.
                        2. The contrastive phonological units of a language.
                        3. The underlying representation.

ALLOPHONE means ...   1. The way in which sounds are pronounced.
                          2. The predictable variants of the language's phonological units.
                          3. The surface representation.

WHEN SOUNDS ARE SEPARATE PHONEMES, THEY ARE

1. contrastive/distinctive
2. in unpredictable distribution
3. easily perceived as different
4. not necessarily phonetically similar

WHEN SOUNDS ARE ALLOPHONES OF THE SAME PHONEME, THEY ARE

1. non-contrastive/rule-governed
2. in predictable distribution
3. not easily perceived as different
4. always phonetically similar

PROBLEM SOLVING FLOWCHART

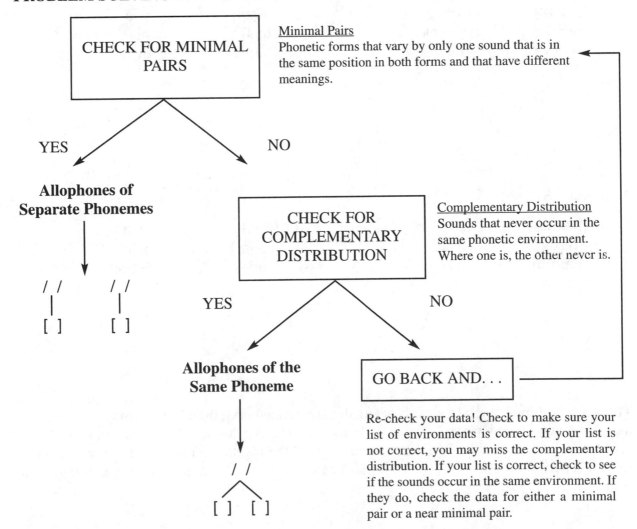

Some data to try. . .

1. Arabic: [h] and [ʔ]

    a. [ʔuruːb]   wars   e. [huruːb]   flight
    b. [fahm]   understanding   f. [faʔm]   coal
    c. [habba]   gust, squall   g. [ʔabba]   grain, seed
    d. [haːl]   cardamom   h. [ʔaːl]   condition

2. Hebrew: [θ] and [t]   ([x] represents a voiceless velar fricative)

    a. [tafar]   saw   e. [tannur]   stove
    b. [ʃtaim]   two   f. [oθax]   you
    c. [iθi]   with me   g. [teʃaʔ]   nine
    d. [raiθa]   you saw   h. [tamid]   always

3. Slovak: [f] and [v]

    a. [vatra]   campfire   d. [vɔlk]   wolf
    b. [farba]   paint   e. [feltʃar]   paint
    c. [faːdni]   monotonous   f. [vedro]   bucket

Think. . . Different languages may contain the same sounds, but these sounds may not pattern in the same way. Think about [t] and [θ] in English. Are these sounds in complementary distribution, or can they be found in a minimal pair? Put together a representation of how these sounds pattern in English. How is the English pattern different from how these sounds pattern in Hebrew?

SOME PHONOLOGY PROBLEMS

The following pages contain data sets from a number of different languages. Some of the data may have been regularized. Each data set contains sufficient data to make valid conclusions about the sounds under consideration. For each data set, do the following:

- State your conclusion (i.e., separate phonemes or allophones of the same phoneme).
- Provide evidence to support your conclusion (i.e., minimal or near minimal pair, complementary distribution).
- Provide a representation of the phoneme(s).

1. Russian: [a] and [ɑ]

      [a]   This symbol represents a low central lax unrounded vowel.

Remember, you want to look for minimal pairs involving the sounds that you have been asked to investigate. There may be other minimal pairs in the data, but you only want those that contain the sounds you are asked to examine.

1.	[atəm]	'atom'	6.	[pɑɫ]	'he fell'
2.	[dva]	'two'	7.	[dɑɫ]	'he gave'
3.	[pɑɫkə]	'stick'	8.	[dar]	'gift'
4.	[mas]	'ointment'	9.	[matə]	'mint'
5.	[ukrɑɫə]	'she stole'	10.	[brɑɫ]	'he took'

2. Korean: [l] and [ř]

      [ř]   This symbol represents a flapped [r].
      [ʉ]   This symbol represents a high central rounded vowel.

1.	[kal]	'dog'	9.	[onelppam]	'tonight'
2.	[kenel]	'shade'	10.	[silkwa]	'fruit'
3.	[iřumi]	'name'	11.	[mul]	'water'
4.	[kiři]	'road'	12.	[seul]	'Seoul'
5.	[pal]	'leg'	13.	[kəřiřo]	'to the street'
6.	[ilkop]	'seven'	14.	[sařam]	'person'
7.	[ipalsa]	'barber'	15.	[tatʉl]	'all of them'
8.	[uři]	'we'	16.	[vəřʉm]	'summer'

3. Inuktitut: [u] and [a]

  [q]   This symbol represents a voiceless uvular stop.

1.	[iglumut]	'to a house'	6. [aniguvit]	'if you leave'
2.	[ukiaq]	'late fall'	7. [ini]	'place, spot'
3.	[iglu]	'(snow)house'	8. [ukiuq]	'winter'
4.	[aiviq]	'walrus'	9. [ani]	'female's brother'
5.	[pinna]	'that one up there'	10. [anigavit]	'because you leave'

4. English: [g], [gʲ] and [gʷ]

  [gʲ]   This symbol represents a 'fronted [g]' made with the back of the tongue
         at or near the hard palate.
  [gʷ]   This symbol represents a 'rounded [g]' made with simultaneous lip rounding.

1.	[gɑn]	'gone'	7. [gʲik]	'geek'
2.	[gʷufi]	'goofy'	8. [igər]	'eager'
3.	[gli]	'glee'	9. [gejm]	'game'
4.	[slʌg]	'slug'	10. [gowfər]	'gopher'
5.	[grin]	'green'	11. [gædʒət]	'gadget'
6.	[rægʷu]	'ragout'	12. [gʲis]	'geese'

5. Tojolabal (spoken in Mexico):   [k] and [k']

  [']   This diacritic means the sound has been glottalized.

1.	[kisim]	'my beard'	7. [sak]	'white'
2.	[ʧak'a]	'chop it down'	8. [k'isin]	'warm'
3.	[koktit]	'our feet'	9. [skuʧu]	'he is carrying it'
4.	[k'ak]	'flea'	10. [k'uutes]	'to dress'
5.	[p'akan]	'hanging'	11. [snika]	'he stirred it'
6.	[k'aʔem]	'sugar cane'	12. [ʔak']	'read'

6. <u>English:</u>   [l] and [ɫ]

   Note: The English data presented below has been simplified somewhat. For a more challenging (and more accurate) analysis of English [l] and [ɫ], try problem 12 on p. 96 of the text!

1.	[lɪp]	'lip'	7.	[fɪlθ]	'filth'
2.	[lʌvli]	'lovely'	8.	[waɫgrinz]	'Walgreens'
3.	[sɪɫk]	'silk'	9.	[gɪlt]	'guilt'
4.	[slajm]	'slime'	10.	[tæɫk]	'talc'
5.	[mɪɫk]	'milk'	11.	[hiəl]	'heal'
6.	[kæɫgri]	'Calgary'			

7. <u>Sindhi:</u>   [p], [b], and [pʰ]

   For these three sounds to be allophones of separate phonemes, you must find a minimal pair for each of the following:

   [p] and [b]   [p] and [pʰ]   [b] and [pʰ]

   You may use the same data item in more than one minimal pair.

1.	[pʌnu]	'leaf'	7.	[tʌru]	'bottom'
2.	[vʌʤu]	'opportunity'	8.	[kʰʌto]	'sour'
3.	[ʃʌki]	'suspicious'	9.	[bʌʤu]	'run'
4.	[gʌdo]	'dull'	10.	[bʌnu]	'forest'
5.	[dʌru]	'door'	11.	[bʌʧu]	'be safe'
6.	[pʰʌnu]	'snakehood'	12.	[ʤʌʤu]	'judge'

8. <u>Kenyang (spoken in Cameroon): [b] and [β].</u>

   [q]   This symbol represents a voiceless uvular stop.
   [β]   This symbol represents a voiced bilabial fricative.

1.	[enoq]	'tree'	7.	[uβit]	'person's name'
2.	[eβet]	'house'	8.	[nʧiβu]	'I am buying'
3.	[bag]	'rope'	9.	[etaq]	'town'
4.	[enok]	'tree'	10.	[nab]	'brother-in-law'
5.	[nbat]	'knife'	11.	[pobrin]	'work project'
6.	[etak]	'town'	12.	[ndeβi]	'European'

RULES AND GENERALIZATIONS

When a phonological analysis uncovers allophones belonging to the same phoneme, a rule can be put together to capture where the allophones occur.

Some things to remember. . .

⇒ Allophones belonging to the same phoneme represent a predictable sound change. Such sound changes occur because segments are often affected by the phonetic characteristics of neighbouring sounds. These changes are described using processes such as assimilation. Rules, therefore, are descriptions of articulatory processes.

⇒ The sound changes represented in allophones of the same phoneme usually affect not individual sounds, but groups of sounds that share a common phonetic property—that is, a class of sounds. For this reason, rules are formulated as generally as possible.

The format and function of rules. . .

⇒ Rules are given in phonological notation.

$$\text{e.g.,}\quad /\text{l}/ \rightarrow [\overset{\circ}{\text{l}}] \; / \; \left\{\begin{matrix} p \\ t \\ k \end{matrix}\right\} \underline{\qquad}$$

⇒ Rules link the phonemic and phonetic levels together and consist of the following three parts:

1. the phoneme (e.g., /l/)
2. the change that takes place as captured by the non-elsewhere allophone (e.g., [l̥])
3. the environment in which the change from the phoneme to the non-elsewhere allophone takes place (e.g., $\left\{\begin{matrix} p \\ t \\ k \end{matrix}\right\} \underline{\qquad}$)

The rule is read as the statement "A voiced lateral liquid becomes voiceless after voiceless stops."

See examples (22) and (23) on p. 88 of the text for examples of rules involving deletion and epenthesis.

Now. . . In English, the voiced retroflex liquid also becomes voiceless after voiceless stops, just like the lateral liquid. Write a rule to capture this distribution. Then, combine your rule with the above rule for lateral liquids. Convert your combined rule into one very general statement.

Think. . . What type of assimilation does your combined rule describe? Think about the phonetic property of the phoneme that changed to arrive at the non-elsewhere allophone.

Try This!   Convert these statements into rules. Watch out for classes of sounds!

1. Voiceless stops become voiced at the beginning of words.

2. Alveopalatal affricates become fricatives between vowels.

3. Vowels become nasalized before nasals.

4. Schwa is deleted word finally.

5. A schwa is inserted between a voiceless bilabial stop and a voiced lateral liquid.

Exercise!   Convert the following rules into statements. Make your statements as general as possible.

1.   t ⟶ tʔ / ʔ ____

2. $\begin{Bmatrix} f \\ \theta \\ s \\ \int \end{Bmatrix} \longrightarrow \begin{Bmatrix} v \\ ð \\ z \\ ʒ \end{Bmatrix}$ / V __ V

3. $\begin{Bmatrix} i \\ e \end{Bmatrix} \longrightarrow \begin{Bmatrix} ɪ \\ ɛ \end{Bmatrix}$ / # ____

4. $\begin{Bmatrix} t \\ d \end{Bmatrix} \longrightarrow$ ɾ / V __ V

PHONETIC AND PHONEMIC REPRESENTATIONS

There are two types of representation: phonetic and phonemic.

⇒ **Phonetic Representation.**   The phonetic representation is a representation of normal everyday speech. That is, it is a representation of pronunciation. It includes all phonetic information, including that which is predictable. Phonetic representations are always given in [ ] brackets.

⇒ **Phonemic Representation.**   The phonemic representation is a representation that contains only the phonemes of the language. That is, it is a representation of contrast. All predictable information is excluded. Phonemic representations are always indicated with / / brackets.

See table 3.10 on p. 64 of the text for some examples of phonetic and phonemic representations of English.

To help you understand the difference between phonetic and phonemic representations, go back to the Russian problem on p. 49 of this study guide. Remember that in Russian [a] and [ɑ] are allophones of the same phoneme, with [ɑ] occurring before [ɫ], a velarized lateral liquid, and [a] occurring elsewhere. Given this information, we can convert some of the Russian phonetic forms into Russian phonemic representations.

Phonetic		Phonemic	
[mas]	"ointment"	/mas/	"ointment"
[ukrɑtə]	"she stole"	/ukratə/	"she stole"
[brɑt]	"he took"	/brat/	"he took"

Think. . . Does the phonemic representation of Russian use the phoneme or the allophones? What about the phonetic representation? Where is [ɑ] used in the phonetic representation?

Now. . . There are two levels of representation: phonetic and phonemic. What links phonetic and phonemic information together? Think about how you go from the phonemic level (knowledge) to the phonetic level (speech).

Try This! Given the rule /t/ → [θ] / V___V, convert the Hebrew phonetic transcriptions (from p. 48 of this study guide) [iθi] 'with me' and [tamid] 'always' into phonemic transcription.

MORE PHONOLOGY PROBLEMS

For each of the following data sets, do the following:

- Determine whether the sounds under consideration are allophones of the same phoneme or whether they are separate phonemes. Provide evidence to support your conclusion, along with a representation of the phoneme.

- If the sounds are allophones of the same phoneme, then provide a phonological rule.

While the data are from hypothetical languages, they exemplify phenomena found in real languages.

1. Storish: [ʃ] and [ʒ]

   1. [gasaʃ]   "mistake"   5. [trutuʃ]   "dive"
   2. [ʒipaʃ]   "head"   6. [tolʒog]   "crash"
   3. [seʒor]   "board"   7. [naʒut]   "hospital"
   4. [tʌʒəkəʃ]   "ambulance"   8. [tʃisoʃ]   "operation"

2. Nonamb: [i] and [ĩ]

   1. [θikig]   "weasel"   5. [apĩŋk]   "fox"
   2. [gorĩm]   "parrot"   6. [nuret]   "knife"
   3. [seyit]   "arrow"   7. [ʌlĩnd]   "ferret"
   4. [kĩŋglɔn]   "cave"   8. [kutʃis]   "deer"

3. Skatik: [p] and [f]

   1. [pʊnt]   "scale"   5. [lɔnik]   "scone"
   2. [akog]   "scatter"   6. [jɪptu]   "scold"
   3. [zifug]   "skelter"   7. [fʊnt]   "skate"
   4. [jɪftu]   "scare"   8. [sipək]   "skin"

4. Severenese: [i] and [u]

   1. [ubren]   "table"   5. [ublet]   "never"
   2. [lezun]   "clock"   6. [seti]   "blue"
   3. [gunob]   "arm"   7. [iplet]   "stop"
   4. [setu]   "moss"   8. [ibren]   "snow"

5. Luru: [u] and [ʊ]

1.	[luska]	"stone"	8.	[sunbu]	"melon"
2.	[holu]	"fly"	9.	[umʊlo]	"they have"
3.	[sʊrak]	"left"	10.	[rukoru]	"singing"
4.	[ketʊl]	"arm"	11.	[uzmaluk]	"road"
5.	[sumbu]	"melon"	12.	[ketuǰ]	"summer"
6.	[ambʊl]	"yellow"	13.	[ʊrkʊl]	"spark"
7.	[mastuf]	"puppy"	14.	[mustʊr]	"wine"

6. Silliese: [t] and [d]

1.	[matan]	"joke"	5.	[dar]	"chip"
2.	[dortalu]	"club"	6.	[bontel]	"laugh"
3.	[antar]	"sneeze"	7.	[gotu]	"funny"
4.	[dili]	"drink"	8.	[doko]	"light"

7. Breakie: [p] and [b]

1.	[tiktæpe]	"juice"	5.	[lobop]	"milk"
2.	[dob]	"sugar"	6.	[θupaz]	"egg"
3.	[fæbe]	"table"	7.	[bagur]	"bread"
4.	[sepita]	"food"	8.	[gitip]	"salt"

Now... Go back over the above problems and wherever allophones of the same phoneme were found, convert the first few words in the data set from their phonetic to their phonemic representation. See if you can identify the predictable phonetic property that is missing from the phonemic representation.

REMINDER! REMINDER!

When you find allophones of the same phoneme, there is a quick way to determine if your solution is in all likelihood correct. If your rule and statement describe an articulatory process such as assimilation, which is the result of neighbouring sounds interacting with each other, then your solution is probably correct. If your rule and statement do not describe such a process, then you might want to rethink your analysis!

Don't forget to use / / brackets to indicate phonemes and [ ] brackets to indicate allophones.

SYLLABLES

A syllable is another phonological unit of representation. Sounds can be grouped together to form a syllable, which consists of a syllabic element (usually a vowel) plus any preceding or following sounds.

Syllable Structure

Syllables have internal structure, which is represented above the individual sounds making up the syllable. A syllable (σ) consists of an onset (O) and a rhyme (R). The rhyme consists of a nucleus (N) and a coda (C). The elements that can make up these constituents are defined below:

⇒ The **nucleus** of a syllable contains a vowel (including diphthongs) or a syllabic consonant (either a syllabic liquid or a syllabic nasal).

⇒ The **onset** contains consonants occurring before the nucleus.

⇒ The **coda** contains consonants occurring after the nucleus.

In any syllable, the nucleus—and therefore, the rhyme—must be included. This is true for all languages. Onsets and codas may not be present in every syllable, although this will depend on individual languages. See figure 3.6 on p. 67 of the text for an example of the constituents making up a basic syllable.

Basic Syllables

Basic syllables contain the structure outlined above. In addition, there are two restrictions on the structure of basic syllables in languages that allow more than one consonant in either the onset or the coda.

1. **Sonority Requirement.** Not all sounds have the same degree of sonority. Vowels are the most sonorant, while obstruents (stops, fricatives, and affricates) are the least sonorant. Of the sonorant consonants, glides are the most sonorant, followed by liquids, and finally nasals. This can be diagrammed as follows:

increasing sonority

→

0	1	2	3	4
Obstruents	Nasals	Liquids	Glides	Vowels

Sonority provides the basis for the following two restrictions on syllable structure:

- Consonants must rise in sonority before the nucleus (i.e., in the onset).
- Consonants must fall in sonority after the nucleus (i.e., in the coda).

See figure 3.11 on p. 69 for an example of a syllable in English that meets this requirement. See table 3.15 on p. 70 for examples of some English onsets that meet the Sonority Requirement.

2. **Binarity Requirement.** Each constituent can, at the most, be binary (branching). This means that an onset can have a *maximum* of two consonants. That is, an onset can consist of zero, one, or two consonants. The same is true for codas.

Try This!   Examine the words below. For each word, determine how many syllables are in the word. For each syllable in the word, determine whether it is or is not a basic syllable. Remember to put the words into their phonemic representation first!

1. garden	4. beauty	7. understand	10. angry
2. parks	5. twinkle	8. triangle	11. cleanser
3. trained	6. lovely	9. tent	12. splashdown

Syllable Representations

There are three steps to putting together a representation of a basic syllable. These are illustrated for the word *blackboard* /blækbord/.

1. Assign the nucleus, the rhyme, and the syllable node. Vowels (including diphthongs) and syllabic consonants may occupy the nucleus position. Remember every syllable (σ) must have a nucleus (N) and a rhyme (R).

2. Assign the onset. These are sounds to the left of the nucleus. Assign the longest possible string of sounds that can begin a word to the onset. Do this for every syllable in the word. Remember that a syllable does not have to have an onset (O).

3. Assign the coda. These are sounds to the right of the nucleus. Do this for every syllable in the word. Remember that a syllable does not have to have a coda (C).

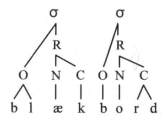

See figures 3.7 to 3.9 on pp. 68 and 69 of the text for another example of the procedure for setting up syllable representations.

Complex Syllables

Complex syllables are those that fail to meet either the Sonority Requirement or the Binarity Requirement. For example, in the word *stop*, the onset *st* does not rise in sonority, since both consonants are obstruents. In *scratch*, the onset (*scr*) contains three sounds, not two. Similarly, in *kept*, the coda does not fall in sonority (again, both consonants are obstruents), while in *tanks*, the coda (*nks*) contains three sounds.

Sounds that do not meet either the Sonority Requirement or Binarity Requirement are not part of either the onset or the coda. Rather, they are sometimes called **appendices**. Appendices are typically found at either the beginning or end of a word.

When representing a complex syllable, a fourth step in the procedure outlined on the previous page is necessary:

4. Assign any sounds that violate either sonority or binarity to the syllable node.

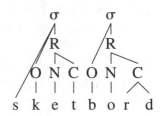

Think. . . why is /s/ assigned to the syllable node in the above example? What requirement does it violate and why?

See figure 3.13 on p. 71 of the text for an example of the representation of a complex syllable. See table 3.16 on p. 71 of the text for some examples of complex syllables in Russian.

Now. . . Go back and construct a syllable representation for each of the 12 words in the previous exercise. Remember to always assign onsets before codas. This reflects a universal preference for onsets over codas.

Some Definitions

⇒ An open syllable is a syllable that does not include a coda—that is, the rhyme only consists of the nucleus.

⇒ A closed syllable is a syllable that includes a coda—the rhyme consists of the nucleus plus the coda.

⇒ A heavy syllable is a syllable whose rhyme contains a vowel plus either a glide or a consonant.

⇒ A light syllable is a syllable whose rhyme contains only a vowel or a syllabic consonant.

The difference between heavy and light syllables is linked to how stress is assigned in English. See tables 3.17 to 3.18 on pp. 72 to 73 of the text for some examples.

Syllable-Based Phonology

In addition to stress, syllables are often relevant to stating generalizations about the distribution of allophones. For example, in English:,

⇒ Voiceless aspirated stops are found at the beginning of a syllable that is word initial or stressed and unaspirated stops are found elsewhere. See tables 3.20 and 3.21 on p. 74 of the text for some examples of English aspiration, as well as the distribution of aspirated stops in English.

⇒ Vowels are long when followed by a voiced obstruent in the coda position of the same syllable. See tables 3.22 and 3.23 on p. 75 of the text for some examples of long and short vowels in English, including their distribution.

Exercise! Exercise!   The data below is from a hypothetical language. In this hypothetical language, all syllables have the structure CV(C). What this means is that all syllables begin with an onset, but do not have to have a coda.

Stress is predictable in this language and is marked by a [´] over a vowel. Determine (making reference to syllable structure) where stress occurs. You might want to first syllabify some of the words.

1. [fémba]   "foot"
2. [hagút]   "month"
3. [fezók]   "music"
4. [waláp]   "mole"
5. [supóspa]   "gravy"
6. [tugábtʃo]   "stone"
7. [jumanumáp]   "armadillo"
8. [póbzudʒi]   "lizard"
9. [gatʃótfobi]   "knee"
10. [talagubiták]   "cowboy"
11. [páfzuliha]   "thin"
12. [kéllaboga]   "arm"

Remember. . . All languages have syllables, but not all languages have the same syllable structure. All languages allow onsets, but not all languages allow codas (e.g., Hawaiian). Some languages allow only a single sound to occupy the onset position (e.g., Korean), some allow two sounds (e.g., French), and some three (e.g., English). There are also languages that require every syllable to have an onset! But no language requires that every syllable have a coda. Finally, onsets usually allow a greater range and type of consonants than do codas.

FEATURES

Segments are made up of features. Features are the smallest type of phonological representation. A feature is a unit that corresponds to a single piece of either articulatory or acoustic information.

Features are usually divided into four categories, as shown below.

Major Class Features	Manner Features
⇒ [+/-consonantal] ⇒ [+/-syllabic] ⇒ [+/-sonorant]	⇒ [+/-continuant] ⇒ [+/-nasal] ⇒ [+/-lateral] ⇒ [+/-delayed release]
Laryngeal Features	**Place Features**

⇒ [+/-voice]
⇒ [+/-spread glottis (SG)]
⇒ [+/-constricted glottis (CG)]
	⇒ [LABIAL]
	   [+/-round]
	⇒ [CORONAL]
	   [+/-anterior], [+/-strident]
	⇒ [DORSAL]
	   [+/-high], [+/-low], [+/-back],
	   [+/-tense], [+/-reduced]

Each sound, or segment, is a bundle, or matrix, of some of the above features. See tables 3.30 and 3.31 on pp. 84 and 85 of the text for the feature matrices of English consonants and vowels.

Some important information

⇒ Since features represent articulation, they are always enclosed in phonetic (i.e., [ ]) brackets.

⇒ Features are binary and are specified either as plus (+) or minus (-).

⇒ [LABIAL], [CORONAL], and [DORSAL] are not specified as either plus or minus, but rather are used to represent the articulator that is active in executing the articulation.

- [LABIAL] for the lips
- [CORONAL] for the tongue tip or blade
- [DORSAL] for the body of the tongue

⇒ Place features are used to represent place of articulation features specific to the active articulator. That is, [LABIAL] sounds are [+/-round]; [CORONAL] sounds are [+/-anterior] and [+/-strident]; and [DORSAL] sounds are [+/-high], [+/-low], [+/-back], [+/-tense], and [+/-reduced]. See table 3.28 on p. 82 of the text for the representation of place of articulation features in some English consonants, and table 3.29 on p. 83 of the text for the representation of place of articulation features in some English vowels.

Features are used. . .

⇒ **To capture natural classes.** Natural classes are classes of sounds that share a feature or features and that pattern together in sound systems. For example, voiceless stops can be considered a natural class, as can rounded vowels. See tables 3.24 and 3.25 on p. 77 of the text for examples of how features capture different natural classes.

⇒ **To define contrast.** When sounds contrast they are responsible for meaning differences. However, it is not the sound that contrasts, but one property of the sound that contrasts: that is, a feature. This is called the distinctive feature: the only feature that distinguishes between the sounds. For example [nasal] is a distinctive feature for the /b/ and /m/ contrast in English. See table 3.26 on p. 78 of the text for another example of a distinctive feature in English.

⇒ **To understand the nature of allophonic variation.** Allophonic variation is not the substitution of one allophone for another, but a change in the specification of a feature of the allophone. For example, voiceless sounds often change and become voiced when near other voiced sounds. This can be captured with the single feature [voice].

Features and Rules

Allophones are the predictable variants of phonemes and their distribution can be described using a rule. Remember that rules have three parts: an individual phoneme or class of contrastive sounds, the allophone or change, and the environment in which the change occurs. Include features for each component of the rule. Rules can be written using phonological notation, or more formally using feature notation.

For example, the rule (given here as a statement) "voiceless unaspirated stops become aspirated syllable initially" can be formulated using feature notation as shown below.

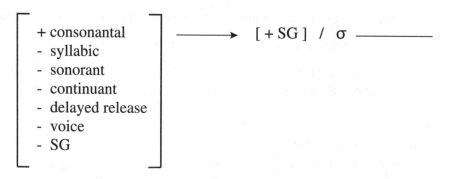

$$\begin{bmatrix} + \text{ consonantal} \\ - \text{ syllabic} \\ - \text{ sonorant} \\ - \text{ continuant} \\ - \text{ delayed release} \\ - \text{ voice} \\ - \text{ SG} \end{bmatrix} \longrightarrow [\,+\,\text{SG}\,] \;/\; \sigma \underline{\hspace{2cm}}$$

Try This! In many dialects of Canadian English, [ʌj] and [ʌw] are allophones of /aj/ and /aw/, respectively. [ʌj] and [ʌw] occur before voiceless consonants and [aj] and [aw] occur elsewhere. This is called Canadian Raising. See table 3.3 on p. 60 of the text for some examples of words containing the allophones. Put together a rule using features to capture how these sounds pattern in English. For the non-elsewhere allophone, only include the feature that changed from the phoneme(s).

FEATURE EXERCISES

1. State the feature that distinguishes each of the following pairs of sounds. (There may be more than one correct answer.)

    a. [θ] / [ð]   _____

    b. [p] / [f]   _____

    c. [s] / [θ]   _____

    d. [b] / [m]   _____

    e. [ʧ] / [ʃ]   _____

2. Each of the following sets contains three sounds that belong to the same natural class. Add one other segment to each set, making sure that the natural class is preserved. Indicate the feature (including its value) that distinguishes the natural class.

	Segment Added	Distinguishing Feature
a. [l̩ ə n̩]	[ ]	_____
b. [θ s f]	[ ]	_____
c. [i e u]	[ ]	_____
d. [t g n]	[ ]	_____
e. [j r n]	[ ]	_____
f. [i æ ɛ]	[ ]	_____

3. Name the natural class described by each of the following feature matrices.

    a. $\begin{bmatrix} - \text{consonantal} \\ - \text{syllabic} \end{bmatrix}$ b. $\begin{bmatrix} + \text{consonantal} \\ - \text{syllabic} \\ - \text{sonorant} \\ + \text{continuant} \\ + \text{voice} \end{bmatrix}$

4. In each of the sets below, all the sounds except one constitute a natural class. Draw a circle around the sound that does not belong and state the feature that the remaining sounds share.

    a. [t   g   v   ʤ] _____

    b. [b   m   r   w] _____

    c. [n   t   g   j] _____

    d. [i   ɛ   u   æ] _____

5. In each consonant system below, some segments are boxed. Determine if the boxed segments constitute a natural class. If they do, then state the feature(s) that make them a natural class.

    a.

p	t	k
f	s	
m	n	ŋ
	l	
w		j

    b.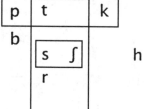

    c.

i	ɪ		u
	ɛ		o
	æ		a

    d.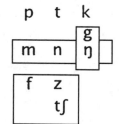

6. Provide a feature matrix for each of the following groups of sounds.

    a. [ð θ f v]   c. [u o]

    b. [g ʤ]   d. [i ɪ e ɛ æ]

DERIVATIONS

Derivations are a representation of how phonemes and allophones are related. Phonetic forms are derived from phonemic forms by applying processes in the form of a rule. There are three parts to a derivation. These parts are very similar to the components of a phonological rule.

⇒ **Underlying Representation (UR).** The underlying representation is a representation of native speaker knowledge and is always in phonemic transcription.

⇒ **Rules.** Remember that phonemes and allophones are linked by a rule. The rule applies to change the phoneme into the allophone. This, of course, only occurs when the structural description (environment) specified in the rule is found in the underlying representation.

⇒ **Phonetic Representation (PR).** The phonetic representation is also called the surface representation. Since the surface representation always represents pronunciation, it is in phonetic transcription.

An example

In English, liquids become voiceless after a voiceless stop at the beginning of a syllable. This is an example of devoicing.

The derivation below illustrates how the phonetic form is derived from the phonological form using this rule.

UR	/pliz/	'please'	/læf/	'laugh'
Liquid Devoicing	pl̥iz			
PR	[pl̥iz]		[læf]	

- In the word *please*, liquid devoicing applies because [l] occurs after a voiceless consonant (i.e., [p]). The structural description of the rule has been met. Notice that after the rule has applied, [l] has become voiceless (i.e., [l̥]).

- In the word *laugh*, the rule does not apply, as indicated by the dashed line, since the structural description necessary for the rule to apply was not met: [l] occurs at the beginning of the word and not after a voiceless consonant. The phonetic form, therefore, remains the same as the underlying form.

See figure 3.15 on p. 86 of the text for an example of a derivation involving aspiration and vowel lengthening in English.

EVEN MORE PHONOLOGY PROBLEMS

For each data set, do the following:

- Determine if the sounds are separate phonemes or allophones of the same phoneme. Remember to provide evidence in support of your conclusion, along with a representation of the phoneme(s).

- For all allophones of the same phoneme, provide a rule. Wherever possible, try to write one rule for all the sounds you have investigated. Watch out for natural classes!

- For all allophones of the same phoneme involving natural classes, write a rule using feature notation.

- For all allophones of the same phoneme, identify the process that your rule describes.

- Provide derivations as indicated.

1. <u>Canadian French:</u>   [t] and [ts]

[ts]	This symbol represents a voiceless alveolar affricate.
[y]	This symbol represents a high front tense rounded vowel.
[ʏ]	This symbol represents a high front lax rounded vowel.

1.	[tu]	'all'	7. [telegram]	'telegram'
2.	[abutsi]	'ended'	8. [trɛ]	'very'
3.	[tɛl]	'such'	9. [kyltsyr]	'culture'
4.	[tab]	'stamp'	10. [minʏt]	'minute'
5.	[tsimɪd]	'timid'	11. [tsy]	'you'
6.	[tsɪt]	'title'	12. [tsʏb]	'tube'

  - Provide a derivation for #5, #10, and #12.

2. <u>Burmese:</u>   [m] and [m̥],   [n] and [n̥],   [ŋ] and [ŋ̊]

Hint: Given that you have been asked to investigate three sets of nasals, would you expect all the nasals to pattern in the same way?

1.	[mi]	'five'	8. [hm̥i]	'to lean against'
2.	[mwej]	'to give birth'	9. [hm̥wej]	'fragrant'
3.	[mji?]	'river'	10. [hm̥jaj?]	'to cure'
4.	[ne]	'small'	11. [hn̥ej]	'slow'
5.	[nwe]	'to bend'	12. [hŋa]	'to lend property'
6.	[ŋa]	'five'	13. [hn̥wej]	'to heat'
7.	[ŋou?]	'tree stump'	14. [hŋe?]	'bird'

  - Provide a derivation for #5, #11, and #14.

3. Malay: [t] and [tʲ]

    [ʲ]   This diacritic represents a sound that has been palatalized.

    1. [tarek]   'pull'   6. [tʲampah]   'tasteless'
    2. [kətʲut]   'shrivelled'   7. [kətil]   'pinch'
    3. [pitər]   'disk'   8. [tʲarek]   'rip'
    4. [tʃomel]   'cute'   9. [lawat]   'visit'
    5. [batʲa]   'steel'   10. [tʃampah]   'tasteless'

4. Tamil: [p] and [b],   [k] and [g],   [ṭ] and [ḍ],   [t̪] and [d̪]

    [.]   This diacritic means that a sound is retroflex.
    [̪]   This diacritic means that a sound is dental.
    [ɨ]   This symbol represents a high central unrounded vowel.

    Remember: When looking for complementary distribution, you must record the imme-
                diate surrounding phonetic environment around *each occurrence* of a
                sound.

    1. [pal]   'tooth'   11. [id̪ɨ]   'this'
    2. [abayam]   'refuge'   12. [ad̪ɨ]   'that'
    3. [kappal]   'ship'   13. [katti]   'knife'
    4. [saabam]   'curse'   14. [kud̪i]   'jump'
    5. [kaakkaaj]   'crow'   15. [patti]   'ten'
    6. [mugil]   'cloud'   16. [paaḍam]   'foot'
    7. [t̪ugil]   'veil'   17. [iḍam]   'place'
    8. [t̪attɨ]   'plate'   18. [kaaṭpaaḍi]   'name of a town'
    9. [padɨ]   'lie down'   19. [pattɨ]   'silk'
   10. [t̪uukkɨ]   'carry'

    • Provide a derivation for #3, #6, and #14.

5. Igbirra: [e] and [a]

    1. [mezi]   'I expect'   5. [mazɪ]   'I am in pain'
    2. [meze]   'I am well'   6. [mazɛ]   'I agree'
    3. [meto]   'I arrange'   7. [matɔ]   'I pick'
    4. [metu]   'I beat'   8. [matʊ]   'I send'

    • Are there minimal pairs?
    • [e] and [a] both occur between m _ z and m _ t. What significance does this have for
      your analysis?
    • Pay attention to syllable structure when looking for complementary distribution.

6. Gascon: [b] and [β],   [d] and [ð], [g] and [ɣ]

Hint: Think about what process you would expect, given pairs of stops and fricatives.

[ɣ]   This symbol represents a voiced velar fricative.

1.	[brẽn]	'endanger'	10.	[ʒuɣɛt]	'he played'
2.	[dilys]	'Monday'	11.	[krãmbo]	'room'
3.	[taldepãn]	'leftover bread'	12.	[eʃaðo]	'hoe'
4.	[ʃiβaw]	'horse'	13.	[gat]	'cat'
5.	[pũnde]	'to lay eggs'	14.	[aβe]	'to have'
6.	[agro]	'sour'	15.	[biɣar]	'mosquito'
7.	[puðe]	'to be able'	16.	[ũmbro]	'shadow'
8.	[riɣut]	'he laughed'	17.	[dudze]	'twelve'
9.	[noβi]	'husband'	18.	[lũŋg]	'long'

- Examine the Gascon data again, paying attention to the oral and nasal vowels. Can you make any conclusions about nasalized vowels in this language? Write one statement involving classes of sounds, describing their behaviour.

- Provide a derivation for #5, #9, and #18.

Some reminders. . .

⇒ To solve phonology problems, you need to understand minimal pairs, near minimal pairs, complementary distribution, and phonemes and allophones.

⇒ To put together rules, you need to be able to spot natural classes, and to do that you need to be familiar with the articulatory descriptions of sounds.

⇒ To put together derivations, you need to understand phonemic transcriptions, phonetic transcriptions, underlying representations, rules, and surface representations.

REVIEW! REVIEW!   Make sure you can do the following:

- define phonemes and allophones
- spot minimal and near minimal pairs
- determine complementary distribution
- construct representations of phonemes
- construct syllable representations
- identify basic and complex syllables
- identify consonantal and vowel features
- spot classes of sounds
- put together feature matrices
- put together rules
- put together rules using feature notation
- construct derivations
- solve phonology problems

QUESTIONS? PROBLEMS? DIFFICULTIES?

CHAPTER 4. MORPHOLOGY: THE ANALYSIS OF WORD STRUCTURE

Morphology is the study of words: their categories, their internal structure, and the operations that form them. Important topics and concepts found in this chapter include the following:

1. Morphological terminology
2. Identifying morphemes
3. Identifying lexical categories
4. Analyzing word structure
5. Derivation
6. Compounding
7. Inflection
8. Morphological processes
9. Morphology problems
10. Morphophonemics

MORPHOLOGICAL TERMINOLOGY

The following terms are crucial to understanding morphology. You should know them!

Term	Definition
Word	Words are the smallest free forms found in language. Free forms are elements that can ap pear in isolation or whose position is not fixed. Words can be simple or complex. See table 4.1 on p. 102 of the text for some examples.
Morpheme	A morpheme is the smallest meaningful or functional unit found in language. Morphemes can be free or bound.
Allomorphs	Allomorphs are the different pronunciations of a morpheme.
Root	A root is the core of a word. It is the portion of the word that carries most of the word's meaning. The majority of English words are built from roots that are free morphemes, making English a word-based language. Some English words, though, are built from roots that are bound morphemes (e.g., unkempt). Try and think of some more examples.
Affixes	Affixes are different types of bound morphemes. There are three types of affixes found in language: prefixes, suffixes, and infixes. See tables 4.3 and 4.4 on p. 105 for some examples.
Base	A base is any form to which an affix is added. The base may be the same as the root, but it can also be larger than the root. See figure 4.3 on p. 104 of the text for an illustration of the difference between roots and bases.

IDENTIFYING MORPHEMES

Morphemes are the building blocks of words. A word can contain only one morpheme, making it a simple word, or a word may contain more than one morpheme, making it a complex word. Below are some hints for determining the number of morphemes that a word contains.

⇒ A morpheme carries information about meaning or function. Think . . . can the word *haunt* be divided into the morphemes *h* and *aunt*? To do so, both *h* and *aunt* must have meaning. Do they? What about the word *bats*? What meaning does *s* have in this word?

⇒ The meanings of individual morphemes should contribute to the overall meaning of the word. Think . . . can the word *pumpkin* be divided into the morphemes *pump* and *kin*? To do so, the meaning of *pumpkin* must have something to do with the meaning of both *pump* and *kin*. Does it?

⇒ A morpheme is not the same as a syllable. A morpheme can consist of one or more syllables, but a morpheme does not have to be a syllable. Think . . . how many syllables are found in the morpheme *treat*? What about in the morpheme *Dracula*? What about the *s* found in *bats*? It is a morpheme, but is it a syllable?

⇒ Often as words are built, changes in pronunciation and/or spelling occur. These do not affect a morpheme's status as a morpheme. Think . . . when *y* is added to the morpheme *scare*, it becomes *scary*, and when *er* is added to *scary*, it becomes *scarier*. Is the root the same in both *scary* and *scarier*? Is the root *scare* or *scar*? What is the base for *scary*? What about for *scarier*? Is the base the same in both?

Exercise!   Identify the number of morphemes in each of the following words.

1. insert _____

   memory _____

3. format _____

   flowchart _____

5. bug _____

   debug _____

2. supply _____

   supplies _____

   supplier _____

4. faster _____

   power _____

   processor _____

Practice! Practice! For each of the following words, identify the number of morphemes and write the free and bound morphemes in the appropriate blanks. A free morpheme can be a word by itself, while a bound morpheme must be attached to another element. Remember, a word may have more than one bound morpheme. The first is done for you.

WORD	TOTAL # OF MORPHEMES	FREE	BOUND
eraser	2	erase	-er
wicked	2	wick	-ed
invalid (A)	2	valid	in-
invalid (N)	1	invalid	
Jack's	2	Jack	-'s
optionality	4	option	-ion, -al, -ity
refurnish	2	furnish	re-
inabilities	4	able	in-, -ity, -s
denationalize	4	nation	de-, -al, -ize
present	1	present	
activation	4	act	-ive, -ate, -ion
rewinding	3	wind	re-, -ing

Think. . . What type of bound morpheme is found in the complex words *optionality* and *activation*? Prefix? Suffix? Infix? Remember that for an affix to be an infix, it must be found inside another morpheme and not between two morphemes.

IDENTIFYING LEXICAL CATEGORIES

In morphology, we are concerned with four lexical categories: nouns, verbs, adjectives, and prepositions. Nouns typically refer to people and things (both concrete and abstract). Verbs typically denote actions, sensations, and states. Adjectives usually name properties. Prepositions generally encode spatial relations.

For each of the words below, state the number of morphemes found in the word, and identify the root, the lexical category of the root, and the lexical category of the entire word. Remember, the root is the core of the word and carries most of the word's meaning. Be careful: the root's lexical category and the word's lexical category may or may not be the same. The first is done for you.

WORD	# OF MORPHS	ROOT	ROOT CATEGORY	WORD CATEGORY
healthiest	3	health	noun	adjective
amazement		amaze		
reusable				
dishonest				
Calgary				
lovelier				
historical				
uncontrolled				
impersonal				
trees				
faster				
rereads				
beautiful				
child				

WORD TREES

A word tree is a representation of a word's internal structure. To put together a word tree, you need to be able to determine the number of morphemes in a word, identify roots and affixes, and assign lexical categories. Remember, prefixes are attached to the front of a base, while suffixes are attached to the end of a base. Infixes are affixes that occur inside another morpheme; they are not found in English.

Below are some examples of how to draw a word tree.

1. Words with a single affix

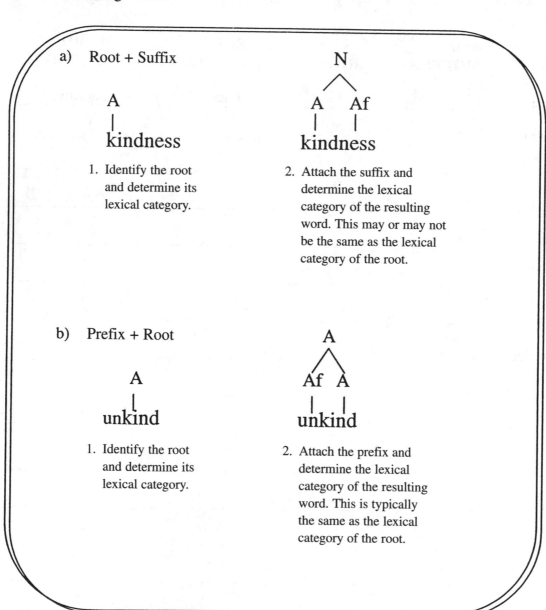

a)   Root + Suffix

A
|
kindness

1. Identify the root and determine its lexical category.

N
/\
A   Af
| |
kindness

2. Attach the suffix and determine the lexical category of the resulting word. This may or may not be the same as the lexical category of the root.

b)   Prefix + Root

A
|
unkind

1. Identify the root and determine its lexical category.

A
/\
Af   A
| |
unkind

2. Attach the prefix and determine the lexical category of the resulting word. This is typically the same as the lexical category of the root.

2. Words with multiple suffixes.

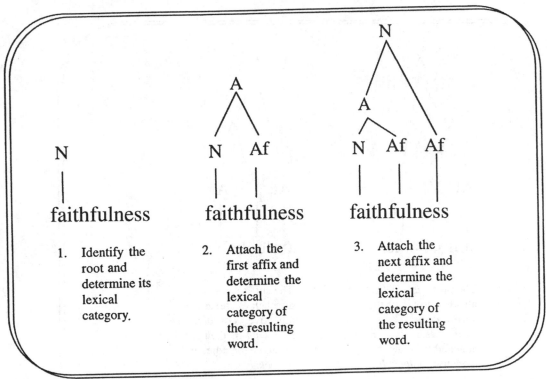

3. Words with both a prefix and a suffix

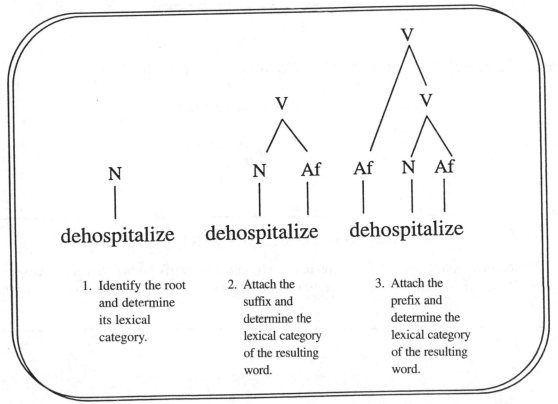

Think. . . in the above example, does the suffix have to be attached before the prefix? Why?

4. Words that are structurally ambiguous

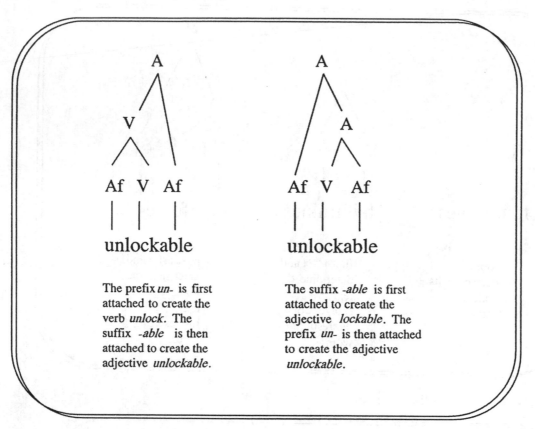

The prefix *un-* is first attached to create the verb *unlock*. The suffix *-able* is then attached to create the adjective *unlockable*.

The suffix *-able* is first attached to create the adjective *lockable*. The prefix *un-* is then attached to create the adjective *unlockable*.

Exercise! Exercise! To practice, draw trees for the following words:

- trees
- lovelier
- dishonest
- beautiful

- amazement
- reusable
- impersonal
- Calgary

REMINDER! REMINDER!

To be able to draw word trees correctly, you need to be able to identify nouns, verbs, adjectives, and prepositions. If you are having difficulty with these, refer to Chapter 5, section 5.1 to get some help!

DERIVATION

Derivation is a process of affixation. Affixation is a morphological process that adds affixes to words. Derivational affixes are affixes that build a word having a different (but usually related) meaning from that of its base. The resulting word may also belong to a different lexical category from its base.

⇒ English has many derivational suffixes. These suffixes typically cause both a meaning and category change to the base. For example:

- The suffix *-ity* combines with an adjective such as *stupid* to create the noun *stupidity*, meaning the result of being stupid.

- The suffix *-en* combines with an adjective such as *hard* to create the verb *harden*, meaning to become hard.

- The suffix *-ous* combines with a noun such as *poison* to create the adjective *poisonous*, meaning producing or possessing poison.

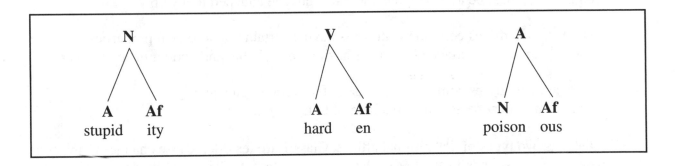

Think of some more derivational suffixes. What lexical category of words do they combine with? What lexical category of words do they create?

⇒ English also has many derivational prefixes. These cause a meaning change to the base, but usually do not change the lexical category of the base. It is the meaning change that makes them derivational. For example:

- The prefix *ex-* combines with a noun such as *friend* to create the noun *ex-friend*, meaning someone who is no longer a friend.

- The prefix *re-* combines with a verb such as *think* to create the verb *rethink*, meaning to think again.

- The prefix *in-* combines with an adjective such as *complete* to create the adjective *incomplete*, meaning not complete.

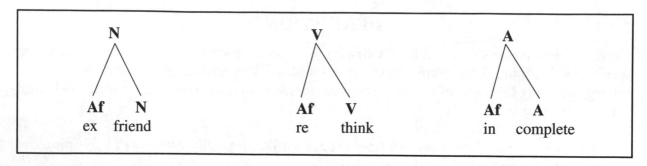

Think of some more derivational prefixes. What lexical category of words do they combine with and create? What meaning change occurs to the base when these are added?

More examples of English derivational prefixes and suffixes can be found in table 4.6 on p. 108.

⇒ Derivational affixes (including those found in English) are often subject to restrictions. For example:

- Derivational affixes combine with bases of particular lexical categories.
  e.g.,   *-ize* must be attached to a noun; *-er* must be attached to a verb

- Derivational affixes combine with bases having certain phonological properties.
  e.g.,   *-en* must be attached to a base having one syllable and ending in an obstruent

- Derivational affixes combine with bases of specific linguistic origin.
  e.g.,   *-ant* must be attached to a base of Latin origin

⇒ English has two types of derivational affixes. Class 1 affixes often cause changes to the consonant or vowel sounds in the base. Class 2 affixes do not. Class 1 affixes may also cause changes to which syllable is stressed. Class 2 affixes do not. See tables 4.9 and 4.10 on p. 111 for examples of both types of English derivational affixes.

Try This! Draw trees for the following words. Remember that a word can contain more than one derivational affix.

- disappear
- homeless
- electricity

- unbreakable
- instructional
- lodger

Now. . . Go back over the above words and identify which affixes are Class 1 affixes and which belong to Class 2.

Remember. . . Derivation builds words having a meaning different from their base. If a word already exists (e.g., cook) with the same meaning as one that would result from derivation (e.g. cook-er), then derivation is blocked: It does not create the word. Try and think of some other examples in which derivation is prevented from taking place.

COMPOUNDING

Compounding is another process used to build words. Compounding involves the combination of two or more already existing words into a new word. Most English compounds are nouns, verbs, and adjectives. See figure 4.9 on p. 112 for some examples.

There are four important concepts about English compounds that you should know.

⇒ **Headedness.** The head of a compound is the morpheme that determines the category of the entire compound. Most English compounds are right-headed. That is, the category of the entire compound is the same as the category of the rightmost member of the compound. For example, since the rightmost member *board* is a noun, the compound *blackboard* is a noun. What is the head of *nation-wide*? (to) *dry-clean*?

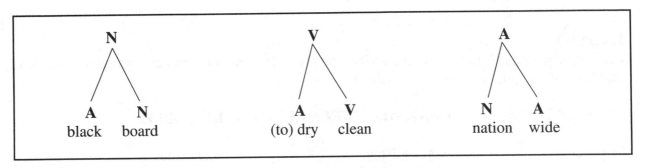

See table 4.14 on p. 115 of the text for some examples of noun compounds in other languages. Notice that not all of these languages have right-headed compounds.

⇒ **Stress Patterns.** Even though compounds can be spelled as one word, two words, or with a hyphen separating the morphemes, a generalization can be made about the stress patterns found on them. Stress tends to be more prominent on the first member of the compound than on the second: for example, *greénhouse* (a garden centre) versus *green hoúse* (a house that is green).

⇒ **Tense/Plural.** Tense and plural markers are usually added to the compound as a whole and not to the first member of the compound. For example, the plural of *fire engine* is *fire engines* and not *fires engine*. What is the past tense of *drop kick*?

⇒ **Meaning Relationships.** Compounds can be classified as either endocentric or exocentric. This classification is based on the meaning relationship between the members of the compound. In an endocentric compound, the entire compound denotes a subtype of the head. For example, a *teacup* is a type of *cup*, and a *lunchroom* is a type of *room*. In an exocentric compound, the meaning of the compound does not come from the head. For example, a *redneck* is not a type of *neck*, but a type of person.

Compounds can be formed from smaller compounds. Compounding can also be used in conjunction with derivation to build words. For example, the compound *blackboard* can combine with the derived word *eraser* to create the larger compound *blackboard eraser*.

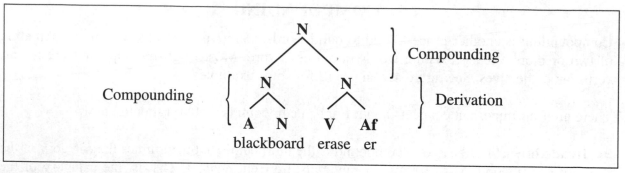

See figures 4.10 and 4.11 on p. 112 of the text for some additional examples of larger compounds and compounds interacting with derivation.

Exercise!

For each compound below, state the lexical categories making it up and give another example of that type of compound. The first is done for you.

COMPOUND	LEXICAL CATEGORIES	EXAMPLE
bathroom	Noun + Noun	movie star
scarecrow	V + N	
skin deep	N + A	
bittersweet	A + A	
upstairs	A + N (+)	downtown

Now. . . Go back and draw a word tree for each compound. **Then. . .** Draw a word tree for each of the following compounds:

- (an) undertaking
- washer-dryer

- election night
- overgrown

Remember. . . Compounding is an excellent source of new words in a language. See table 4.11 on p. 113 of the text for some examples of recent compounds in English. Try and think of some additional examples.

INFLECTION

Inflection involves modifying the form of a word to indicate grammatical information, such as singular versus plural or past versus non-past.

Inflection is most commonly a process of affixation. Inflectional affixes do not change the lexical category of the base.

⇒ English has eight inflectional affixes. These are found on nouns, verbs, and adjectives, and provide the following grammatical information: plural (-s) and possessive (-'s); third person singular non-past tense (-s), past tense (-ed), progressive (-ing) and past participle (-en/-ed); comparative (-er) and superlative (-est).

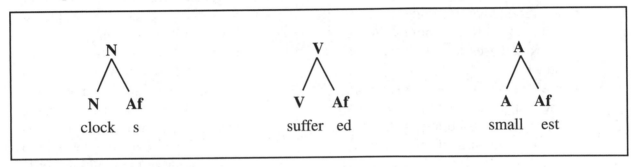

See table 4.15 on p. 116 for some examples of English inflectional affixes.

Practice! For each of the following words, identify the lexical category of the root and the type of inflectional information found (i.e., past tense, superlative, plural, etc.). The first is done for you.

WORD	LEXICAL CATEGORY	INFLECTIONAL INFORMATION
watched	verb	past tense
runs	*verb*	*present tense*
sorriest	*adj*	*superlative*
lamps		
playing		
driven		
lovelier		

INFLECTION VERSUS DERIVATION

It can sometimes be hard to determine whether an affix is an inflectional affix or a derivational affix. The boxes below provide some criteria for helping determine whether an affix is inflectional or derivational.

Inflectional affixes. . .	Derivational affixes. . .
• do not change the lexical category or meaning of the base. • are attached after derivational affixes have been attached. • are productive, meaning there are relatively few exceptions on the class of bases to which they can attach. • are semantically transparent, meaning that it is easy to determine the contribution of the affix to the meaning of the resulting word.	• typically change both the lexical category and meaning of the base. • occur closer to the root than inflectional affixes. • are less productive than inflectional affixes, meaning there are restrictions on the class of bases to which they can attach. • are less semantically transparent than inflectional affixes, meaning that it is not always easy to determine the contribution of the affix to the meaning of the resulting word.

Identify the Affix! Each of the following English words contains at least one affix. For each word, identify all the affixes, and for each affix, state whether it is inflectional (IA) or derivational (DA). For inflectional affixes, identify the type of information. The first is done for you.

WORD	AFFIX(ES)	IA / DA
trucks	-s	IA (plural)
insanity		
reuse		
girl's		
smaller		
delightful		
nationalize		
watched		
mistreat		
unhealthiest		

It can get even more complicated! Many affixes have the same form but can be either inflectional or derivational, or they can be different inflectional or different derivational affixes. To correctly identify an affix as inflectional or derivational, you need to pay attention to how the affix is functioning in the word rather than to its form. Use the four criteria outlined in this section to help you decide if an affix is functioning as an inflectional or a derivational affix.

Form versus Function! In each group of four words below, two words have affixes of the same type, one word has a different affix, and one word has no affix at all. Next to each word, write S (same), D (different), or N (none) based on the other words in the data set. You may want to use a dictionary. The first is done for you.

1.	ovens	S		2.	greener	___
	lens	N			farmer	___
	hens	S			colder	___
	listens	D			water	___

3.	greedy	___		4.	friendly	___
	ivory	___			slowly	___
	jealousy	___			intelligently	___
	dirty	___			early	___

5.	leaven	___		6.	intelligent	___
	harden	___			inhale	___
	spoken	___			incongruous	___
	thicken	___			inhuman	___

7.	rider	___		8.	candied	___
	colder	___			shopped	___
	silver	___			cleaned	___
	actor	___			candid	___

PRACTICE WITH WORD TREES

Draw one tree for each of the words listed below and identify whether inflection, derivation, and/or compounding was used to build the word. Remember that more than one process can be used in a single word. Use the context sentence to help you determine the lexical category of the entire word!

For example, the word *creamiest* might be diagrammed as follows.

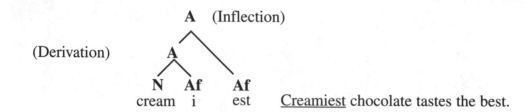

Creamiest chocolate tastes the best.

	WORD	CONTEXT SENTENCE
1.	taken	The baby has <u>taken</u> his first steps.
2.	spoonfeeding	Mother is <u>spoonfeeding</u> the baby.
3.	retry	She should <u>retry</u> the recipe.
4.	silkiest	Sandra used the <u>silkiest</u> material.
5.	introductions	Mary performed the <u>introductions</u>.
6.	steps	John <u>steps</u> up the ladder.
7.	steps	I hate those steep <u>steps</u>.
8.	thickener	Flour is a type of <u>thickener</u>.
9.	skiers	The <u>skiers</u> were rich.
10.	insightful	Your answer is rather <u>insightful</u>.
11.	stone-cold	Your French fries are <u>stone-cold</u>.
12.	making	Jill is <u>making</u> candy.
13.	boxing	We watched the <u>boxing</u>.
14.	unbreakable	Joan always buys <u>unbreakable</u> dishes.

15. attractive   That room is very <u>attractive</u>.

16. moonrocks   The astronauts collected many <u>moonrocks</u>.

17. blessing   Give me your <u>blessing</u>.

18. blessing   She is <u>blessing</u> the bread.

19. school teacher   My mother was a <u>school teacher</u>.

20. clumsiness   I detest <u>clumsiness</u>.

21. ex-Albertan   George is an <u>ex-Albertan</u>.

22. hammered   John <u>hammered</u> on the door.

23. overthink   Don't <u>overthink</u> the problem.

24. unlocked   We <u>unlocked</u> the door.

25. impure   <u>Impure</u> water is dangerous.

26. criticize   You <u>criticize</u> too much.

27. treatment centre   He needs to go to a good <u>treatment centre</u>.

28. defrosting   The steaks are <u>defrosting</u>.

29. stringier   Her hair is <u>stringier</u> than yours.

30. selfishness   <u>Selfishness</u> is not very attractive.

QUICK REMINDER!

Remember that *all* English prefixes are derivational even though they do not cause a lexical category change!

OTHER INFLECTIONAL PROCESSES

In addition to affixation, inflection can also be marked using internal change, suppletion, reduplication, and tone placement.

Process	Definition
Internal Change	This process provides grammatical information by substituting a portion of the morpheme. In English, the tense of a word can be marked by replacing the vowel with another vowel (e.g., r<u>u</u>n → r<u>a</u>n). See table 4.17 on p. 119 for more examples.
Suppletion	This process provides grammatical information by replacing one morpheme with an entirely different morpheme. In English, the tense of a word can be marked in this way (e.g., *go* → *went*). See table 4.18 on p. 120 of the text for more examples. Partial suppletion is sometimes used to describe the change in words such as *think* → *thought*, in which more than a segment has been changed, but not the entire morpheme.
Reduplication	A process that repeats all (full) or a portion (partial) of the base to mark a semantic or grammatical contrast. This process is not very productive in English. See tables 4.19 and 4.20 on p. 121 for some non-English examples.
Tone Placement	This process is found in tone languages where differences in tone can be used to mark grammatical information such as a change in tense or number. See table 4.21 on p. 121 for some examples from Mono-Bili (spoken in the Congo).

Exercise! Exercise!   Each of the following words has been inflected. For each, identify the type of inflectional process (including affixation) that has been used to mark the grammatical contrast. The first has been done for you.

WORD   **TYPE OF INFLECTION**

drove   <u>internal change</u>

was   _____

(is) jumping   _____

anak anak
'all sorts of children'
_____

better
_____

lovelier
_____

George's
_____

tatakbuh
'will run'
_____

mice
_____

Reminder! Many more inflectional phenomena, including case and agreement, are widely used in language. For more information on these and other inflectional phenomena, visit www.pearsoncanada.ca/ogrady.

MORE MORPHOLOGICAL PROCESSES

Process	Definition
Cliticization	Clitics are morphemes that behave like words in terms of meaning and function. Clitics differ, though, in that they cannot stand alone as a word. Cliticization attaches these elements to either the beginning of a following word or the end of a preceding word. E.g., _re_ from _are_ is attached to _they_, as in _they're_
Conversion	A process that assigns an existing word to a different lexical category. The lexical category and meaning change that occur make this process a type of derivation. E.g., _butter (N) → (to) butter (V)_ See table 4.22 on p. 122 for more examples. In two-syllable words, conversion can also be accompanied by a change in stress placement. See table 4.23 on p. 123 for some examples.
Clipping	A process that shortens a polysyllabic word by removing one or more syllables. E.g., _condominium → condo_
Blends	A process that creates a new word by combining non-morphemic portions of two existing words. E.g., _spiced + ham → spam_

Backformation	A process that creates a word by removing a real or supposed affix from an existing word in the language. E.g., *enthuse* ← *enthusiasm* See table 4.24 on p. 125 for more English examples.
Acronyms & Initialisms	A process that creates new words using the initial letters of the words in a phrase or title and pronouncing them as a word. E.g., *scuba, UNICEF, BOGO* Acronyms are different from initialisms, in which each letter making up the word is pronounced. E.g., *IBM, NHL, PEI*
Onomatopoeia	A process that creates new words that sound like the thing they name. E.g., *buzz, hiss, sizzle* See table 4.25 on p. 126 for some examples from various languages.

Other ways to form new words include the following:

- Word manufacture (coinage), in which a totally new word is created. This process commonly occurs with product names.
- Creating words from names (called eponyms). See table 4.26 on p. 127 for some examples.
- Borrowing words from other languages.

Practice! Practice! Identify the process responsible for the formation of each of the following English words. Choose any of the morphological phenomena from the above table, as well as derivation, compounding, and any of the inflectional processes on p. 86. The first is done for you.

infomercial   blending_____

(to) ship   _____

swam   _____

support-hose   _____

chirp   _____

MADD   _____

healthy   _____

demo   _____

export   _____

sadness   _____

he's   _____

headline   _____

beep   _____

ATM   _____

jumped   _____

There are many examples of different word formation processes in the following passage. Find all the examples of ACRONYM, BACKFORMATION, BLENDING, CLIPPING, COINAGE, COMPOUNDING, and INITIALISM.

> John didn't enthuse about UCLA, as he probably expected his profs to spoonfeed him. He preferred to avoid the smog by taking sandwiches to the beach, where he would laze around and go scuba diving in his new dacron dry suit. One day he was suffering from a headache and dizziness, which he thought might be caused by sunstroke or the flu, so he went to the doctor. The doc sent him to the lab for a urinalysis and a blood test and suggested that he should see an ENT specialist as well. He is now OK, having returned from the USA, and he is learning about ohms, watts, and volts at MIT.

Get ready for morphology problems . . .

INTRODUCTION TO MORPHOLOGY PROBLEMS

The goal in morphology problems is to isolate and identify all the morphemes in the data given. To do this, you must identify recurring strings of sounds and match them with recurring meanings. Here are a few easy ones to try!

All data is given in phonetic transcription.

1. Mende (Sierra Leone)

1.	[pɛlɛ]	'house'	9.	[pɛlɛi]	'the house'
2.	[mɔm]	'glass'	10.	[mɔmi]	'the glass'
3.	[dɔmi]	'story'	11.	[dɔmii]	'the story'
4.	[kali]	'hoe'	12.	[kalii]	'the hoe'
5.	[hele]	'elephant'	13.	[helei]	'the elephant'
6.	[kaamɔ]	'teacher'	14.	[kaamɔi]	'the teacher'
7.	[navo]	'boy'	15.	[navoi]	'the boy'
8.	[numu]	'person'	16.	[numui]	'the person'

   a.   What is the morpheme meaning 'the'?

   b.   Given [sale] meaning 'proverb', what is the form for 'the proverb'?

   c.   If [kpindii] means 'the night', then what does [kpindi] mean?

2. Ganda (Uganda)

1.	[omukazi]	'woman'	6.	[abakazi]	'women'
2.	[omusawo]	'doctor'	7.	[abasawo]	'doctors'
3.	[omusika]	'heir'	8.	[abasika]	'heirs'
4.	[omuwala]	'girl'	9.	[abawala]	'girls'
5.	[omulenzi]	'boy'	10.	[abalenzi]	'boys'

   a.   What is the morpheme meaning 'singular'?

   b.   What is the morpheme meaning 'plural'?

   c.   Given [abalanga] meaning 'twins', what is the form for 'twin'?

3. Kanuri (Nigeria)

1. [gana]	'small'	6. [nəmgana]	'smallness'
2. [kura]	'big'	7. [nəmkura]	'bigness'
3. [kurugu]	'long'	8. [nəmkurugu]	'length'
4. [karite]	'excellent'	9. [nəmkarite]	'excellence'
5. [dibi]	'bad'	10. [nəmdibi]	'badness'

a. What type of affix is shown (i.e., prefix, suffix, infix)?

b. What is the affix?

c. Given [kəji] meaning 'sweet', what is the form for 'sweetness'?

d. Given [nəmgəla] meaning 'goodness', what is the form for 'good'?

e. What morphological process was used to form the words in the second column?

f. Draw a word-tree for [nəmkurugu] 'length'.

REMINDER!

For more tips on identifying morphemes in unfamiliar languages (i.e., solving morphology problems), see pp. 129 and 130 of the text.

MORE MORPHOLOGY PROBLEMS

The following pages contain a number of data sets from different languages. These data sets are intended to give you practice in doing morphological analysis. Each contains sufficient data to make valid conclusions; however, the data may have been regularized somewhat. All data is in phonetic transcription.

1. Turkish

1.	[deniz]	'an ocean'	9.	[elim]	'my hand'
2.	[denize]	'to an ocean'	10.	[eller]	'hands'
3.	[denizin]	'of an ocean'	11.	[disler]	'teeth'
4.	[eve]	'to a house'	12.	[disimizin]	'of our tooth'
5.	[evden]	'from a house'	13.	[dislerimizin]	'of our teeth'
6.	[evcikden]	'from a little house'	14.	[elcike]	'to a little hand'
7.	[denizcikde]	'in a little ocean'	15.	[denizlerimizde]	'in our oceans'
8.	[elde]	'in a hand'	16.	[evciklerimizde]	'in our little houses'

Give the Turkish morpheme that corresponds to each of the following English translations.

ocean	_deniz-_	my	_-im_
house	_evd_	our	_-imiz-_
hand	_el-_	of	_-in_
tooth	_dis_	little	_-cik-_
plural	_-ler-_	from	_-den_
to	_-e_	in	_-de_

What is the order of morphemes in a Turkish word in terms of noun, preposition, plural, possessive determiner, and adjective? (Don't assume that this order will be the same as it is in English.)

$$N - A - Pl - Pd - Pp$$

What would be the Turkish word meaning 'of our little hands'? (HINT: Use the order you determined above.)

elciklerimizin

2. Bontoc (Philippines)

1.	[fikas]	'strong'	5.	[fumikas]	'he is becoming strong'
2.	[kilad]	'red'	6.	[kumilad]	'he is becoming red'
3.	[bato]	'stone'	7.	[bumato]	'he is becoming stone'
4.	[fusul]	'enemy'	8.	[fumusul]	'he is becoming an enemy'

What is the affix used to form the verbs?

—um—

What type of affix (i.e., prefix, suffix, infix) is used to form the verbs?

infix

What morphological process is used to build the verbs?

3. Michoacan Aztec (also known as Nahuatl—Mexico)

1.	[nokali]	'my house'	8.	[mopelo]	'your dog'
2.	[nokalimes]	'my houses'	9.	[mopelomes]	'your dogs'
3.	[mokali]	'your house'	10.	[ipelo]	'his dog'
4.	[ikali]	'his house'	11.	[nokwahmili]	'my cornfield'
5.	[kali]	'house'	12.	[mokwahmili]	'your cornfield'
6.	[kalimes]	'houses'	13.	[ikwahmili]	'his cornfield'
7.	[nopelo]	'my dog'	14.	[ikwahmilimes]	'his cornfields'

Fill in the blanks with the corresponding Michoacan morphemes:

house   *kali*   my   *no*

dog   *pelo*   your   *mo*

cornfield *kwahmili*   his   *i*

                          plural   *mes*

What does [pelomes] mean in this language?

dogs

What would be the form for 'my cornfields' in this language? For 'his dogs'?

nokwahmilimes   *ipelomes*

4. Lebanese Arabic

1.	[hamalt]	'I carried'		10.	[hibbt]	'I loved'
2.	[hamal]	'he carried'		11.	[hibba]	'he loved her'
3.	[hamaltak]	'I carried you (masc)'		12.	[hibbni]	'he loved me'
4.	[hamaltik]	'I carried you (fem)'		13.	[hibbak]	'he loved you (masc)'
5.	[hamaltu]	'I carried him'		14.	[hibbik]	'he loved you (fem)'
6.	[hamalta]	'I carried her'		15.	[hibbu]	'he loved him'
7.	[hamaltkun]	'I carried you (pl)'		16.	[hibbbna]	'he loved us'
8.	[hamaltun]	'I carried them'		17.	[hibbkun]	'he loved you (pl)'
9.	[hibb]	'he loved'		18.	[hibbun]	'he loved them'

Give the Lebanese Arabic morpheme for each of the following English pronouns.

I	_____		me	_____
he	_____		us	_____
you (masc)	_____		him	_____
you (fem)	_____		her	_____
you (pl)	_____		them	_____

What is the order of morphemes in terms of subject pronoun, object pronoun, and root?

5. Turkish

Below are some examples of compounds in Turkish. For each, the Turkish word is given a literal translation followed by the English equivalent. For each, identify the type of compound.

1.	[bas-parmak]	head finger	thumb	_____
2.	[orta-ca]	middle epoch	Middle Ages	_____
3.	[deniz-alti]	sea underside	submarine	_____
4.	[bas-bakan]	head minister	Prime Minister	_____
5.	[on-ajak]	front leg	pioneer	_____

6. Isleta (a dialect of Southern Tiwa—New Mexico, USA)

1.	[temiban]	'I went'	4. [mimiay]	'he was going'
2.	[amiban]	'you went'	5. [tewanban]	'I came'
3.	[temiwe]	'I am going'	6. [tewanhi]	'I will come'

List the morphemes corresponding to the following English translations:

I	_____	present progressive	_____
you	_____	past progressive	_____
he	_____	past	_____
go	_____	future	_____
come	_____		

What type of affixes are the subject morphemes?

What type of affixes are the tense morphemes?

What is the order of morphemes in this language?

How would you say the following in this language?

he went	_____
I will go	_____
you were coming	_____

SOME HINTS. . .

1. The term 'progressive' refers to an ongoing action.

2. In English, the progressive is formed by adding the inflectional affix *-ing* to a verb and adding the present (*am, are, is*) or past tense (*was, were*) of the auxiliary verb 'be'. So *I am going* is present progressive, and *he was going* is past progressive.

3. The progressive may be formed differently in different languages, so don't expect to find all of the elements in the English glosses in Isleta.

4. Morphemes can have the same form but different meanings!

7. Isthmus Zapoteco (Mexico)   Note: [ñ] is a palatal nasal

1. [ñee]   'foot'
2. [kañee]   'feet'
3. [ñeebe]   'his foot'
4. [kañeebe]   'his feet'
5. [ñeeluʔ]   'your foot'
6. [kañeetu]   'your (pl) feet'
7. [kañeedu]   'our feet'
8. [kazigi]   'chins'
9. [zigibe]   'his chin'
10. [zigiluʔ]   'your chin'
11. [kazigitu]   'your (pl) chins'

12. [kazigidu]   'our chins'
13. [zike]   'shoulder'
14. [zikebe]   'his shoulder'
15. [kazikeluʔ]   'your shoulders'
16. [diaga]   'ear'
17. [kadiagatu]   'your (pl) ears'
18. [kadiagadu]   'our ears'
19. [bisozedu]   'our father'
20. [bisozetu]   'your (pl) father'
21. [kabisozetu]   'your (pl) fathers'

List the morphemes of Isthmus Zapoteco that correspond to each of the following words:

foot   _____   your   _____

shoulder   _____   our   _____

father   _____   his   _____

chin   _____   plural   _____

ear   _____

your (pl)   _____

What is the order of morphemes in Isthmus Zapoteco in terms of nouns, possessive determiners, and plural?

TWO REMINDERS!

1. An affix is an infix only when it is inserted inside a morpheme.
2. Don't forget to use a hyphen to indicate that a morpheme is bound (i.e., an affix, either a prefix, suffix, or infix). Root words do not need a hyphen.

8. Fore (Papua New Guinea)

1. [natuwi]	'I ate yesterday.'	8. [natuni]	'We ate yesterday.'
2. [nagasuwi]	'I ate today.'	9. [nagasuni]	'We ate today.'
3. [nakuwi]	'I will eat.'	10. [nagasusi]	'We (dual) ate today.'
4. [nataːni]	'You ate yesterday.'	11. [nakuni]	'We will eat.'
5. [nataːnaw]	'You ate yesterday?'	12. [nakusi]	'We (dual) will eat.'
6. [nakiyi]	'He will eat.'	13. [nataːwi]	'They ate yesterday.'
7. [nakiyaw]	'He will eat?'	14. [nataːsi]	'They (dual) ate yesterday.'

- Don't forget that what are inflectional affixes in many languages can be translated into separate words in English.

- In the glosses, 'yesterday', 'today', and 'tomorrow' are translations of the English past, present, and future tenses, respectively.

Identify the Fore morphemes that correspond to the following English words, as well as the question and statement markers:

I	_____	eat	_____
he	_____	yesterday	_____
we	_____	today	_____
they	_____	will	_____
we (dual)	_____	question	_____
they (dual)	_____	statement	_____

Describe the order of the morphemes in terms of personal pronouns, question/statement markers, verbs, and adverbs.

Give the Fore words for the following:

He ate yesterday?   _____

They (dual) will eat?   _____

They ate today.   _____

MORPHOPHONEMICS

Morphemes do not always have the same form. Allomorphs are the different forms of a morpheme. Consider the following English example.

⇒ **The Allomorphs...** The English plural morpheme *-s* has three different phonetic forms:

> [-s] in words like *cats*
> [-z] in words like *dogs*
> [-əz] in words like *dishes*

⇒ **The Conditioning Environment...** Which phonetic form is realized depends on the phonological characteristics of the final segment in the preceding word:

> [-s] occurs after a base ending in a voiceless consonant that is not strident.
> [-z] occurs after a base ending in a voiced consonant that is not strident.
> [-əz] occurs after a base ending in a strident consonant.

The specific environment in which the different allomorphs occur is often referred to as the distribution of the allomorphs. This interaction between morphology and phonology is called **morphophonemics**.

For more information on morphophonemics, visit www.pearsoncanada.ca/ogrady and select Chapter 4, Morphophonemics.

Practice!   Identify morphemes in the following data from Luiseño. Watch out for allomorphs in the plural morpheme.

Luiseño (Southern California)

1.	[nokaamay]	'my son'	13.	[pokaamay]	'his son'
2.	[ʔoki]	'your house'	14.	[poki]	'his house'
3.	[potaanat]	'his blanket'	15.	[notaanat]	'my blanket'
4.	[ʔohuukapi]	'your pipe'	16.	[pohuukapi]	'his pipe'
5.	[ʔotaanat]	'your blanket'	17.	[nohuukapi]	'my pipe'
6.	[noki]	'my house'	18.	[ʔokaamay]	'your son'
7.	[ʔokim]	'your houses'	19.	[pompeewum]	'their wives'
8.	[nokaamayum]	'my sons'	20.	[camhuukapim]	'our pipes'
9.	[popeew]	'his wife'	21.	[ʔotaanatum]	'your blankets'
10.	[ʔopeew]	'your wife'	22.	[pomkaamay]	'their son'
11.	[camtaanat]	'our blanket'	23.	[campeewum]	'our wives'
12.	[camhuukapi]	'our pipe'	24.	[pomkim]	'their houses'

List the Luiseño morphemes that correspond to the following English words:

son   _____   my   _____

house   _____   his   _____

blanket   _____   your   _____

wife   _____   their   _____

pipe   _____   our   _____

What are the two allomorphs of the Luiseño plural marker?

_____

State the conditioning environment that determines which allomorph occurs. Be very general!

a. _____

b. _____

REVIEW! REVIEW! Make sure you know how to do the following:

- define morphological terms
- divide a word into its morphemes
- assign lexical categories
- build word trees
- identify inflection and derivation
- construct compound words
- recognize endocentric and exocentric compounds
- recognize morphological processes used to build words
- do morphological analysis
- identify morphemes and morphological processes in unfamiliar languages
- find allomorphs

QUESTIONS? PROBLEMS? DIFFICULTIES?

_____

_____

_____

_____

_____

_____

_____

_____

_____

_____

_____

_____

CHAPTER 5. SYNTAX:
THE ANALYSIS OF SENTENCE STRUCTURE

Syntax is the study of how speakers of a language combine words into phrases and phrases into grammatical sentences in order to convey any and all thoughts. Important topics and concepts found in this chapter include the following:

1. Lexical and non-lexical categories
2. Phrases
3. Phrase structure and phrase structure tests
4. Sentences
5. Complement clauses
6. Complement options
7. Merge and Move
8. *Yes/no* and *wh* questions
9. Deep and surface structure
10. Verb Raising
11. Relative clauses, modifiers, and passives
12. VP Internal Subjects

WORDS

Words are an important part of a language's grammar. Words can be grouped together into a small number of syntactic categories (parts of speech).

There are two types of syntactic categories: lexical and non-lexical. Some of the major characteristics of each include the following:

Lexical:
- words that have meaning
- words that can be inflected
- includes nouns (N), verbs (V), adjectives (A), prepositions (P), and adverbs (Adv)

Non-Lexical:
- words whose meaning is harder to define
- words that have a grammatical function
- includes determiners (Det), auxiliary verbs (Aux), conjunctions (Con), and degree words (Deg)

See table 5.1 on p. 141 of the text for some examples of lexical (content) and non-lexical (function) words.

The lexical category to which a word belongs can be determined by examining (1) its meaning, (2) the type of inflectional affixes that it can take, and (3) the non-lexical category words with which it can co-occur. Words can often belong to more than one category, so you also need to pay close attention to how the word is being used in a sentence.

Practice! Each sentence below contains some underlined words. Identify the category of each underlined word. Note that the underlined word can be either lexical or non-lexical.

1. Pamela's heart <u>beat</u> <u>really</u> fast and her hands trembled as she <u>listened</u> to <u>the</u> <u>intermittent</u> <u>knocking</u> on the front <u>door</u> of her shanty located <u>near</u> the railroad <u>tracks</u> <u>beside</u> a hobo jungle, and she <u>thought</u>, "That's a <u>bum</u> rap, if ever I <u>heard</u> one."

2. The railroad <u>agent</u> told the <u>Navajo</u>, "The <u>coming</u> of the Iron Horse <u>may</u> <u>bring</u> great <u>prosperity</u> to your people."

3. "The <u>leg</u>, he is <u>fractured</u>," he <u>said</u> <u>in</u> broken English.

4. The Great Barrier Reef is 900 miles <u>long</u>, <u>and</u> Wilmer Chanti, the <u>great</u> explorer, <u>says</u> it <u>could</u> <u>be</u> <u>circumnavigated</u> in 40 days.

5. When I <u>turned</u> the <u>key</u> to open <u>my</u> lab door, I thought that it <u>would</u> be a <u>very</u> <u>dull</u> day, until I noticed that my little cucaracha <u>had</u> <u>flopped</u> over on <u>his</u> back and <u>was</u> waving his <u>little</u> legs <u>frantically</u>, and I <u>realized</u> that someone had <u>bugged</u> my bug.

6. It was <u>a</u> <u>rather</u> dark, <u>but</u> calm night, its <u>green</u> clarity <u>diluted</u> by my roommates, who, as usual, <u>were</u> <u>making</u> <u>cutting</u> remarks as they drank <u>that</u> bottle <u>of</u> old Scotch.

7. "I <u>hate</u> <u>pineapples</u>," said Tom <u>dolefully</u>.

8. Here's how to make a <u>fortune</u>. <u>Buy</u> 50 female <u>pigs</u> and 50 male deer. Then you <u>will</u> have a hundred sows and bucks.

Reminder! There are two types of auxiliary verbs: modal and non-modal. Modal auxiliary verbs include *will, would, can, could, may, must, should, might*. Non-modal auxiliary verbs include all the different forms of *be* (*am, are, is, was, were, been, being*) and *have* (*has, had*).

Go back over the above exercise, and for any word that you identified as an auxiliary verb, determine if it is a modal or non-modal auxiliary verb.

PHRASES

Words are grouped together to form phrases. There are three important components to a phrase.

⇒ **Heads.** A phrase must have a head. The head of a phrase is the obligatory nucleus around which the phrase is built. Four lexical categories usually function as the head of a phrase, thereby allowing for four types of phrases:

1. **NP** – noun phrase
2. **AP** – adjective phrase
3. **VP** – verb phrase
4. **PP** – prepositional phrase

The head of a noun phrase, of course, is a noun; the head of an adjective phrase, an adjective; the head of a verb phrase, a verb; and the head of a prepositional phrase, a preposition.

⇒ **Specifiers.** A phrase can optionally contain a specifier. Specifiers occur at the edge of a phrase. In English, specifiers occur before the head, thus indicating the beginning of a phrase. There are three types of specifiers.

1. Determiners
   – specify a noun
   e.g., *the, a, these, that*

2. Preverbal Adverbs
   – specify a verb
   e.g., *always, often, never*

3. Degree words
   – specify an adjective or a preposition
   e.g., *very, quite, really*

⇒ **Complements.** A phrase can also optionally contain a complement. Complements provide information about entities and locations implied by the meaning of the head of the phrase. In English, complements come after the head, thus marking the end of a phrase. Complements are always phrases.

A phrase can consist of a single word or many words. If a phrase consists of a single word, that word must be the head of the phrase. If a phrase consists of a number of words, the phrase may consist of:

- a specifier and a head;
- a head and a complement; or
- a specifier, a head, and a complement.

Below are some possibilities for each type of phrase.

1. Noun Phrase (NP)

a. *mud*   – contains only the head noun (*mud*)

b. *the mud*   – contains a specifier (*the*) and the head noun (*mud*)

c. *mud*   – contains the head noun (*mud*) and a complement
    on the floor   prepositional phrase (*on the floor*)

d. *the mud*   – contains a specifier (*the*), the head noun (*mud*),
    on the floor   and a complement prepositional phrase (*on the floor*)

The prepositional phrase *on the floor* consists of a head preposition (*on*) and a complement noun phrase (*the floor*). The noun phrase *the floor* then consists of a specifier (*the*) and a head noun (*floor*).

In addition to the noun phrases shown above, noun phrases can also contain pronouns (e.g., *I, you, them*) and proper nouns (i.e., names). When these are used to indicate possession, they are called possessive noun phrases. Possessive noun phrases function as specifiers for nouns. Some examples are shown below.

a. *Bob's*   – contains a specifier (*Bob's*) and a head noun
    coat   (*coat*)

b. *his*   – contains a specifier (*his*) and a head noun (*coat*)
    coat

c. *the boy's*   – contains a specifier (*the boy's*) and a head noun
    coat   (*coat*)

In (a) and (b), the specifier is a noun phrase consisting only of the head noun (*Bob's* in (a) and *his* in (b)), while in (c) the specifier noun phrase *the boy's* consists of a specifier (*the*) and a head noun (*boy's*).

2. Adjective Phrase (AP)

a. *happy*   – contains only the head adjective (*happy*)

b. *very happy*   – contains a specifier (*very*) and the head adjective (*happy*)

c. *happy with*   – contains the head adjective (*happy*) and a complement
    the results   prepositional phrase (*with the results*)

d. *very happy*   – contains a specifier (*very*), the head adjective (*happy*),
    with the results and a complement prepositional phrase (*with the results*)

3. Verb Phrase (VP)

a. *sings*   – contains only the head verb (*sings*)

b. *often sings*   – contains a specifier (*often*) and the head verb (*sings*)

c. *sings a song*   – contains the head verb (*sings*) and a complement noun phrase (*a song*)

d. *often sings*   – contains a specifier (*often*), the head verb (*sings*), and a
    a song   a complement noun phrase (*a song*)

The complement noun phrase *a song* consists of a specifier (*a*) and a head noun (*song*).

4. Prepositional Phrase (PP)

a. *in the car*   – contains the head preposition (*in*) and a complement noun phrase (*the car*)

b. *almost in*   – contains a specifier (*almost*), the head preposition (*in*),
    the car   and a complement noun phrase (*the car*)

The complement noun phrase *the car* contains a specifier (*the*) and a head noun (*car*).

Think. . . How are prepositional phrases different from the other types of phrases discussed? Do they require a complement? Is this complement always the same?

Now. . . Think of an example of each of the following:

⇒ a noun phrase containing a specifier, a head, and a complement. Then make the specifier a possessive noun phrase.
⇒ an adjective phrase containing a specifier and a head adjective
⇒ a verb phrase containing a head verb and a complement
⇒ a prepositional phrase containing a head preposition and a complement

---

REMINDER! REMINDER!

Specifiers can help determine the category to which a word belongs. This is because the type of specifier found in a phrase depends on the category of the head. So, if a word can occur with a determiner, it is a noun; if it can occur with an adverb, it is a verb; and if it can occur with a degree word, it is an adjective.

Practice!

For each of the following phrases, determine the head of the phrase, the specifier, and the complement. Remember that every phrase must have a head, but that specifiers and complements are optional! The first is done for you.

	SPECIFIER	**HEAD**	**COMPLEMENT**
the rat	the	rat	none
George			
in the barn			
really mean			
worked			
worked at the station			
extremely boring			
that house on the corner			
never walks to the park			
very small			
in the room			
awfully cute			
seldom smiles			
swept the floor			
the poem about love			
pancakes			

Now. . . Go back and determine the type of each phrase. Remember: the lexical category of the head determines the type of phrase. If you're having trouble identifying the lexical category of the head, refer to pp. 140 to 143 of the text.

PHRASE STRUCTURE TESTS

A number of tests can be done to determine whether a group of words is a phrase. Three frequently used tests are the Substitution Test, the Movement Test, and the Coordination Test. Be careful, though: not every test works for every phrase.

Substitution Test

The Substitution Test states that a group of words is a phrase if you can substitute words such as *they*, *there*, or *do so*, and still be grammatical. The word used as a substitute also tells you the type of phrase you have.

NP: A noun phrase can be substituted with a pronoun:
e.g.,   **The boys** played in the mud. **They** played in the mud.
(they = the boys)

VP: A verb phrase can be substituted with *do so*:
e.g.,   The girls will **play in the mud**, if the boys **do so**.
(do so = play in the mud)

PP: A prepositional phrase can often be substituted with *there*:
e.g.,   The girls played **in the mud** and the boys played **there** too
(there = in the mud)

Movement Test

The Movement Test states that a group of words is a phrase if it can be moved to another position in the sentence and still be grammatical.

e.g.,   The children bought candy **at the store**. ⟶
At the store, the children bought candy.

Coordination Test

According to this test, a group of words is a phrase if it can be joined to another group of words using a conjunction (*and, but, or*) and still be grammatical.

e.g.,   The children **bought candy** and **left the store**.
– two verb phrases joined with the conjunction *and*

Try This!

1. Apply the Substitution Test to determine which of the bracketed sequences of words in the following sentences are phrases.

   a. [Juanita and Juan] arrived [in San Juan] [on Epiphany].
   b. The cabbage [rolls were] salty.
   c. They moved [the desk with the wooden top].
   d. Little Andrew swallowed [all the pills].
   e. The polar bears [were swimming across] the lake.

2. Apply the Movement Test to determine which of the bracketed sequences in the following sentences are phrases.

   a. The [army was surrounded] by the enemy.
   b. Leona likes [Viennese waltzes and Argentinian tangos].
   c. Jean ate his lunch [in the revolving restaurant].
   d. Eat, drink, and [be merry for] today will become yesterday.

3. Use a conjunction (*and, but, or*) to join each of the following phrases with a phrase of the same type. You might want to first use the Substitution Test to determine the type of phrase!

   a. the new desk
   b. assembled the new desk
   c. new
   d. in a hole
   e. rather huge
   f. worked on a movie
   g. beside the fence
   h. really lovely
   i. talked to the girls
   j. a dentist

PHRASE STRUCTURE TREES

Specifiers, heads, and complements are arranged using the X' (X-bar) schema, in which X stands for any head.

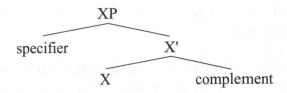

The representation of a phrase using the above schema is often referred to as a tree diagram.

⇒ Some things to remember about tree diagrams:

- All phrases have a head (X).
- The X' level is usually omitted from the tree diagram if there is no specifier and/or complement.
- If there is a specifier and a complement, specifiers are always attached higher (XP) in the tree than are complements (X').

⇒ See figures 5.4 to 5.6 on p. 145 of the text for examples of tree diagrams of phrases containing heads, specifiers, and complements; specifiers and heads; and heads and complements. Figures 5.7 and 5.8 on p. 146 of the text illustrate tree diagrams of noun phrases without specifiers or complements, and of noun phrases functioning as specifiers.

Exercise!   Draw tree diagrams for each of the following phrases. Remember that specifiers come before the head, and complements come after the head. You will not always need to include the X' level.

1. the rat	8. many trucks	15. the poem about love
2. George	9. the house on the corner	16. silly
3. really mean	10. very small	17. read your poem
4. ran	11. under the stove	18. really happy with him
5. in the barn	12. seldom smiles	
6. ran into the shed	13. swept the floor	19. usually eats lunch
7. rather boring	14. George's hand	20. looks good

QUICK REMINDER!

Use the Substitution Test to help you determine the type of phrase you are dealing with. Remember: the Substitution Test not only tells you if a group of words is or is not a phrase; it can also tell you the type of phrase you have. Refer back to p. 107 in this guide for more information.

SENTENCES

A sentence is the largest unit of syntactic analysis. Sentences have the same structure as do phrases in that they consist of a specifier, head, and complement.

⇒ **NP.** The noun phrase is typically referred to as the subject. The subject is the specifier of T. Every T will have a specifier.

⇒ **T (Tense).** This is the obligatory head of the sentence and is used to refer to tense. There are two possibilities for T: +pst (past) and -pst (non-past); +pst is used for sentences in the past tense, and -pst is used for sentences in either the present or future tense.

Modal auxiliaries occur under T. This is because modals have an inherent tense (usually non-past), so T is a natural place for them to occur. T, then, has two possibilities:

- tense (either +pst or -pst) *or*
- a modal auxiliary (+/-pst is not necessary, as tense is inherent in the modal auxiliary)

⇒ **VP.** The verb phrase is the complement of T. Every T will have a verb phrase.

Sentences, like phrases, are built according to the X' schema. Since T is the head of a sentence, TP is used to represent the sentential phrase.

Below are two examples of diagrammed sentences, the first without a modal auxiliary and the second with a modal auxiliary. For another example of each possibility, see figures 5.10 and 5.11 on pp. 147 and 148 of the text.

(1) *The children saw a deer.*

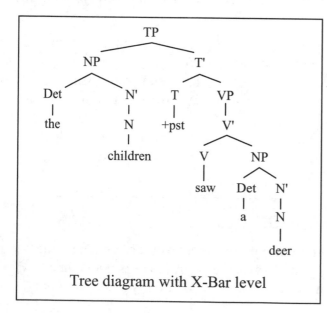

Tree diagram with X-Bar level

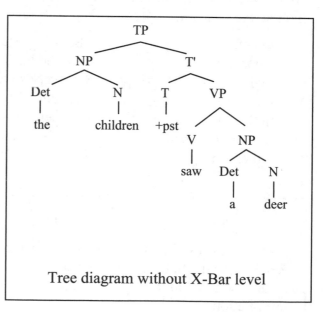

Tree diagram without X-Bar level

(2) *The children will see a deer.*

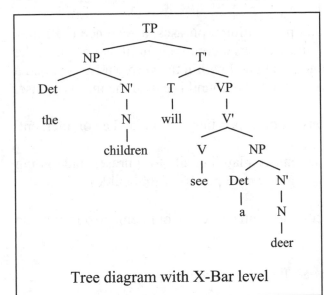

Tree diagram with X-Bar level

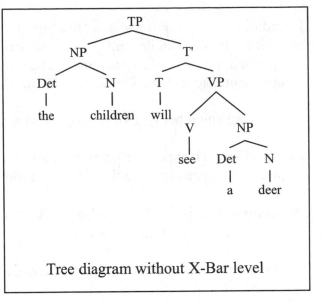

Tree diagram without X-Bar level

Practice! Draw a tree diagram for each of the following sentences.

1. Abner should conceal the document.
2. They usually watch the sunset.
3. A penguin walked into the room.
4. Carla might sell her car.
5. The air smells really fresh.
6. Grandparents often live in condominiums.
7. That house across the street sold.
8. Those monsters never hide under Daniel's bed.
9. Gerard may seem tired of studying.
10. Dogs will sometimes run in the park.

Remember. . . A noun phrase (NP), a prepositional phrase (PP), or an adjective phrase (AP) are all potential complements of a verb. The particular complement that occurs depends on the verb. Some verbs can take more than one complement! See figure 5.13 on p. 151 of the text for an example.

COMPLEMENT CLAUSES

In addition to noun phrases, adjective phrases, and prepositional phrases, a sentence (TP) may also function as a complement. When a sentence functions as a complement, it can occur in the complement position of a verb phrase. The sentence contained within the verb phrase is called a complement clause (CP). The sentence within which the CP is found is called the matrix clause.

A CP is like any other type of phrase in that it consists of a specifier, a head, and a complement.

⇒ **Specifier.** The specifier position of a CP functions as a landing site for phrases undergoing the Move operation (see the section on Move beginning on p. 116 of this guide).

⇒ **Complementizer.** The head of a CP is a complementizer (C). Complementizers include words such as *that*, *if*, and *whether*.

⇒ **TP.** The complement of a complementizer is a TP (i.e., a sentence).

Below is a tree diagram of the sentence *John thinks that Mary might sing*, which contains a CP inside the VP. See figure 5.15 on p. 153 of the text for another example. See table 5.9 on p. 153 of the text for examples of verbs that can have CP complements.

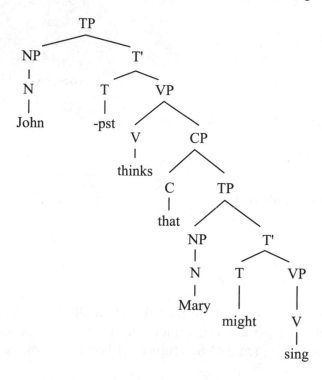

Think. . . Does the tense (either +pst or –pst) of the matrix clause have to be the same as that of the complement clause? Think of an example where they are the same and where they are different.

Practice! Practice! Draw a tree diagram for each of the following sentences.

1. Nancy hopes that Sean will become a pilot.
2. Kasey wondered whether aliens exist.
3. Sailors know that ships can sink at sea.
4. He thought that the plane would never land.

SOME HINTS FOR DRAWING PHRASE STRUCTURE TREES

1. Every sentence (TP) has the following structure.

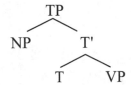

2. Every sentence contains T. Identify the tense of the sentence. Use +pst if a sentence is in the past tense, and -pst if the sentence is in either the present or future tense. If the sentence contains a modal auxiliary, this auxiliary occurs under T, and tense is not specified.

3. Every sentence has a verb. Identify the verb. Check if this verb has a specifier and/or a complement. Remember that the specifier of a verb is a preverbal adverb and marks the beginning of the phrase. If there is a complement, it can be either a phrase or a sentence.

   - If the complement is a phrase, identify the type of phrase and then diagram the phrase using the X' schema. Remember you can omit the intermediate (X-Bar) level.
   - If the complement is a sentence, it will begin with the following structure.

   Identify the complementizer. Since a CP contains a TP, you will also need to identify and diagram the NP, T, and VP for this embedded TP.

4. Every sentence has a subject NP. Identify the noun. Check if this noun has a specifier and/or a complement. Remember that the specifier of a noun is a determiner and that this determiner marks the beginning of this noun phrase. If there is a complement, it will be a prepositional phrase. Diagram this phrase using the X' schema. You can omit the intermediate (X-Bar) level.

   For more hints on drawing tree diagrams of phrases and sentences, see the Appendix to Chapter 5 on pp. 173 to 176 of the text.

MORE PRACTICE WITH SENTENCES

The following exercise contains many examples of sentences with and without complement clauses. Draw a tree diagram for each.

1. The repairman fixed the watch.

2. Neighbours can be unfriendly.

3. She never complains.

4. The train often leaves on time.

5. The castle fell into the sea.

6. The rabbit might eat those lilies.

7. Children are very curious.

8. Sally's friend lives in a house by the sea.

9. The secretary should mail the proposal.

10. Your soup tastes really great.

11. The rabbit may sometimes hide under the bridge.

12. Sandra is almost at the restaurant.

13. Those men on the shore saw a signal.

14. The doctor's team was quite correct in their diagnosis.

15. The driver of that car sped through many streets.

16. George hoped that Fred would win a car.

17. The salesman wondered if those customers might buy that sofa.

18. Kayleigh usually thinks that playing at home is fun.

19. The media reported that no candidate won the election.

20. The captain hoped that the tourists would perhaps see a whale.

MERGE

Merge is a syntactic operation that is responsible for building the phrase structure in a manner compatible with the X' schema. Essentially, Merge combines words together to make phrases, phrases to make sentences, and sentences to make larger sentences.

The following example illustrates how Merge operates.

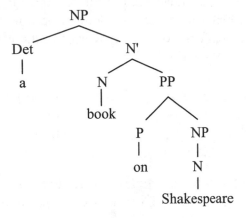

Merge created the above complex phrase by combining the noun phrase *Shakespeare* with the preposition *on* to create the prepositional phrase *on Shakespeare*. This phrase was then combined with the noun *book* and the specifier *a* to create the noun phrase *a book on Shakespeare*. Merge continues to operate in this way to create entire sentences.

Complement Options

In addition to using the X' schema, Merge must combine words into phrases and sentences in a manner consistent with the complement options of the individual words. Essentially, individual words in a sentence must occur with complements of the right type for the sentence to be grammatical. The complement(s) with which a word can occur are called its complement options. Information about a word's complement options is often referred to as subcategorization.

Think. . . Does the verb *throw* require a complement or can it occur without a complement? If it requires a complement, what type of complement is needed? If it is used without this complement or with a complement of a different type, is the resulting sentence grammatical or ungrammatical? What about the verb *become*? What type of complement does it require? What about the verb *arrive*? Does it require a complement? Which of the verbs *throw, become, arrive* is transitive? Which is intransitive? What is the structural difference between transitive and intransitive verbs?

Try This! Determine the complement options that the verbs listed below require. Do this by thinking of grammatical and ungrammatical sentences containing the verb.

- panic
- watch
- imagine

- write
- wonder
- play

Nouns, adjectives, and prepositions also have restrictions on the types of complements with which they can and cannot occur. Determine the complement options that the following words require. Start by identifying the lexical category of the word and then think of grammatical and ungrammatical sentences containing the word.

- pleasure
- with
- contribution

- intelligent
- out
- upset

See table 5.5 on p. 150 of the text for some examples of different verb complements in English. See tables 5.6, 5.7, and 5.8 on pp. 151 and 152 of the text for some examples of complement options for nouns, adjectives, and prepositions.

MOVE

Move is another syntactic operation. Move transports elements from one position in a sentence to another. This is all that a Move operation can do: Move cannot change the categories of words, nor can it eliminate any part of the structure.

There are three important points to remember about how Move operates.

⇒ **CP.** Move transports elements to positions within a CP. For this to occur, every TP must be found within a larger CP. This CP is a 'shell' that contains a TP.

Remember that C is the head of CP. The C in a CP shell contains information on whether the sentence is a question or a statement: if C contains +Q, the structure is a question, and if C contains -Q, it is a statement. It is the +Q that can trigger a Move operation. See figure 5.16 on p. 155 of the text for an example of a TP within a CP shell.

⇒ **Trace.** Moved elements leave behind a trace (*t*). A trace records (1) that a movement has occurred and (2) where in the structure the moved element originated. Leaving a trace is necessary, as Move cannot change the structure that Merge builds.

⇒ **Levels of Representation.** Two levels of representation result: deep and surface structure.

- Merge occurs first to build the syntactic structure. The structure that Merge generates is called the deep structure (D-structure).

- Move may then apply. The surface structure (S-structure) is the result of applying Move.

If a Move operation has taken place, then the deep and surface structures are not the same. If no Move operation takes place, then the deep and surface structures are the same.

Remember. . . A CP can also function as a complement clause, in which case it is embedded in a larger sentence. When a CP is embedded within a larger sentence, C contains a complementizer such as *that*, *if*, or *whether*. Refer to figure 5.15 on p. 153 of the text for an example of a sentence with an embedded CP.

QUESTIONS

Merge is responsible for building the structure of a sentence using both subcategorization information (i.e., complement options) and the X' schema. However, Merge cannot create all the structures of a language. Some structures require a second operation. Move transforms an existing structure (e.g., a statement) into another type of structure (e.g., a question) by transporting elements from one position in a sentence to another.

Move operates to create both *yes-no* and *wh* questions.

Yes-no Questions

⇒ *Yes-no* questions are so named because the response to such a question is usually 'yes' or 'no'.

Yes-no questions are formed by moving an auxiliary verb from its position in T to the complementizer position within a CP. This is informally called Inversion.

Inversion: Move T to the C position

e.g., Mary **will** sing → **Will** Mary *t* sing
       (D-structure)   (S-structure)

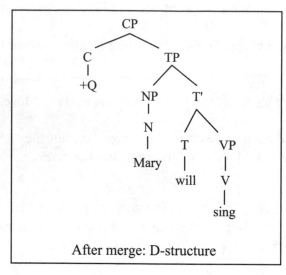

After merge: D-structure

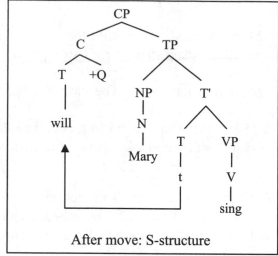

After move: S-structure

Wh Questions

⇒ *Wh* questions are so named because they begin with a *wh* word. These are question words that typically begin with a *wh*. *Who, what, which, where, when, why,* and *how* are all examples of *wh* words. See table 5.10 on p. 157 of the text for the syntactic categories of *wh*-words.

Wh questions are the result of *Wh* Movement. *Wh* Movement is normally followed by Inversion.

Wh Movement: Move a *wh* phrase to the specifier position under CP.

e.g., Mary **should** buy *what* → *What* **should** Mary *t* buy *t*
(D-structure)   (S-structure)

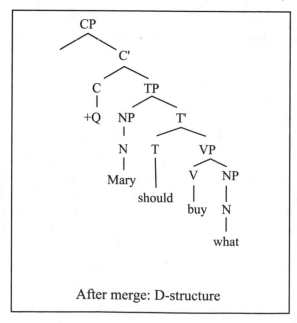

After merge: D-structure

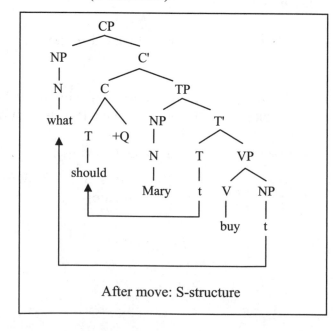

After move: S-structure

⇒ *Wh* Movement can

- move a *wh* phrase occurring as the complement of the verb (as in the previous example)

- move a *wh* phrase occurring in the subject position (as in the following example)

e.g.,   *Who* will sing → *Who t* will sing
(D-structure)   (S-structure)

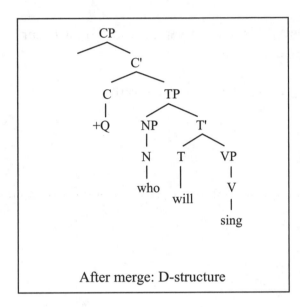

After merge: D-structure

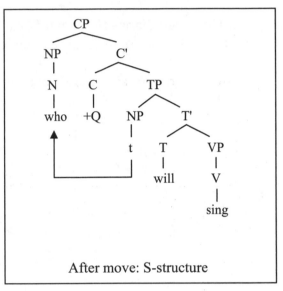

After move: S-structure

Think. . . Compare the above deep and surface structures. Is the word order in the deep and surface structure the same? Is Inversion required when *Wh* Movement moves a subject NP?

See figures 5.17 to 5.21 on pp. 155 to 160 of the text for more examples of tree diagrams of the deep and surface structures of sentences in which Inversion and *Wh* Movement have taken place.

Try This! For each of the following sentences, draw a tree diagram for both the deep and surface structures. On the surface structure, indicate with arrows the elements that have moved and where they have moved.

1. Will Paul enjoy the trip?
2. What could the spy uncover?
3. Who saw the lion?
4. Should Joan visit that museum?
5. Who might Leyna play with?

VERB RAISING

Move can also transport a verb to a new position in the sentence. This is often called Verb Raising. In English, Verb Raising affects auxiliary verbs.

⇒ Remember there are two types of auxiliary verbs:

- Modal auxiliaries (e.g., *will, could, should, would,* etc.) occur in T and are not specified for either + pst or -pst.

- Non-modal auxiliaries (*have* and *be*) are a special type of verb. As such, they occur in V and they take a verb phrase as a complement.

Below is a tree diagram of a sentence containing a non-modal auxiliary verb.

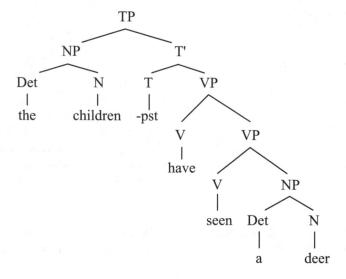

Think. . . A sentence can have more than one auxiliary. For example, the sentence *The choir has been singing many songs* contains two non-modal auxiliaries. How would you diagram the verb phrase of this sentence? What about the sentence *The choir will be singing more songs,* which contains both a modal and a non-modal auxiliary? How would you diagram the verb phrase for this sentence?

Remember. . . Non-modal auxiliaries can also occur as the only verb in the sentence. (e.g., *Mary is happy,* or *John has a cat*). They still occur in V, but they take a noun phrase, adjective phrase, or prepositional phrase rather than a verb phrase as a complement.

⇒ Both modal and non-modal auxiliaries can be inverted when forming a *yes-no* question:

- Modal auxiliaries occur in T and are moved from T to C using Inversion.

- Non-modal auxiliaries occur in V. Before moving from T to C, they must first be moved from V to T. The move from V to T is called Verb Raising.

Verb Raising: Move V to T.

e.g.,   Mary **is** leaving → Mary **is** *t* leaving → **is** Mary **t** *t* leaving
        (D-structure)   (S-structure)

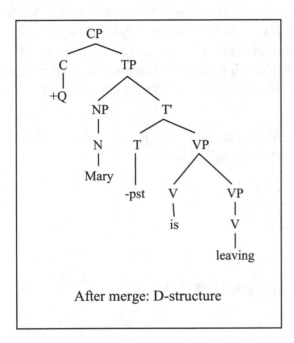

After merge: D-structure

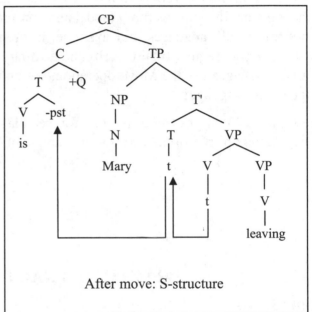

After move: S-structure

Think! Verb Raising can also occur during the formation of *wh* questions.

E.g., Sylvia **was** thinking *what* → *What* Sylvia **was** thinking *t* →

What Sylvia **was** *t* thinking *t* → *What* **was** Sylvia *t* *t* thinking *t*

Try drawing a tree diagram of both the deep structure and surface structure for the above sentence. Indicate with arrows all of the movements. Do this on the surface structure.

Does Verb Raising take place if *Wh* Movement moves a subject NP, as in the sentence *Who has been eating the cake?* Why or why not? Draw a tree diagram of both the deep structure and surface structure for the above sentence. Indicate with arrows all of the movements. Do this on the surface structure.

Try This!   For each of the following sentences, draw a tree diagram of both the deep and surface structures.

1. Had the elves washed in the tub?
2. Are the neighbours moving?
3. What was Sally painting?
4. Which restaurant is the city closing?

Variation

Verb Raising is a good example of the variation that occurs across languages. In English, only auxiliary (non-modal) verbs can move to T; regular (main) verbs cannot move. What this means is that only auxiliary verbs (both modal and non-modal) can be inverted to create questions. This is not true of all languages. For example, in French, any type of verb can move into T. This means that both regular (main) verbs and auxiliary verbs can be inverted in French. The idea is that all languages use the Move operation, but how this operation is instantiated can vary from language to language!

See figure 5.23 on pp. 163 of the text for tree diagrams illustrating Verb Raising in French and figure 5.26 on p. 165 of the text for an example of Verb Raising in English.

PRACTICE! PRACTICE! PRACTICE!

Some Hints

You need to be able to determine the deep structure for any sentence you are given, and to do so, you need to be able to identify any of the movements that have occurred. Remember, Inversion, *Wh* Movement, and Verb Raising are all applications of the Move operation.

On the next page are some clues to help you identify which movements have occurred and to put surface structure sentences back into their deep structure. Remember: You may also have to construct a tree diagram of the deep and surface structures.

You See:	You Think:	You Do:
A modal auxiliary verb before the subject	Inversion has taken place.	Put the modal auxiliary back into its deep structure position (T).
A non-modal auxiliary verb before the subject	Inversion has taken place. Verb Raising has taken place.	Put the non-modal auxiliary back into its deep structure position (V).
A *wh* word or phrase	*Wh* Movement has taken place.	Examine each verb in the sentence. Determine if a verb is missing either a subject or an object. Put the *wh* word or phrase into that position.

See the Appendix to Chapter 5 on pp. 175 to 176 of the text for more hints on how to analyze sentences involving the Move operation.

Some Reminders

- You are trying to determine which elements have already been moved; therefore, you must **never** move any additional words or phrases!
- No movements may have occurred, only one movement may have occurred, or more than one movement may have occurred. To find the deep structure, you need to find all instances of Move. Remember the deep structure is the result of Merge and therefore follows the phrase structure rules of the language.
- Include a trace (t) for every movement.

Now. . . Draw a tree diagram of both the deep and surface structures for each of the following sentences. Identify any movements that have occurred to derive the surface structure. Be careful: for some sentences, the deep structure and surface structure will be the same.

1. Can the clown amuse that boy?
2. Which coat should Hilary wear?
3. Who broke my lamp?
4. Margo dreamt that Frances flew to England.
5. Has the player left the team?

6. What was Joanne eating?

7. Could the vandals destroy the billboard?

8. Christopher hopes that he has discovered the treasure.

9. Who might these clothes fit?

10. Were the maids cleaning the house?

11. Will the winner be claiming the prize?

12. What might Mary's sister want?

13. The jury believed that the prisoner was guilty.

14. Who prepared the meal?

15. Colin was wondering whether George would order pizza.

MORE SYNTACTIC STRUCTURES

Some other syntactic structures include modifiers, relative clauses, passives, and VP internal subjects. Each of these structures builds on the basic syntactic system (i.e., Merge and Move) for forming sentences.

Modifiers

Modifiers are words and phrases that denote properties of heads. There are two main types of modifiers.

⇒ Adjective phrases modify nouns in that they indicate a property of the noun.

E.g., A **very cold** wind is blowing.

⇒ Adverb phrases modify verbs in that they can provide information on the manner (for example) of the verb.

E.g., The ballerina danced **gracefully**.

Modifiers attach at the X-Bar (intermediate) level, as the tree diagrams on the next page illustrate. See figure 5.27 on p. 166 of the text for some more examples of diagrams of noun and verb phrases containing modifiers.

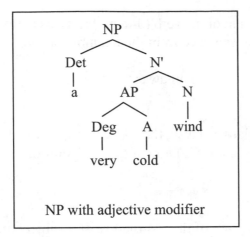

NP with adjective modifier

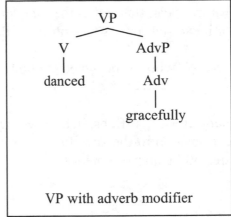

VP with adverb modifier

Relative Clauses

A relative clause is a special type of CP that modifies nouns; that is, it is a clause that provides more information about a noun. A relative clause occurs after the noun that it modifies. A relative clause is like a *wh* question in two ways:

⇒ It begins with a *wh* word (e.g., *who* or *which*) called a relative pronoun.

    e.g.,   The house [**which** Jerry designed]$_{CP}$ won an award.

⇒ The *wh* word occurs within the sentence and is moved to the specifier position of C, leaving a trace behind. This is *Wh* Movement.

    e.g.,   The house [**which** Jerry designed *t*]$_{CP}$ won an award.

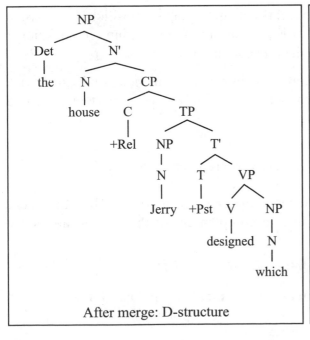

After merge: D-structure

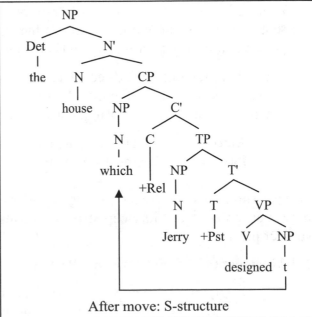

After move: S-structure

⇒ The *wh* word can start out as the complement of the verb (direct object), as in the above example, or it can start out as the subject of the sentence as in the example below.

e.g.,   Jerry [**who**   t   designed the house]CP won an award.

As with subject *wh*-questions, in a subject relative clause, the *wh*-word is assumed to move from the subject position to the specifier position under C. Draw a tree diagram of both the D- and S-structures of the above sentence.

See figure 5.30 on p. 168 of the text for a diagram of the S-structure of a subject relative clause. See figures 5.28 and 5.29 on pp. 167 and 168 of the text for another example of a tree diagram of the deep and surface structures of an object relative clause.

Think. . . The presence of +Q in C triggers *Wh* Movement during the formation of *wh* questions. What triggers *Wh* Movement during the formation of relative clauses?

Passives

A sentence may be either active or passive. Active and passive sentences differ in the following ways:

⇒ In an active sentence, the agent (doer of the action) occurs in the subject position. In a passive sentence, this agent is often absent. If the agent is present, it is found within a prepositional phrase that occurs after the verb and contains the preposition *by*.

⇒ In a passive sentence, the direct object of the corresponding active sentence usually functions as the subject of the sentence. Verbs that cannot occur with a direct object in an active sentence can also not occur in passive sentences.

e.g., **Active:**   The chef prepared the meal.
       Passive: The meal was prepared. The meal was prepared by the chef.

Passive sentences are formed using NP Movement, another type of Move. NP Movement moves an object from its deep structure position as a complement of the verb to an empty subject position.

NP Movement: Move an NP into the specifer position under TP

e.g., was prepared **the meal** → **the meal** was prepared **t**
         (D-structure)   (S-structure)

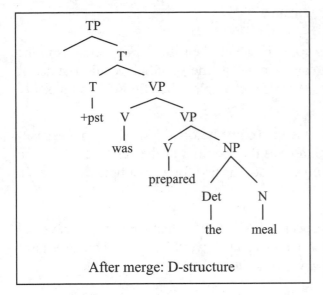

After merge: D-structure

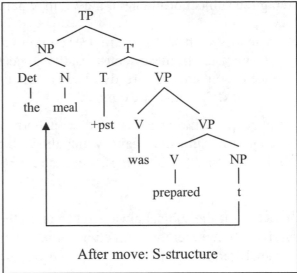

After move: S-structure

See figures 5.31 and 5.32 on pp. 169 to 170 of the text for another example of a tree diagram of the D-structure and S-structure of a passive sentence.

VP Internal Subjects

In a passive sentence, the subject starts out as the complement of a verb and moves to the subject position via NP movement. This may also be true for active sentences: the subject starts out in the specifier position under VP and moves to the specifier position under TP using NP movement. The following example illustrates this movement.

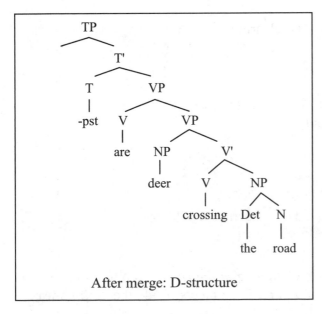

After merge: D-structure

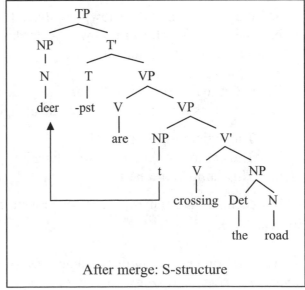

After merge: S-structure

Having the subject originate in the VP may help explain:

⇒ Sentences such as *There are deer crossing the road,* in which the subject *deer* remains in the verb phrase. In these sentences, the subject cannot move to the specifier position under T, since this position is already filled: it contains *there* (for example). See figure 5.35 on p. 171 of the text for another example.

⇒ Languages whose basic word order pattern has the verb come before the subject. In these languages, the subject remains within the verb phrase (as the specifier of the verb), and the verb raises to tense (verb raising). See figure 5.36 on p. 172 of the text for an example from Welsh.

Think. . . If the subject always starts out as the specifier of the verb, what happens to preverbal adverbs? Remember these function as the specifer of a verb. How would preverbal adverbs have to be analyzed in a sentence such as *The deer always cross the road*?

Exercise! The following exercises will give you some practice with identifying relative clauses, modifiers, and passives.

1. Each of the following sentences contains at least one modifier. Identify all the modifiers. For each modifier, determine if it is modifying a noun or a verb. Identify the noun or verb that is being modified.

    a. The musicians often play music loudly.
    b. The really awful movie won top prize.
    c. The undercover police car drove away speedily.

2. Each of the following phrases contains a relative clause. Identify the relative clause and determine its deep structure.

    a. the roads which the snowplows have finished clearing
    b. the roads which were plowed yesterday
    c. the trucks which the city uses

3. Decide if each of the following sentences is active or passive. Remember: a passive sentence does not necessarily include an agent.

    a. Those tigers were trained.
    b. The company should make a donation.
    c. That lamp could be fixed.

    For each passive sentence, determine what the deep structure would be.

Now. . . try diagramming the sentences *Dogs are swimming in the river, There are dogs swimming in the river,* and *Dogs sometimes swim in the river* with subjects inside the verb phrase.

REVIEW! REVIEW! If you can do the following, then you've conquered syntax:

- describe the differences between lexical and non-lexical categories
- assign words to their syntactic category
- determine if a group of words is or is not a phrase
- identify and diagram phrases
- diagram sentences, including those with complement clauses
- determine complement options
- understand the Merge and Move operations
- spot *yes-no* and *wh* questions
- spot Inversion, *Wh* Movement, and Verb Raising
- find the deep structure of a sentence
- recognize relative clauses, modifiers, and passives
- understand how NP movement works in both passives and VP internal subjects

QUESTIONS? PROBLEMS? DIFFICULTIES?

CHAPTER 6. SEMANTICS:
THE ANALYSIS OF MEANING

Semantics is the study of meaning in human language. Meaning refers, very generally, to the content of an utterance.

Important concepts and topics in this chapter include the following:

1. Semantic relations
2. Meaning
3. Concepts
4. Constructional Meaning
5. Lexicalization and Grammaticalization
6. Lexical and structural ambiguity
7. Thematic roles
8. Pronoun interpretation
9. Role of pragmatics
10. Conversation

SEMANTIC RELATIONS

Determining the semantic relations that exist between words, phrases, and sentences constitutes one of the basic notions used in evaluating meaning.

⇒ **Between words**

- Synonymy: Words that have similar meanings
- Antonymy: Words that have opposite meanings
- Polysemy: One word with two or more related meanings
- Homophony: Two words with the same pronunciation, but different meanings

See tables 6.1 to 6.4 on pp. 182 and 183 of the text for some English examples of the above relations.

Think. . . Polysemy and homophony can result in lexical ambiguity—a single form that has two or more meanings. Try and think of some examples. Keep in mind. . .

- Different words with the same spelling are called homographs.
- Homophones may or may not have the same spelling.
- Homographs, therefore, may or may not be homophones.

⇒ **Between sentences**

- • Paraphrase: Two sentences that have very similar meanings
    - e.g.,   The cat ate the mouse.
      The mouse was eaten by the cat.
- • Entailment: Two sentences in which the truth of the first implies the truth of the second, but the truth of the second does not necessarily imply the truth of the first
    - e.g.,   George killed the burglar.
      The burglar is dead.
- • Contradiction: Two sentences such that if one is true, then the second must be false
    - e.g.,   George is rich.
      George is a pauper.

Try This! For each of the following, identify the relation that exists between either the words or the sentences. The first is done for you.

1. test
   exam   synonyms _____

2. Mary sang a solo.
   A solo was sung by Mary.   _____

3. bug (insect)
   bug (microphone)   _____

4. Sam is a widower.
   Sam's wife is alive.   _____

5. The bear attacked a camper.
   The camper is injured.   _____

6. parent
   offspring   _____

7. George gave Sally the book.
   George gave the book to Sally.   _____

8. Nancy brought salmon for dinner.
   There is nothing to eat for dinner.   _____

9. hungry
   famished   _____

10. steak (a piece of meat)
    stake (a sharp piece of wood)   _____

MEANING

As native speakers of a language, we all know the meaning of a great many words in our language. It is actually difficult to determine the precise meaning of a word. Without using a dictionary, try and determine the meaning of the words *spring, bridge,* and *Hawaii*. Some of the theories of meaning outlined below might help.

⇒ **Connotation.** This theory states that the meaning of a word is simply the set of associations that the word evokes. Think about what connotations the words *spring, bridge,* and *Hawaii* evoke.

⇒ **Denotation.** This theory states that the meaning of a word is not the set of associations it evokes, but rather the entity to which it refers: that is, its denotation or referent. Think about what denotations the words *spring, bridge,* and *Hawaii* have.

⇒ **Extension and Intension.** This theory attempts to combine the first two. Extension refers to the referent of a word, and intension to the associations it evokes. Thus, the meaning of a word includes both its extension and its intension. What are the extensions and intensions of *spring*, *bridge*, and *Hawaii*?

⇒ **Componential Analysis.** This theory is based on the idea that meaning can be decomposed into smaller semantic units. These units of meaning are called features. Semantic features can be combined to group entities into classes. For example, the semantic features [+living, +human, -adult] give us the category of children. Think about how you might decompose the meaning of the words *spring*, *bridge*, and *Hawaii* into semantic features.

⇒ **Verb Meaning and Subcategorization.** Features of a verb's meaning can be relevant when it comes to choosing the phrases to go along with that verb to form a verb phrase. Componential analysis helps us to capture such features.

Think. . . What difficulties do connotation, denotation, extension, intension, and componential analysis have in determining the meaning of the words *spring*, *bridge*, and *Hawaii*?

Practice! Practice!

1. For each of the following words, attempt to define their meaning according to the theories of connotation, denotation, and extension and intension.

    a. summer
    b. a linguistics instructor
    c. grass

2. Identify the types of phrases with which the verbs in A and B can occur. What difference in meaning between the verbs in A and the verbs in B determines the type of complement the verbs require?

A	B
sweep	crawl
kick	fall

3. Examine the following two groups of words and determine the semantic feature(s) each group has in common. What semantic feature(s) are different between members of each group? What about between the two groups?

Group A: grandmother / mother / daughter / widow
Group B: grandfather   / father /   son   / widower

Now. . . Try doing a componential analysis for   ⇒ ewe and lamb
⇒ mare, filly, and colt

CONCEPTS

Linguists use the term 'concepts' to refer to the system we use to identify, classify, and organize all elements of our many and varied experiences. Our conceptual system reveals how meaning is expressed through language.

⇒ **Fuzzy Concepts.** Fuzzy concepts are concepts that can differ from person to person. They have no clear boundaries. Think about how much something has to cost before you would consider it expensive.

⇒ **Graded Membership.** Concepts have internal structure. The members of a concept can be graded according to how typical they are within that concept. The most typical member is selected as the prototype. Other members are arranged around the prototype, with members sharing more properties closer to the prototype. Members sharing fewer properties are farther from the prototype. See figure 6.2 on p. 191 of the text for a diagram of the internal structure of the concept *bird*. Think. . . Does the concept of *house* have a graded membership? If so, what might the prototype be? Could this prototype vary from person to person?

⇒ **Metaphor.** The concepts expressed by language do not exist in isolation but are interconnected and associated. Metaphor, the understanding of one concept in terms of another, can be used to make these connections. Metaphors can be based on perceptions, physical experiences, culture, and shared feelings. See table 6.6 on p. 192 of the text for some examples of the metaphorical use of spatial terms.Think of a metaphor that attributes animal-like properties to people. What might be the basis of such a metaphor?

Exercise! Exercise! For each of the following concepts, determine whether they are fuzzy or graded.

1. cats
2. mountains
3. time
4. vegetables

For any of the above that exhibit a graded membership, determine the member that is prototypical for you. How might this differ from person to person?

Languages can differ in terms of how they organize and express different concepts. This can be done using processes of lexicalization and grammaticalization.

⇒ **Lexicalization.** Lexicalization refers to the process whereby concepts (e.g., snow, light) are encoded into the meanings of words. Languages may differ in terms of how many words they use to convey a concept. How concepts are encoded also varies from language to language. See tables 6.9, 6.10, and 6.11 on pp. 194 to 195 for some examples of systematic differences in how motion is encoded into English, French, and Atsugewi verbs.

⇒ **Grammaticalization.** Grammaticalization refers to concepts that are expressed as affixes or functional categories. See table 6.12 on p. 196 for some examples of concepts in English that have been grammaticalized. Concepts that are grammaticalized can vary from language to language. See table 6.13 on p. 197 for an example in Hidatsa in which evidence for the truth of a statement has been grammaticalized. Think about the different ways in which negation has been grammaticalized in English.

Try This!

1. Quite often, languages contain different forms of grammaticalized affixes or functional categories. Consider the data below from Cree involving possession and answer the questions that follow.

	Noun	My Noun	Gloss
1.	mispiton	nispiton	'arm'
2.	tʃima:n	nitʃima:n	'canoe'
3.	miski:sik	niski:sik	'eye'
4.	mo:htawiya	no:htawiya	'father'
5.	mo:ka:wiya	no:ka:wiya	'mother'
6.	astotin	nitastotin	'cap'

What are the two different (morphological) ways of indicating possession? What is the semantic basis for this difference? Think about different kinds of possession: which of the above could you give away and which could you not?

2. The language data below illustrates differences in the use of singular and plural prefixes in Swahili. Group the nouns into classes based on their use of the different prefixes. What is the semantic basis for your grouping?

	Sg.	Pl.	Gloss
1.	mtoto	watoto	'child'
2.	mhindi	mihindi	'corn'
3.	kikombe	vikombe	'hair'
4.	mkindu	mikindu	'date palm'
5.	mfigili	mifigili	'radish'
6.	mwalimu	wawalimu	'teacher'
7.	kioo	vioo	'mirror'
8.	mume	waume	'husband'
9.	kikapu	vikapu	'basket'
10.	mboga	miboga	'pumpkin'

3. German neuter nouns can occur in a prepositional phrase in either the dative case (definite article *dem*) or the accusative case (definite article *das*). Examine the following sentences and determine the semantic basis for the choice of either the dative or accusative case.

1. Monika arbeitet in dem Kaffeehaus. (Monika works in the coffeehouse.)
   Stefan kommt in das Kaffeehaus. (Stefan comes into the coffeehouse.)

2. Ritas Stuhl steht neben dem Fenster. (Rita's stool stands next to the window.)
   Jan stellt seinen Stuhl neben das Fenster. (Jan puts his chair next to the window.)

3. Ein Schuh steht unter dem Bett. (A shoe is under the bed.)
   Kurt stellt den anderen Schuh unter das Bett. (Kurt puts the other shoe under the bed.)

4. Ilsa ist in dem Wohnzimmer. (Ilsa is in the living room.)
   Armin geht in das Wohnzimmer. (Armin goes into the living room.)

What concept is contained in the German articles that is not found in English articles?

THE ROLE OF SYNTAX

Not only do the words and phrases that make up a sentence contribute to its meaning, but the position of words and phrases in the syntactic structure also has a role.

The contribution of syntax to sentence interpretation includes constructional meaning, structural ambiguity, thematic roles, and pronoun interpretation.

Constructional Meaning

⇒ The meaning of a sentence goes beyond the meaning of the individual words and phrases that it is composed of. The syntactic structure, or construction, also contributes to the meaning of the sentence.

⇒ Two common constructions are the following:

- The caused-motion construction: X causes Y to go somewhere
- The ditransitive construction: X causes Y to have Z

Think. . . What construction is found in the sentence *Joe sold Sabrina a car*? What about in the sentence *Joe flew the airplane to Red Deer*? Is there anything in the verb that implies 'caused motion'? What about 'causes another person to have something'? If not, then where do these meanings come from?

Structural Ambiguity

Structural ambiguity occurs when a group of words in a sentence can be combined in more than one way. Each different combination is associated with a different meaning. Ambiguity can be found in both noun and verb phrases.

⇒ **Noun Phrases.** In the sentence *The surface was painted with red flowers and leaves*, the noun phrase *red flowers and leaves* can be combined in two ways. Each combination corresponds to a particular grouping of words in syntactic structure. Each grouping has its own meaning.

Meaning One: red [flowers and leaves]
            —Both the flowers and the leaves are red.

Meaning Two: [red flowers] and [leaves]
            —Only the flowers are red.

⇒ **Verb Phrases.** In the sentence *Sam ate the cake in the kitchen,* the phrases contained within the verb phrase *ate the cake in the kitchen* can be grouped together in two ways. As with noun phrases, each grouping corresponds to a particular syntactic structure and meaning.

Meaning One: ate [the cake in the kitchen]
            —Sam ate the cake that was in the kitchen.

Meaning Two: ate [the cake] [in the kitchen]
            —Sam was in the kitchen eating cake.

Remember. . .   A sentence can also be lexically ambiguous. This type of ambiguity results from one word in the sentence having more than one meaning. Think about the ambiguity in the sentence *The glasses are on the table.* Which word has more than one meaning? What are the two different meanings? Why would we typically not notice this ambiguity during a conversation?

Each of the sentences below is either lexically or structurally ambiguous. Remember that lexical ambiguity comes from a single word, while structural ambiguity comes from more than one possible combination of a group of words.

Try This!

1. Cool beer and wine are what we want.
2. Fred was cool.
3. I met the woman standing by the water cooler.
4. Parliament passed a dangerous drug bill.
5. George and Harry or Fred will draw the picture.
6. I want to look at the pictures in the attic.
7. The instructor left his key in the office.

Now. . .   Go back over the sentences, and for all those that are structurally ambiguous, determine which words need to be grouped together for each possible interpretation or meaning. You might want to start by first identifying which phrase (noun or verb) contains the ambiguity. Remember that each interpretation will have a different grouping!

Thematic Roles

To interpret sentences, we need to know who is doing the action, what is undergoing the action, the starting point of the action, etc. Thematic, or theta, roles capture the relations between a sentence and the situation the sentence describes.

There are three important things to know about thematic roles.

⇒ **Common Thematic Roles.**   Some of the common thematic roles include the following:

- agent (the entity performing the action)
- theme (the entity undergoing the action or movement)
- source (the starting point of a movement)
- goal (the end point of a movement)
- location (the place where an action occurs)

Think. . . What thematic role would be assigned to the noun phrases in the sentence *The gardener planted flowers by the front door*? What about the noun phrases in the sentence *John drove the car to Vancouver*? Does a sentence have to contain all the thematic roles outlined above?

⇒ **Thematic Role Assignment.** Thematic roles are assigned to noun phrases based on their position within the sentence. Typically, verbs and prepositions assign thematic roles.

- A verb assigns the agent role (if it has one) to its subject noun phrase.
- A verb assigns the theme role (if it has one) to its complement noun phrase.
- A preposition assigns a thematic role to its complement noun phrases. The specific role that is assigned depends on the specific preposition.

Knowledge of the thematic roles that individual verbs and prepositions assign is stored in our mental lexicon.

See figures 6.4, 6.5, and 6.6 on pp. 202 and 203 for examples of thematic role assignment by prepositions and verbs.

Think. . . How do the noun phrases in the sentences *The gardener planted flowers by the front door* and *John drove the car to Vancouver* receive their thematic roles?

⇒ **Thematic Roles and Deep Structure.** Thematic roles are assigned at deep structure.

- The Merge operation determines the position of the noun phrase within the syntactic structure (i.e., the D-structure). It is the noun phrase's position as a result of Merge that determines its thematic role.
- The operation Move can move noun phrases to other positions in the structure.
- If Move has transported the noun phrase to another position in the structure, this operation must be undone to determine how the noun phrase received its thematic role. That is, the noun phrase must be returned to its originating position.
- The sentence *What should George make*? has the D-structure *George should make what*. In the D-structure, the verb *make* assigns the agent role to *George* and the theme role to *what*. See figure 6.7 on p. 203 of the text for an example of thematic role assignment in a *wh* question.

Think. . . Does *what* retain its role after Move changes the position of *what* in the sentence? How does *the store* receive its thematic role and what role does *the store* receive?

Exercise! For each of the following sentences, identify all the noun phrases and the thematic role assigned to each noun phrase.

1. Sarah drove that bus from Toronto to St. John's.
2. The children are eating their ice cream with spoons.
3. Which shoes did you buy at the store?
4. Alyssa came from work.
5. The boys walked to the park.
6. Sally mailed a parcel to her nephew.
7. What did Bill leave at your house?
8. The letter was sent.
9. Ginger scribbled her address on the paper with a pen.
10. The designer turned that ugly room into a masterpiece.

Now. . . Go back through each sentence and for each thematic role, determine the verb or preposition that assigned the role. Make sure you put any sentences in which Move has applied into the D-structure first. Remember: The D-structure is the result of Merge.

Pronoun Interpretation

Pronouns replace, or stand for, a noun phrase. This noun phrase is called the antecedent, and it is this antecedent that determines how the pronoun is interpreted.

Think. . .

- What is the antecedent of the pronoun *she* in the sentence *Janice's sister bought the dress that she liked*? Could *she* refer to Janice? Janice's sister? Could it refer to someone else not mentioned in the sentence?
- Consider the pronoun *herself* in the sentence *Janice's sister wondered if Fiona liked herself*. Does *herself* refer to Fiona, Janice, or Janice's sister? Can *herself* refer to someone not mentioned in the sentence?

It is the syntactic structure of the sentence that helps determine which noun phrase can or cannot function as the antecedent of a pronoun. The following concepts are important in understanding how the syntactic structure does this for pronominals and reflexive pronouns.

⇒ **Pronominals and Reflexives.** English pronominals and reflexives vary in terms of number (singular and plural), person (1st, 2nd, and 3rd), and gender (masculine, feminine, and neuter) in the 3rd person. See table 6.16 on p. 204 for a complete list of the pronominals and reflexives found in English. For example, *she* is a pronominal (3rd person, singular, feminine) and *herself* is a reflexive (3rd person, singular, feminine).

⇒ **C-Command.** The interpretation of pronominals and reflexive pronouns is based on the idea of c-command. A noun phrase c-commands another noun phrase if it is found in the following structure:

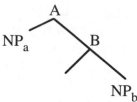

NP$_a$ c-commands NP$_b$ since the first category above NP$_a$ (as indicated by A) contains NP$_b$. NP$_b$ does not c-command NP$_a$ since the first category above NP$_b$ (as indicated by B) does not contain NP$_a$.

⇒ **Principles.** Two principles of interpretation are relevant. The first applies to reflexive pronouns and the second to pronominals. Notice that these principles are opposite to each other.

- Principle A. This principle applies to reflexive pronouns and states that a reflexive pronoun must have an antecedent that c-commands it in the same clause (TP).

  See figure 6.9 on p. 205 for an illustration of how this principle determines which NPs can and cannot serve as an antecedent for a reflexive pronoun. Essentially, if an NP c-commands a reflexive, the NP can serve as the reflexive's antecedent. Conversely, if an NP does not c-command a reflexive, the NP cannot serve as the reflexive's antecedent.

- Principle B. This principle applies to pronominals, and states that a pronominal cannot have an antecedent that c-commands it in the same clause (TP).

  See figure 6.10 on p. 206 for an illustration of how this principle determines which NPs can and cannot serve as antecedents for a pronominal. Essentially, if an NP c-commands a pronominal, the NP cannot serve as the pronominal's antecedent. If an NP does not c-command a pronominal, the NP can serve as the pronominal's antecedent.

Try This! Using Principles A and B, determine the antecedent of either the pronominal or the reflexive in the sentences *Janice bought the dress that she liked, Janice wondered if Fiona liked herself, Janice's sister liked herself,* and *Janice's sister liked her.* To start, you will need to identify where the pronoun in the sentence is a pronominal or a reflexive. You might also want to draw a tree diagram of the TP containing either the pronominal or reflexive. When doing so, use the following structure for the NP *Janice's sister.*

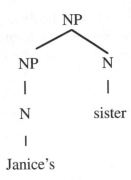

Now. . . In the sentence *Janice's sister bought the dress that she liked,* determine whether *she* can refer to either Janice or Janice's sister. In the sentence *Janice's sister wondered if Fiona liked herself,* determine why *herself* must refer to Fiona and not to either Janice or Janice's sister.

ROLE OF PRAGMATICS

Besides the structure of a sentence and the thematic roles assigned to the noun phrases within a sentence, there are many other factors involved in sentence interpretation. Pragmatics is the study of the role that other necessary information has in sentence interpretation.

⇒ **Beliefs and Attitudes.** Non-linguistic knowledge can be used to interpret elements within a sentence. Think about the sentence *City Council denied the demonstrators a permit because they advocated violence.* Does the pronoun *they* refer to the demonstrators or the council members? Think about how the pronoun reference changes if we change the verb from *advocate* to *abhor*. Who does the pronoun refer to now? How is this difference in pronoun reference related to our beliefs about demonstrators and council members?

⇒ **Presupposition.** Presupposition refers to the assumption or belief implied by the use of a particular word. Think about the meaning of the sentence *John admitted that the soccer team had won the game* in relation to the meaning of the sentence *John said that the soccer team had won the game.* Which verb, *admitted* or *said*, indicates that the speaker is presupposing the truth of the claim being made?

⇒ **Setting and Deictics.** The form and interpretation of some words depends on the location of the speaker and/or hearer within a particular setting. These words are called spatial deictics. Some examples of English deictics include *here there* and *this that*. *Here* and *this* are used to refer to items close to the speaker, while *there* and *that* are used to refer to words close to the listener. See table 6.17 on p. 208 for some examples of how deictic distinctions can vary across languages.

⇒ **Discourse Topic.** Many sentences can only be interpreted in reference to information contained in preceding sentences. **Discourse** is the term used to describe a connected series of utterances. Old (given) information refers to knowledge that speakers assume addressees know, while new information refers to knowledge that is being introduced into the discourse for the first time. **Topic** refers to what a sentence or portion of the discourse is about. Some languages use a special affix (e.g., in Japanese, -wa) to indicate the topic of the discourse.

Practice! Practice! Sentences can be difficult to interpret because they are ungrammatical, because they violate our knowledge of the world, or because they contain words that have no known referent. For each of the following sentences, identify why it is hard to interpret.

1. Our ten-month-old son is six feet tall.
2. Mike red bought car a.
3. Palm trees grow vigorously at the North Pole.
4. Radiculus glautons are found in the soil.
5. The bumblebee picked up the cat and flew back to the hive with it.

Now. . . Reconsider sentence 4. What meaning might you assign to the unknown words in this sentence? What might be the meaning of the overall sentence?

Why might the sentence *His mother wants you to be a doctor* be difficult to interpret if it is not part of a discourse (i.e., as a stand-alone sentence)?

CONVERSATION

We use words and sentences to convey messages. And we often do this by having a conversation with someone. Conversations have rules. These rules refer to our understanding of how language is used in a particular social situation to convey messages. Our knowledge of these rules also contributes to our interpretation of utterances.

⇒ **Cooperative Principle.** This is the general principle guiding all conversations. It requires participants (speakers and addressees) to make their contributions to the conversation appropriate to the conversation.

⇒ **Conversational Maxims.** Conversations also have more specific guidelines. These guidelines are called maxims, and if we follow these maxims, then we have satisfied the Cooperative Principle.

• Maxim of Relevance (Make your contribution relevant.)
• Maxim of Quality (Make your contribution truthful.)
• Maxim of Quantity (Make your contribution only as informative as required.)
• Maxim of Manner (Make your contribution unambiguous, clear, and orderly.)

⇒ **Conversational Implicature.** During the course of a conversation, we are often able to make inferences about what is meant but was not actually said. Consider, for example, the following interaction:

> Mike: How did you do on the last exam?
> Jim: Want to come with me to the Registrar's Office?

Think about which conversational maxim Jim has violated. What can you infer about how Jim did on the exam even though he doesn't actually tell Mike how he did?

Try This!!

You've just missed your bus and are standing at the bus stop waiting for the next bus. The time is 2 p.m. and the next bus is due at 2:15 p.m., but you don't know that. You ask someone at the bus stop when the next bus is due and receive several replies. Each reply you receive may or may not violate one or more conversational maxims. For each reply, identify which maxim(s), if any, has/ have been violated.

1. When's the next bus?
   At 2:30. (He's lying.)

   _____

2. When's the next bus?
   When I was little I was obsessed with buses. I wanted to be a bus driver. I had hundreds of different kinds of buses. Little buses, big buses, red buses, blue buses, and even double-decker buses. Did you know that in England, many buses are double-decker? I have made a study of buses. I think the next bus will be here in 15 minutes. Did you know that in India there are no buses? Did you know I wanted to be a bus driver? Did you know. . .

   _____

3. When's the next bus?
   Let me think! If the last bus was here at 1:50 and if they run every 20 minutes or so, then the next bus should be here at 2:10. (He has no idea.)

   _____

4. When's the next bus?
   At 2:15, but if we were in Newfoundland that would be 2:45.

   _____

5. When's the next bus?
   I don't know. (He's telling the truth.)

   _____

REVIEW! REVIEW! Make sure you can do the following:

- identify the semantic relations between words (4)
- identify the semantic relations between sentences (3)
- define connotation, denotation, extension, and intension
- do componential analysis
- spot fuzzy concepts, grammaticalized concepts, and lexicalized concepts
- spot constructional meanings
- spot lexical ambiguity
- spot and represent structural ambiguity
- identify noun phrases, their thematic roles, and how these are assigned
- determine how pronominals and reflexive pronouns are interpreted
- identify the effect of world knowledge on sentence interpreation
- identify when presupposition occurs in sentence interpretation
- spot the different forms of deictic terms
- identify conversational principles and maxims

QUESTIONS? PROBLEMS? DIFFICULTIES?

_____

_____

_____

_____

_____

_____

_____

_____

_____

_____

_____

CHAPTER 7.
THE CLASSIFICATION OF LANGUAGES

Language classification involves arranging languages into groups based on shared characteristics. Important topics and concepts found in this chapter include the following:

1. language universals
2. markedness theory
3. structural classification
4. phonological classification
5. morphological classification
6. syntactic classification
7. genetic classification
8. the Indo-European family of languages

TERMS AND CONCEPTS

The following terms and concepts are important in understanding how linguists classify languages:

Term	Definition
mutual intelligibility	Mutual intelligibility is a criterion used to determine whether language varieties are dialects of the same language or are different languages altogether. Essentially, if speakers can understand each other, the varieties are considered dialects of the same language, and if the speakers cannot understand each other, they are considered different languages.
language loss	Languages can be lost (become extinct) over time. An extinct language is not a language that evolves over time into one or more languages (e.g., Latin), but a language that ceases to be spoken altogether. For example, Manx (in 1974) and Bo (in 2010) disappeared completely: They have no speakers and no descendant languages.
classic pattern of language loss	Language loss typically takes three generations. Parents are monolingual speakers of a language; their children adopt a new language and become bilingual speakers; and their children's children grow up monolingual in the new language.

TYPOLOGICAL CLASSIFICATION

Linguistic typology groups languages together based on their structural characteristics. This type of classification can be done using phonological properties, morphological systems, and grammatical structures. Typological studies are carried out to uncover universal characteristics of language.

⇒ **Linguistic Universals.** Linguistic universals are structural characteristics that occur in all or most languages.

- An absolute universal is a structural characteristic that is found in all languages.
- A universal tendency is a structural characteristic that is found in most languages.
- An implicational universal outlines a particular relationship between two structural characteristics.
- The presence of characteristic A (e.g., nasal vowels) implies that the language will also have characteristic B (e.g., oral vowels).
- The presence of B (e.g., oral vowels) does not imply that the language will also have A (e.g., nasal vowels).

Implicational universals can be used to determine possible and impossible characteristics of language. If A (e.g., nasal vowels) implies B (e.g., oral vowels), then:

- it is possible for a language to have both B and A, and
- it is possible for a language to have B without having A, but
- it is impossible for a language to have A without having B. This is because if a language has A, it also has to have B.

Think. . . The vowel phoneme /a/ is found in almost all of the world's languages. What type of universal does this statement represent? What about this statement: All languages have syntactic structure.

⇒ **Markedness Theory.** Markedness theory is another way to analyze linguistic universals. Structural characteristics can be identified as being more or less marked in relation to each other.

- Unmarked characteristics are characteristics that are considered to be more basic.
- Marked characteristics are characteristics that are considered to be less basic.

Markedness is closely related to implicational universals. Where the presence of A implies the presence of B, this means that a language cannot have A unless it also has B. B is less marked than is A. Languages will typically not have the more marked characteristic unless they also have the corresponding less marked characteristic.

Try This! Consider the following statement: If a language has derivational affixes, it will also have inflectional affixes. What type of universal does this statement represent? Which would be the more marked type of affix, derivational or inflectional? Which would be the less marked type of affix? Is it possible for a language to have both inflectional and derivational affixes? Only inflectional affixes? Only derivational affixes?

PHONOLOGICAL CLASSIFICATION

Phonological classification is based on the phonemes found in a language.

⇒ **Vowel Systems.** Languages can be classified according to the size and pattern of their vowel system. The most common system has five vowels: /i, u, e, o, a/. Other common vowel systems have three, four, six, seven, eight, or nine different vowels. See figure 7.2 on p. 224 of the text for examples of some of the common vowel systems.

Some universal tendencies include:

- /a/ is the most commonly occurring vowel phoneme. /i/ and /u/ are almost as common.
- Front vowels are generally unrounded, while non-low back vowels are generally rounded.
- Low back vowels are generally unrounded.

Think. . . How many vowel phonemes are found in English? Is this more or less than the average number found across languages? Does English follow each of the universal tendencies shown above?

Some implicational universals include:

- If a language has contrastive nasal vowels, then it will also have contrastive oral vowels.
- If a language has contrastive long vowels, then it will also have contrastive short vowels.

See table 7.4 on p. 225 of the text for some examples of contrastive long and short vowels in Finnish.

Think. . . Which vowels are more marked? Nasal or oral vowels? Long or short vowels? What are the possible and impossible combinations of sounds that these implicational universals predict? See tables 7.3 and 7.5 on pp. 223 and 225 of the text for help if you need it.

⇒ **Consonant Systems.** Languages are not usually classified according to the size of their consonant inventories. This is because there is a great deal of variation in the number of consonant inventories found in the world's languages. Some languages (e.g., Rotokas, spoken in Papua New Guinea) have as few as six, while others (e.g., !Kung spoken in Namibia and Angola) have as many as 96.

Some absolute universals and universal tendencies include:

- All languages have stops, but not all languages have fricatives.
- The most common stop phonemes are /p, t, and k/, with /t/ being the most common.
- The most commonly occurring fricative is /s/, followed by /f/.
- Most languages have at least one nasal phoneme.
- If a language has only one nasal phoneme, it is most likely /n/. If a language has contrasting nasal phonemes, they are most likely /m/ and /n/.
- Most languages have at least one phonemic liquid. (Some languages have none.)

Think. . . How many consonant phonemes are found in English? Does English follow the universals outlined above?

Some universal implications include:

- If a language has voiced obstruent phonemes, then it will also have the corresponding voiceless obstruent phonemes.
- If a language has voiceless sonorant phonemes, then it will also have the corresponding voiced sonorant phonemes.
- If a language has fricative phonemes, then it will also have stop phonemes.
- If a language has affricate phonemes, then it will also have fricative and stop phonemes.

Think. . . Which is more marked? Voiced or voiceless obstruent phonemes (stops, fricatives, affricates)? Voiced or voiceless sonorant phonemes (nasals, liquids, glides)? Is the markedness relationship the same for obstruents and sonorants? What are the possible and impossible combinations of sounds that these universals predict? See tables 7.6 and 7.7 on p. 226 of the text for help if you need it.

Now. . . Think about the relationship between stops, fricatives, and affricates. Which is the least marked of the three? Which is the most marked? Why? What are the possible and impossible combinations of these three sounds in language? See table 7.9 on p. 227 of the text for help if you need it.

⇒ **Suprasegmentals.** Suprasegmentals are prosodic characteristics of a sound independent of the sound's individual articulation.

Tone

- Tone languages (languages in which differences in pitch are used to indicate differences in meaning) can have two, three, or four contrastive level tones. Most tone languages have two.

- If a tone language has contrastive contour tones, then it will also have contrastive level tones. A contour tone is a tone that involves moving pitch.

Think... Which are more marked: level or contour tones? Is it possible for a language to have contour tones without also having level tones? See table 7.12 on p. 228 of the text for help if you need it.

Stress

- In a fixed stress system, the stress is predictable: for example, always on the first syllable, like Hungarian, or always on the last syllable, like Modern Hebrew.
- In a free stress system, stress is not predictable; it must be learned for every word. In these languages (e.g., Russian), a difference in stress placement can cause a meaning difference. See table 7.13 on p. 228 of the text for some examples of the relationship between stress and meaning in Russian.

Syllable Structure

- All languages have CV and V syllable types. This means that all languages allow syllables that begin with an onset, but not all languages have syllables with codas.
- If a language allows sequences of consonants in an onset (i.e., a complex onset) then it will allow onsets with only one consonant (i.e., a simple onset). Similarly, if a language allows sequences of consonants in a coda (i.e., a complex coda), then it will allow codas with one consonant (i.e., a simple coda).

Think... Can a language have complex onsets without having simple onsets? Can a language have complex codas without simple codas? Which are more marked: simple onsets and codas or complex onsets and codas? See tables 7.14 and 7.15 on p. 229 of the text for help if you need it.

Exercise!

1. For each of the following pairs, circle the more marked item of the two.
   a. fricatives   affricates
   b. VC   VCC
   c. voiced obstruents   voiceless obstruents
   d. level tones   contour tones
   e. short vowels   long vowels
   f. CCV   CV

2. Complete the following statements.

   a. The most common vowel system has _____ vowels, which are _____.

   b. The three most common stops are _____, with _____ being the most common.

   c. The two most common fricatives are _____ and _____.

   d. The two most common nasals are _____ and _____.

   e. Front vowels are generally _____, while back vowels are generally _____ _____.

   f. Low vowels are generally _____.

3. Assume that a language contains the following consonants: /p, b, g, z, pf, n, m̥, r̥/. Use your knowledge of implicational universals to predict which other consonants might be found in this language. Note: /pf/ is a labial affricate.

4. Assume that a language contains the following vowels: /eː, oː, uː, iː, aː, ã/. Use your knowledge of implicational universals to predict which other vowels might be found in this language.

5. Examine the data below and answer the questions that follow. (Note: The data are from a hypothetical language.)

     /drong/   "basket"   /sas.gnu/   "foot"
     /ben/   "stove"   /gle/   "sun"
     /a.dupt/   "chicken"   /brit.e.aks/ "chair"

   a. Identify the syllable types present in each of the words. Remember that a period indicates a syllable boundary.

   b. Does this language allow sequences of consonants in an onset? In a coda?

   c. Which other syllable type would be found in this hypothetical language?

   d. Which syllable structure universals (including implicational universals) are evident in the data?

6. Examine the following data and answer the questions below. (Note: The data are from a hypothetical language.)

     H M   H LH   HL M
     | | | ∨   ∨ |
    /t i k u/ "man"   /t i k u/ "woman"   /t i k u/ "child"

   a. Identify the tones as either level or contour.

   b. Use your knowledge of implicational universals to predict which other tones this hypothetical language might have.

7. Using your knowledge of implicational universals, decide whether each of the following corresponds to a possible or impossible combination of sounds in language.

   a. contrastive long vowels without contrastive short vowels   _____

   b. voiced sonorants without voiceless sonorants   _____

   c. affricates without fricatives   _____

   d. contrastive oral vowels without contrastive nasal vowels   _____

   e. voiceless obstruents without voiced obstruents   _____

   f. level tones without contour tones   _____

MORPHOLOGICAL CLASSIFICATION

Morphological classification is based on the different ways in which languages combine morphemes to form words. There are four types of morphological systems.

⇒ **Isolating.** In an isolating language, words consist only of free morphemes. There are no affixes. Information such as tense or plural is contained within separate free morphemes.

   • Mandarin is an example of a language with an isolating morphology.

⇒ **Agglutinating.** In an agglutinating language, words contain many affixes. Each affix typically corresponds to a single piece of grammatical information (e.g., number, tense, possession, etc.).

   • Turkish is an example of a language with an agglutinating morphology.

⇒ **Fusional.** In a fusional (or inflectional) language, words also contain many affixes. However, each affix may contain several pieces of grammatical information at the same time. That is, one affix may contain information on gender, number, case, and so on.

   • Russian is a good example of a language with a fusional morphology.

⇒ **Polysynthetic.** In a polysynthetic language, a single word consists of a number of roots and affixes. These words often express meanings that are associated with entire sentences in other languages.

   • Inuktitut is a good example of a language with a polysynthetic morphology.

Think. . . about the information found in English pronouns such as *he*, *she*, *him*, and *her*; in English derived words such as *activation*, *optionality*, and *denationalize*; and in English phrases such as *John will sing*. What type of system do each of these structures correspond to? Is the same type of system found in each structure? If not, what conclusion can you make about the type of morphological system found in English?

Some universals include:

⇒ If a language has derivational affixes, then it will also have inflectional affixes.

⇒ If a word has both a derivational and an inflectional affix, the derivational affix will be closer to the root. See table 7.16 on p. 231 of the text for some examples of the ordering of inflectional and derivational affixes in English and Turkish.

⇒ If a language has only suffixes, it will only have postpositions (e.g., Turkish). A postposition is the equivalent of a preposition. The difference between the two is that a preposition occurs before its noun phrase complement, while a postposition occurs after its noun phrase complement.

Try This!   Identify the morphological system evident in each of these words. Note that the words are divided into their morphemes (indicated with a hyphen). The meaning of each morpheme is given in English directly underneath. The equivalent English translation is given on the third line.

a. Blackfoot: maːt-jaːk-waːxkaji-waːtsiksi
not-will-go home-he
"He is not going home."

b. Italian: parl-av-o   port-av-ano   trov-av-i
speak-past-I   carry-past-they   find-past-you
"I spoke"   "they carried"   "you found"

Now. . . Which implicational universal related to affixes is evident in the following Latvian words?

lidot-aj-s   rakstit-aj-a
to fly-one who flies-nominative   to write-one who writes-genitive
"aviator (subject)"   "writer's (possessive)"

SYNTACTIC CLASSIFICATION

Much of syntactic classification is based on the word order patterns found in basic declarative sentences (e.g., *The boy kicked the ball*). The three most common word order patterns are described below.

⇒ **SOV.** In this word order pattern, the subject (S) comes first, followed by the object (O) and then the verb (V). Using this pattern, the English sentence *The boy kicked the ball* would have the order *The boy the ball kicked*.

- Turkish and Japanese are examples of languages that follow this pattern.

⇒ **SVO.** In this word order pattern, the subject (S) comes first, followed by the verb (V) and then the object (O). This pattern corresponds to the English sentence *The boy kicked the ball*.

- English and French are examples of languages that follow this pattern.

⇒ **VSO.** In this word order pattern, the verb (V) comes first, followed by the subject (S) and then the object (O). Using this pattern, the English sentence *The boy kicked the ball* would have the order *Kicked the boy the ball*.

- Welsh is an example of a language using this pattern.

Think... What do the three word order patterns have in common? Why might this be so? Are there other word order patterns found in the world's languages that do not follow this generalization? Which word order pattern is the most common?

There are also some universal generalizations that can be made regarding word order. These are related to whether a language places the verb before the object (VO) or after the object (OV).

⇒ VO languages
- have prepositions (e.g., *in* the park, *with* his foot)
- place prepositional phrases after the verb (e.g., The boy <u>ran</u> *in the park*)
- generally place adverbs after the verb (e.g., The boy <u>ran</u> *quickly*)
- place possessors before the noun (e.g., *The boy's* <u>dog</u>)

⇒ OV languages
- have postpositions (e.g., the park *in*, his foot *with*)
- place postpositional phrases before the verb (e.g., The boy *the park in* <u>ran</u>)
- place adverbs before the verb (e.g., The boy *quickly* <u>ran</u>)
- place possessors after the noun (e.g., <u>dog</u> *the boy's*)

Reminder... VO languages tend to be right-branching languages, meaning that the complement occurs to the right of the head. In contrast, OV languages tend to be left-branching languages, meaning that the complement occurs to the left of the head. Figure 7.6 on p. 238 of the text illustrates this structural difference.

Practice!

1. Determine the word order in each of the following sentences. The English translation for each word is given on the line underneath. The equivalent English sentence is given on the third line. (Yuwaalaraay is an Australian language.)

   a. Spanish: Los soldados quebraron las ventanas.
                      the soldiers broke   the windows
                      "The soldiers broke the windows."

   b. Yuwaalaraay: duyugu nama dayn yiy
                      snake   that man bit
                      "The snake bit that man."

2. Would you expect Spanish to have prepositions or postpositions? What about Yuwaalaraay? Would the phrase containing the preposition or postposition come before or after the verb in Spanish? What about in Yuwaalaraay?

3. What is the difference in the ordering of nouns and demonstratives in the following phrases? (Tinrin is an Austronesian language; Limbu is a Sino-Tibetan language spoken in Nepal.)

Tinrin: moo horro ha   Limbu: khɛy nɛpphu cum   ha
          Det   prayer this   that two   friend plural
          "this prayer (going on right now)"   "those two friends"

WHY? WHY?

Why are some patterns found in language? Why are other patterns not found in language? Why are some structural characteristics more common than others? There are no definitive answers to such questions, although some possible explanations have been given:

- Some phonological universals may have a perceptual basis. Others may be motivated by articulatory possibilities (e.g., that languges tend to have more obstruents than sonorants).

- Some morphological universals may be linked to language change (see Chapter 8). Others may be related to the internal structure of words (see Chapter 4).

- Syntactic patterns may be linked to how we process language (see Chapter 13).

GENETIC CLASSIFICATION

Genetic classification groups languages together based on common ancestry. These groups of languages are called "families," since all members of the group are descended from the same ancestor. This common ancestor is usually found using the comparative method of reconstruction discussed in Chapter 8.

There can be many difficulties in doing genetic classification. One is the amount of data that is needed to be sure of the genetic status of a language. Some others are given below.

⇒ **Language Contact.** When languages come into contact with each other, they often borrow sounds, words, morphemes, and syntactic structures from one another. The result is that languages that are unrelated may end up being similar in many ways.

⇒ **Sound Change.** Sound changes can make it difficult to find relationships between languages, since sound changes may render words in related languages very different from one another. The result is that languages that are related may not look similar.

⇒ **Vocabulary Change.** Words that are often good indicators of a genetic relationship between two languages may be lost from the lexicon over time.

THE INDO-EUROPEAN FAMILY

English belongs to the Indo-European family of languages. These languages are found in Europe as well as in the Middle East and India. The Indo-European language family currently has nine branches.

⇒ **Albanian.** Albanian, the only member of this family, is spoken in Albania and in parts of the former Yugoslavia, Greece, and Italy.

⇒ **Armenian.** Armenian, the only member of this family, is spoken in the Republic of Armenia as well as in Turkey, Iran, Syria, Lebanon, and Egypt.

⇒ **Baltic.** Latvian and Lithuanian are the two Baltic languages. They are spoken in Latvia and Lithuania (west of Russia and northeast of Poland).

⇒ **Celtic.** The Celtic languages are divided into the Insular and Continental branches. The Insular branch is further divided into the Brythonic and Goidelic (or Gaelic) sub-branches. Celtic languages are spoken in the British Isles as well as in northwestern France.

⇒ **Germanic.** The Germanic languages are divided into East, North, and West branches. North Germanic languages are spoken in Scandinavia, while the West Germanic languages are spoken in Germany, the Netherlands, Belgium, South Africa, England, and, of course, North America.

⇒ **Hellenic.** This branch has only one member: Greek.

⇒ **Indo-Iranian.** This branch is divided into Indic and Iranian languages. Iranian languages are spoken in Iran, Afghanistan, Iraq, Turkey, the former Yugoslavia, and China. Indic languages are spoken in northern India, Pakistan, and Bangladesh.

⇒ **Italic.** The Italic languages are divided into four branches: Ibero-Romance, Gallo-Romance, Italo-Romance, and Balkano-Romance.

⇒ **Slavic.** The Slavic languages are divided into East, West, and South branches. These languages are spoken in Russia, the Ukraine, Belarus, and the former Yugolsavia.

See figure 7.8 on p. 244 of the text for the approximate locations of the different Indo-European languages.

Now. . . Study the tables 7.20 to 7.25 on pp. 239 to 243 of the text, and construct a diagram of the Indo-European language family by filling in the chart below. Provide (1) the names of the sub-branches in the different branches and (2) the languages of each branch or sub-branch. Extinct languages and their branches have been omitted from the diagram.

DID YOU KNOW...
- The ancestor of the Indo-European language family is a reconstructed language called Proto-Indo-European (PIE).
- The reconstruction of PIE is based on Old English, Old Norse, Latin, Sanskrit, and Attic Greek, among other languages.
- Lithuanian has a case system thought to be similar to that found in PIE.
- English descended from the languages spoken by the Germanic tribes: the Angles, Jutes, and Saxons.
- Frisian is the closest relative to English.
- Some Indo-European languages are extinct. For example, Gothic is an extinct East Germanic language and Cornish is an extinct Celtic (Continental) language.

Remember. . . There are many other language families, including Uralic, Altaic, and Austronesian. You can find more information on these families (and others) on the Companion Website at www.pearsoncanada.ca/ogrady, Chapter 7.

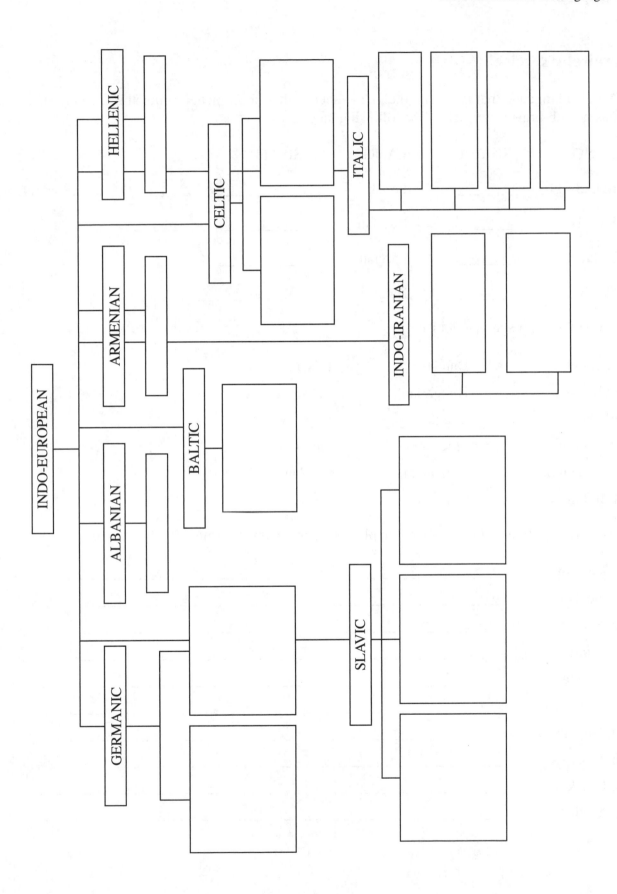

Exercise! Exercise!

1. Name a language that is a sister (i.e., a member of the sub-branch, or branch if the language has no sub-branch) to each of the following languages.

LANG	SISTER	LANG	SISTER
Italian	_____	Polish	_____
Swedish	_____	Russian	_____
Yiddish	_____	Latvian	_____
Catalan	_____	Bulgarian	_____

2. Circle the language that does not fit.

   a. Greek   Danish   Frisian
   b. Russian   Hungarian   Polish
   c. Persian   Bengali   Romany
   d. Portuguese   Macedonian   Sardinian
   e. Albanian   Romanian   Catalan
   f. Italian   German   Spanish

3. Give the sub-branch (and branch if applicable) for each of the following languages.

   a. Danish   _____
   b. Scots Gaelic   _____
   c. Sardinian   _____
   d. Kurdish   _____
   e. Bengali   _____
   f. Slovene   _____
   g. Bulgarian   _____
   h. Czech   _____
   i. Greek   _____
   j. Yiddish   _____

4. Determine whether each of the following statements is true or false.

   a. The genetic relationship between Norwegian and Swedish is the same as that between Latvian and Lithuanian.

TRUE   FALSE

   b. The genetic relationship between Spanish and French is the same as that between Czech and Polish.

TRUE   FALSE

   c. The genetic relationship between Swedish and Slovene is the same as that between Norwegian and German.

TRUE   FALSE

   d. The genetic relationship between Frisian and Danish is the same as the genetic relationship between Italian and Romanian.

TRUE   FALSE

QUICK REMINDER!

There is a third type of classification: areal. This type of classification groups languages according to shared characteristics based on geographical contact. Languages that are geographical neighbours often borrow sounds, morphemes, words, and even syntactic structures from each other. This means that neighbouring languages may resemble each other even though they are not genetically related!

REVIEW! REVIEW!   Make sure you know. . .

- – what mutual intelligibility means
- – the difference between the three types of classification
- – the different types of language universals
- – the difference between marked and unmarked characteristics
- – how to determine possible and impossible phonological, morphological, and syntactic systems
- – the common phonological systems found across the world's languages
- – the four types of morphological systems found across the world's languages
- – the three most common word order patterns found across the world's languages
- – phonological, morphological, and syntactic universals
- – the branches of the Indo-European language family
- – the languages of each branch of the Indo-European language family

QUESTIONS? PROBLEMS? DIFFICULTIES?

_____

_____

_____

_____

_____

_____

_____

_____

_____

_____

_____

_____

CHAPTER 8. HISTORICAL LINGUISTICS: THE STUDY OF LANGUAGE CHANGE

Historical linguistics studies the principles governing language change, including both its description and explanation. Important topics and concepts in this chapter include the following:

1. Phonetic sound change
2. Phonological change
3. Morphological change
4. Syntactic change
5. Lexical change
6. Semantic change
7. Language reconstruction
8. The discovery of Indo-European
9. Naturalness and typology

LANGUAGE CHANGE

Consider the following important points concerning language change:

⇒ **Frequency.** Language is always changing. However, for a particular change to take hold, it must be accepted by the language community as a whole.

⇒ **Regularity.** Language change is regular and systematic. Some changes affect all words without exception. Other changes begin in a small number of words in the speech of a small number of speakers. These changes may gradually spread through both the vocabulary and the population.

⇒ **Acquisition.** Languages change because of the way language is acquired. Children are not born with a complete grammar but must construct a grammar based on the language they are exposed to. Therefore, changes will occur from one generation to the next, and because all children have the same genetic capabilities for language and construct their grammars in similar fashions, the same patterns of change repeat both within and across languages.

⇒ **Cause.** Causes of language change include articulatory simplification (see table 8.2 on p. 251 of the text for some examples), spelling pronunciation, reanalysis, analogy, and borrowing as a result of language contact. Hypercorrections (overgeneralizations about a particular rule) can also cause languages to change.

SEQUENTIAL SOUND CHANGE

While all aspects of a language's structure can change, sound change is often the most noticeable. There are many types of sound change that can occur; however, most sound changes involve sequences of segments. The major types of sequential sound changes are outlined in the boxes below.

⇒ **Assimilation.**   Assimilation involves sounds changing to become more like the nearby sounds. Assimilation increases the efficiency of the articulations involved in producing the sequence of sounds. Such an increase in efficiency results from simplifying articulatory movements.

Some common examples include the following:

Assimilation Processes

a.   Place of Articulation Assimilation
   A sound becomes similar to a nearby sound in terms of place of articulation. See table 8.4 on p. 254 of the text for some examples.

b.   Voicing Assimilation
   A consonant changes its voicing to be like a nearby sound. See the first example in table 8.5 on p. 254 of the text.

c.   Total Assimilation
   A sound assimilates totally to a following sound. See table 8.6 on p. 254 of the text for some examples.

d.   Palatalization
   A non-palatal sound becomes or moves toward a palatal sound. This usually occurs near a sound that is made with the tongue at or near the hard palate—usually [j] or [i]. Palatalization is often the first step in the process of creating an affricate (called affrication) from a stop. See table 8.7 on p. 255 of the text for some examples.

e.   Nasalization
   A vowel becomes nasal near a nasal sound. See table 8.8 on p. 255 of the text for some examples.

Remember. . .   Assimilation most often affects adjacent segments. It can, however, apply at a distance. Umlaut, which is responsible for irregular plurals such as *goose/geese,* is an example of such an assimilatory process. See table 8.9 on p. 255 of the text for some more examples of this process.

⇒ **Weakening and Deletion.** Sounds, both vowels and consonants, tend to weaken over time. They can also delete. Deletion is often the end result of the weakening process.

- Full vowels have a tendency to weaken, or reduce, to a schwa-like vowel. Vowels are often subject to deletion when they occur in unstressed syllables.

  Vowel weakening and deletion processes include the following:

Vowel Weakening	**Vowel Deletion**
a. Vowel Reduction A full vowel reduces to schwa. This process typically affects short vowels in unstressed syllables.	a. Apocope The deletion of a word-final vowel b. Syncope The deletion of a word-internal vowel

See table 8.14 on p. 258 and table 8.15 on p. 259 of the text for some examples of the above processes.

- Consonants tend to weaken along a path determined by the hierarchy shown below.

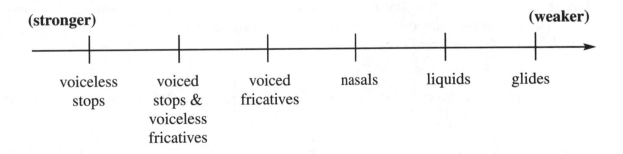

Remember... It is most common for consonants to weaken over time. However, consonants can also strengthen. For example, glides often strengthen to affricates. This process is called glide strengthening and is common in word-initial position. See table 8.19 on p. 261 of the text for some examples.

Consonantal weakening and deletion processes include the following:

Consonantal Weakening	**Consonantal Deletion**

a. Degemination
    A long sound becomes short.
    This is usually the first step in
    the weakening of consonants.
 	
b. Frication
    A stop weakens to a fricative.
    This often occurs between vowels.
 	
c. Voicing
    Voiceless stops or fricatives
    weaken to voiced stops or
    fricatives.
 	
d. Rhotacism
    This is a fairly common type of
    weakening in which [z] weakens
    to [r].
	a. Consonantal Deletion
	    Consonants often delete when
	    they occur as part of a
	    consonant cluster, or as the
	    final consonant in a word, or
	    as the last step after several
	    weakening processes. See
	    table 8.16 on p. 259 of the
	    text for some examples.

See table 8.17 on p. 260 of the text for examples of degemination, frication, voicing, and Deletion in the Romance languages, and table 8.18 on p. 260 of the text for some examples of rhotacism in the Germanic languages.

Remember. . . Geminate (long) consonants are stronger than their non-geminate counterparts. Geminate consonants are often represented using two identical sounds. So, [tt] represents a voiceless alveolar geminate stop.

Now. . . Which is stronger? [t] or [s]? [t] or [d]? [tt] or [t]? [s] or [z]? [s] or [ss]? [v] or [f]?

⇒ **Others.** There are other types of sound changes as well, many of which will be familiar to you from the phonology chapter! These types of sound changes are not as frequent as those already presented, but like assimilation, they tend to have the overall effect of making sequences of sounds easier to articulate. Like assimilation, these changes can also affect adjacent segments or segments at a distance.

Some common examples include the following:

Other Processes

a. Dissimilation

   A sound becomes less like a nearby sound. This often occurs so that a sequence of sounds is easier to articulate or perceive.

b. Epenthesis

   A sound is inserted. This usually occurs to break up a consonant cluster that is hard to pronounce. See table 8.10 on p. 256 of the text for some examples from Old English, and table 8.12 on p. 257 of the text for some examples from the development of Spanish.

c. Metathesis

   The position of two sounds changes relative to each other. See table 8.13 on p. 257 of the text for some examples from Old English.

OTHER TYPES OF SOUND CHANGE

There are two other common types of sound change, segmental and auditory, which do not involve segments changing under the influence of nearby segments.

⇒ **Segmental Change.**   Segmental change involves a change within the segment itself. Segmental change often involves affricates. Affricates are considered a complex segment, since they consist of a stop and a fricative. Complex segments often simplify over time.

One common example is given below:

Segmental Change Processes

Deaffrication

   An affricate becomes a fricative by eliminating the stop portion of the affricate. See tables 8.20 and 8.21 on p. 261 of the text for an example of this process in the change from Old French to French, and how this process influenced the pronunciation of French words borrowed into English.

⇒ **Auditory Change.** In addition to the articulatory considerations typically involved in sound change, auditory factors can also have an influence.

One common example is given below:

Auditory Change Processes

Substitution
  One segment is replaced with a similar sounding segment. See table 8.22 on p. 262 of the text for an example of substitution in the change from Middle English to English.

NAME THAT SOUND CHANGE

Each of the following exemplifies one or more sound changes. The older form is on the left, and the more recent form is on the right. Identify the sound change that has taken place for each of the underlined sound(s).

1. Proto-Quechua   [cum<u>p</u>i]   >   Tena   [cum<u>b</u>i]

   _____

2. Old English   [<u>hl</u>af]   >   Modern English   [<u>l</u>of]

   _____

3. Latin   [mar<u>e</u>]   >   Portuguese   [mar]

   _____

4. Proto-Slavic   [<u>k</u>emerai]   >   Russian   [<u>tʃ</u>emer]

   _____

5. Proto-Tupi-Guaraní   [puʔ<u>am</u>]   >   Guaraní   [puʔ<u>ã</u>]

   _____

6. Latin   [orn<u>a</u>mentum]   >   Old French   [orn<u>ə</u>ment]

   _____

7. Old English   [knotta]   >   Mod. English   [nɑt]

_____

8. Proto-Germanic   [doːmaz]   >   Old Icelandic   [doːmr]

_____

9. Latin   [venre]   >   Spanish   [vendre]

_____

10. Early Latin   [inpossibiliss]   >   Latin   [impossibilis]

_____

11. Proto-Bantu   [mukiːpa]   >   Swahili   [mʃipa]

_____

12. Proto-Romance   [sekuru]   >   Spanish   [seguru]

_____

13. Latin   [pekkatum]   >   [pekaθo]   >   [pekaðo]

_____

14. Proto-Romance   [biskɔktu]   >   Latin   [biskotto]

_____

Think. . . Sound change tends to occur in a step-by-step fashion, so a single sound can often be subject to a number of different sound changes. But these multiple sound changes are often not visible in the resulting form.

For example, the word meaning "good" underwent several changes as it developed from Proto-Germanic to Old Icelandic. See if you can identify all the changes, including any intermediate but not visible changes that affected the underlined sounds.

Proto-Germanic   [goːdas]   Old Icelandic   [goːðr]

PHONOLOGICAL SOUND CHANGE

All of the sound changes described in the previous sections can influence a language's phonological inventory. They can add, eliminate, or rearrange the phonemes within a language.

⇒ **Phonological Splits.**   A phonological split adds phonemes to a language's phonological inventory. In a phonological split, allophones of the same phoneme come to contrast with each other. They split into separate phonemes. This is often caused by a loss of the conditioning environment making sounds that were once predictable no longer predictable and therefore phonemic.

Consider the following example in the development of English.

Old English: In Old English, /n/ had two allophones:

          – [ŋ] occurred before velar stops
          – [n] occurred elsewhere

          So a word like *sing* was pronounced as [sɪŋg].

Middle English: Consonant deletion removed [g] at the end of a word (after a nasal consonant). This created a minimal pair between *sing*, now pronounced as [sɪŋ], and *sin*, pronounced as [sɪn]. And minimal pairs tell us that sounds contrast.

This split can be diagrammed as follows:

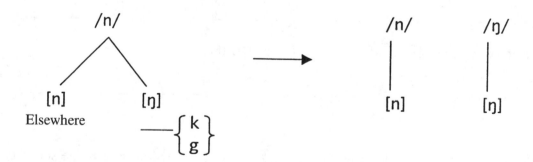

    So. . . what phoneme was added to the language?

Think. . . Spelling often lags behind sound change. We still spell *sing* with the final *g* even though it is now silent. Many silent letters in our English spelling system are a reflection of older pronunciations! Think of other words that have silent letters. Were these silent letters pronounced at one time?

⇒ **Phonological Mergers.** While a phonological split adds phonemes to a language, a phonological merger reduces the number of contrasts.

A phonological merger occurred in the development of German. At one time, /s/ and /z/ were contrastive sounds: They could occur in the same environments. Later [z] was only found between vowels. This merger can be diagrammed as follows:

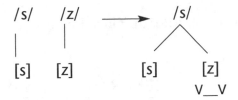

So. . . What phoneme was lost from the language? What type of sound change is most likely responsible for this merger?

See figure 8.7 on p. 264 of the text for an example of a phonological merger that happened in Cockney English. Think about what phonemes were lost as a result of this merger. What type of sound change is most likely responsible for this merger?

⇒ **Phonological Shifts.** A phonological shift does not add to or reduce a language's phonemic inventory. Rather, some of the phonemes are reorganized with respect to each other.

The Great English Vowel Shift, beginning in Middle English, is an example of a phonological shift affecting vowels. The chart below shows the Middle English long vowels before the vowel shift occurred.

	FRONT	CENTRAL	BACK
HIGH	i:		u:
MID	e:		o:
	ε:		ɔ:
LOW		a:	

The Great English Vowel Shift affected only the long vowels. It probably began with the diphthongization of [i] and [u]. The creation of the diphthongs [aj] and [aw] reduced the number of simple vowels from seven to five. The remaining vowels then shifted upward in their articulation.

The vowel shifts are summarized below.

1. Long [i] became the diphthong [aj]   3. Long [e] became [i]   6. Long [o] became [u]
2. Long [u] became the diphthong [aw]   4. Long [ɛ] became [i]   7. Long [ɔ] became [o]
                                          5. Long [a] became [e]

See figure 8.8 on p. 264 of the text for a diagram outlining how the vowels shifted.

As the vowels shifted, length was lost. After the Great English Vowel Shift, the long vowels now looked like this:

	FRONT	CENTRAL	BACK
HIGH	i		u
MID	e	aj aw	o
LOW			

Compare the two vowel charts. What was the overall effect of the vowel shift in terms of the number of vowels?

Think. . . Many of our vowel spellings reflect Middle English pronunciation. For example, the word *goose* is spelled with *oo* because this orthographic symbol represented [o:]. *Goose* continues to be spelled this way, even though as a result of the Great English Vowel Shift, [o:] became [u], changing the pronunciation of *goose* to [gus]. One reason for this mismatch between spelling and pronunciation is that spelling was standardized before the vowels had finished shifting.

Try This! For each of the Middle English words below, state the vowel change that would have occurred as a result of the Great English Vowel Shift, and then give the spelling of the corresponding Modern English word.

Middle English	Vowel Change	Modern English Word
[no:n]	_____	_____
[li:fə]	_____	_____
[swe:t]	_____	_____
[bɔ:st]	_____	_____
[gu:n]	_____	_____

GRIMM'S LAW

Phonological shifts can also affect consonants. One famous example is Grimm's Law, named for Jacob Grimm (of Grimm's Fairy Tables). In 1822, Jacob Grimm noticed some regular correspondences between the Germanic languages and the non-Germanic, Indo-European languages. The correspondences he noticed are listed below:

Non-Germanic Consonant	As in these Non-Germanic Words	Corresponding Germanic Consonant	As in these Germanic Cognates
[p]	pater (Latin)	[f]	father (German – Vater)
[t]	tonare (Latin)	[θ]	thunder
[k]	canis (Latin)	[x] → [h]	hound (German – Hund)
[b]	kannabis (Greek)	[p]	hemp
[d]	duo (Latin)	[t]	two
[g]	ager (Latin)	[k]	acre
[bh]	bhrata (Sanskrit)	[b]	brother (German – Bruder)
[dh]	vidhava (Sanskrit)	[d]	widow
[gh]	ghansas (Sanskrit)	[g]	goose (German – Gans)

Grimm explained these correspondences using three sound changes.

(1) Voiceless stops became voiceless fricatives (i.e., weakening – frication).

PIE		Proto-Germanic (PG)
[p]	>	[f]
[t]	>	[θ]
[k]	>	[x] → [h]

This first sound change involved frication: the weakening of stops to fricatives, a sequential sound change. The result of this weakening process left Proto-Germanic without voiceless stops.

(2) Voiced stops became voiceless stops.

PIE		PG
[b]	>	[p]
[d]	>	[t]
[g]	>	[k]

This second sound change involved devoicing the voiced stops. This most likely happened because it is rare for a language to completely lack voiceless stops. The reintroduction of voiceless stops in turn created a lack of voiced stops.

(3) Voiced aspirated stops became voiced unaspirated stops.

PIE		PG
[bh]	>	[b]
[dh]	>	[d]
[gh]	>	[g]

This third sound change involved deaspirating the voiced aspirated stops and filled the gap left by (2). This third change, of course, created yet another gap: a lack of voiced aspirated stops. This gap was not filled!

Try This! For each bolded sound in the reconstructed Proto-Indo-European (PIE) word, give the Germanic sound that resulted from Grimm's Law. Then give the Modern English equivalent of the proto-form.

PIE WORD	GERMANIC SOUND (IN IPA)	ENGLISH WORD IN REGULAR SPELLING
1. *gel	_____	_____ool
2. *leb	_____	li_____
3. *grebh	_____	_____ra_____
4. *ghreib	_____	_____ri_____
5. *pulo	_____	_____oul
6. *koimo	_____	_____ome
7. *swad	_____	swee_____

Remember. . . Grimm's Law is part of the body of research that led to the discovery of the Indo-European language family, and developed the methods of comparative reconstruction (discussed later in this chapter). Read the discussion on pp. 293 to 297 of the text and think about the following:

- Why did Jacob Grimm (and other historical linguists) work with ancient languages such as Sanskrit and Latin?

- Why are there exceptions to Grimm's Law?

- What is the relationship between the sound changes of Grimm's Law and typology? What about between Proto-Indo-European consonants and typology?

MORPHOLOGICAL CHANGE

Morphological change affects the structure of words within a language. Morphological change involves either the addition or the loss of affixes. Recall from morphology that affixes are bound morphemes that attach to a base. Affixes provide grammatical information (inflection) or are used to create new words (derivation).

⇒ **The Addition of Affixes.** Affixes can be added to a language through

- borrowing
- grammaticalization (creating new grammatical forms from lexical forms)
- fusion (developing an affix from two words that are frequently adjacent to each other). see table 8.28 on p. 267 of the text for some examples from English, and table 8.29 on p. 267 of the text for some examples from Italian.

⇒ **The Loss of Affixes.**   Affixes can also be lost, through

- lack of use: see table 8.30 on p. 267 of the text for some English examples.
- sound change: see tables 8.31 and 8.32 on p. 268 of the text for an example of how sound changes caused the loss of Old English case affixes.

The Effect of Adding or Losing Affixes.   The loss of affixes can result in a synthetic morphological system becoming analytic, while the addition of affixes can result in an analytic morphological system gradually becoming synthetic. An analytic language has very few inflectional affixes (e.g., Modern English). In contrast, a synthetic language has many inflectional affixes (e.g., Old English).

Reanalysis and Analogy. Reanalysis and analogy can also affect the morphological structure of a language. Reanalysis adds new morphemes to a language, while analogy can change an existing morphological pattern. See table 8.35 on p. 271 of the text for an example of reanalysis in the development of English.

Try This! Folk etymology refers to the analysis of a word based on an incorrect historical division of that word into its apparent morphemes. This is usually done without reference to the word's origins. Hence the use of the word "folk"! See table 8.34 on p. 270 of the text for some English examples.

Identify the base and affix for each of the following words:

- yearling
- duckling
- gosling

- underling
- hireling
- nursling

Are the words in the second column as common as those in the first? Do they have the same meaning?

Think... Historically, each of the above words consists of a base plus the affix -ling. This German affix has the meaning "having the quality of." What has happened to this affix in terms of its form? Why would such a reanalysis occur? What happened to the affix in terms of its meaning? What might have caused this shift?

Now... What about the word *earthling*? How does this relate to the original German affix as well as the above words? What about the word *darling*?

SYNTACTIC CHANGE

Change can also affect the syntactic component of a language's grammar. Two types of change are briefly discussed below.

⇒ **Word Order.** Languages can change their basic word order pattern. One common change involves the change from an SOV (subject-object-verb) order to an SVO (subject-verb-object) order. This is a change that happened in the development of English. English descended from a Germanic language having an SOV order.

⇒ **Inversion.** *Yes-no* questions in English are formed using inversion. In Old English, both main verbs and auxiliary verbs could be inverted. In Modern English, though, only auxiliary verbs can be inverted. Now, any sentence that does not contain an auxiliary must be made into a *yes-no* question by inserting *do*.

Try This! Below are some sentences from sixteenth-century English along with their modern counterparts. Examine the sentences, and determine how negatives were formed. How does this differ from today's English?

1. A kinder gentleman treads not the Earth.
   A kinder gentleman doesn't tread the Earth.
2. Hate counsels not in such a quantity.
   Hate doesn't counsel in such a quantity.
3. Clamber not you up to the casement then.
   Don't climb up to the casement then.

THE EFFECT OF CHANGE

Changes can have far-reaching effects. A change that affects the phonology of a language can eventually affect the morphology, which in turn can affect the syntax of a language.

Consider an example (somewhat simplified) from the development of English.

⇒ Old English was an analytical language. Old English inflectional affixes included the following:

1. case: nominative, accusative, dative, genitive
2. number: singular, dual, plural
3. person: first, second, third
4. gender: masculine, feminine, neuter
5. tense: past, present

Inflectional affixes were found on pronouns, nouns, articles, adjectives, verbs, etc. As in many highly inflected languages, Old English had a fairly free word order. Sentences with SVO, VSO, and SOV orders could all be found.

⇒ During Middle English, sound changes started happening in unstressed syllables. These sound changes included the following three:

- m → n / _____#   (a bilabial nasal became alveolar at the end of a word)
- n → Ø / _____#   (alveolar nasals were deleted at the end of words)
- a, o, u, i, e → ə / _____#   (short vowels reduced to schwa at the end of words)

These three sound changes affected the inflectional system since inflectional affixes in Old English were suffixes, and suffixes are typically not stressed.

The following two examples illustrate the application of the above rules:

Old English   **Middle English**

foxum   >   foxun   >   foxu   >   foxə
helpan >   helpan >   helpa >   helpə

As a result of these sound changes, all the affixes became the same: ə. Since it was now impossible to tell what information was contained in an affix, the Old English affixes were dropped. The language's morphology became more analytic!

Think. . . Just like with phonological rules, sound changes also often require an order to their application. The three sound changes presented in the last section occurred in a certain order. [m] had to first change to [n] before it could be deleted. If this change had not occured first, then [n] would not have been deleted and the affixes would not have all become [ə].

Now. . . Why doesn't it matter when the vowel reduction change occurred?

⇒ But speakers still needed to know what the subject of a sentence was, what the object of a sentence was, and what noun an adjective referred to. To get this information, speakers of English began to:

1. rely on prepositions
2. rely on fixed word order (SVO)

So sound change can have a drastic effect on the structure of a language over time!

LEXICAL CHANGE

Lexical change involves modifications to the lexicon, usually in one of two ways.

Addition of Lexical Items

New lexical items are typically added to a language's vocabulary in one of two ways.

⇒ **Word Formation.** Some of the morphological phenomena found in the morphology chapter are frequently used to add new words to a language. These new words often fill a lexical gap resulting from technological innovations. Compounding, derivation, acronyms, backformation, blending, clipping, and conversion can all be used to add new words to a language. See table 8.38 on p. 275 of the text for some Old English examples of compounding and derivation.

⇒ **Borrowing.** As languages come into contact, they often borrow words from each other. Borrowed words are often called loan words. There are three types of influences that languages can have on each other: substratum, superstratum (see table 8.40 on p. 277 of the text for some examples), and adstratum (see tables 8.42 and 8.43 on pp. 278 and 279 of the text for some examples).

Loss of Lexical Items

Words can also be lost from the vocabulary of a language. Loan words, non-loan words, compounds, and derived words can all be lost. The most common reason for the loss of a lexical item is some societal change that has rendered an object, and therefore its name, obsolete. See table 8.46 on p. 280 of the text for some words no longer used in English. See table 8.39 on p. 276 of the text for some Old English compounds and derived forms that are no longer used.

Exercise!

1. Identify the word-formation processes responsible for the recent addition of words such as Facebook, BOGO, tase, LOL, spork, app, and (to) friend into the English language. Think of other recent additions using the same processes.

2. Identify the type of influence responsible for the addition of each of the following groups of words into English.

   a. cake, egg, husband, score, window, ugly
   b. Thames, Dover, London
   c. prayer, government, revenue, fashion, army
   d. toboggan, moccasin, potlatch, chipmunk

SEMANTIC CHANGE

In addition to the addition and loss of lexical items, the meanings of existing words can also change over time. There are seven main types of semantic change.

Type	Definition
Broadening	The meaning of a word becomes more general or inclusive over time. See table 8.47 on p. 280 of the text for some examples.
Narrowing	The meaning of a word becomes less general or inclusive over time. See table 8.48 on p. 280 of the text for some examples.
Amelioration	The meaning of a word changes to become more positive or favourable. See table 8.49 on p. 281 of the text for some examples.
Pejoration	The meaning of a word changes to become less positive or favourable. See table 8.50 on p. 281 of the text for some examples.
Weakening	The meaning of a word weakens over time. See table 8.51 on p. 281 of the text for some examples.
Semantic Shift	A word loses its former meaning and takes on a new, but related, meaning. See table 8.52 on p. 282 of the text for some examples.
Metaphor	A word with a concrete meaning takes on a more abstract meaning, without losing the original meaning. See table 8.53 on p. 282 of the text for some examples.

Practice! Practice! For each of the following words, identify which of the processes in the above table best captures the semantic change that has occurred.

Word	Earlier Meaning	Later Meaning	Semantic Change
1. aisle	passage between pews of a church	passage between rows of seats	_____
2. mischievous	disastrous	playfully annoying	_____
3. blue	a colour	being melancholy	_____
4. spill	shed blood	waste of liquid	_____
5. fond	foolish	affectionate	_____
6. butler	male servant in charge of the wine cellar	male servant in charge of a household	_____
7. passenger	traveller	one who travels by vehicle or vessel	_____
8. wretch	exile	unhappy person	_____
9. notorious	widely known	widely and unfavourably known	_____
10. chair	a seat	head of a university or college department	_____

Quick Reminder. . . Language change must spread through both the vocabulary of the language and its speakers. Read the discussion on pp. 282 to 285 of the text to learn more about this process.

COMPARATIVE RECONSTRUCTION

By comparing languages with each other, it can be determined if they are or are not genetically related. Genetically related languages are languages that have descended from a common ancestor. Using the comparative method, this ancestor can be reconstructed. This is typically done by comparing later forms to determine what the earlier form must have looked like. Although it is possible to reconstruct all aspects of a language's grammar, the focus here is on phonological reconstruction.

Some Important Terms

⇒ **Cognates** are phonetically and semantically similar words that have descended from a common source. Cognates are compared to reconstruct what this common source must have looked like.

⇒ A **proto-language** is a language that has been reconstructed using a comparative method. Written evidence of what this language actually looked like typically doesn't exist.

⇒ A proto-language consists of **proto-forms**. These are the individual reconstructed words of the proto-language. Proto-forms are usually indicated with an asterisk (*).

Some Important Strategies

⇒ The **phonetic plausibility strategy** requires that any change posited to account for the differences between the proto-form (the ancestor) and the cognates must be phonetically plausible. That is, a sound change that has been found to occur in the course of language development must be able to account for these differences. For our purposes, the sound changes listed under the heading **sequential change**, as well as under **segmental** and **auditory change**, are all plausible.

⇒ The **majority rules strategy** operates in the absence of a phonetically plausible sound change. This strategy states that when no phonetically plausible sound change can be determined, we may reconstruct the segment that occurs in the majority of the cognates. This strategy should only be used as a last resort.

An Example:

Reconstruct the proto-forms for the data below.

<u>Lang A</u>	<u>Lang B</u>	<u>Lang C</u>
(1) [hauda]	[hauta]	[hauta]
(2) [sav]	[ʃive]	[sav]

⇒ **First.** Determine the number of sounds that need to be reconstructed. This is straightforward for (1) in that all the cognates have the same number of sounds: five. The situation is different in (2). In (2), two of the cognates contain three sounds, and one contains four. If four sounds are reconstructed, then deletion must have occurred in Langs A and C. If three sounds are reconstructed, then epenthesis must have occurred in Lang B. It is more plausible for deletion rather than epenthesis to occur at the end of words. (2), therefore, requires the reconstruction of four sounds.

⇒ **Second.** Look for any total correspondences. These are sounds that have not changed; they are the same for all the cognates. Reconstruct these sounds. The proto-forms after this step are *hau?a and *??v?.

⇒ **Third.** Examine alternations between the different languages and determine phonetic plausibility.

- (1) exhibits an alternation between [t] and [d]. Either [t] or [d] can be reconstructed in the proto-form.

    - If [d] is reconstructed, then the change from the proto-form to the form in Langs B and C ([d] > [t]) does not correspond to a sound change. Therefore, this has a low phonetic plausibility.
    - If [t] is reconstructed, then the change from the proto-form to Lang A ([t] > [d]) can be explained as an instance of weakening (a voiceless stop weakens to a voiced stop). This has a high phonetic plausibility.

  Reconstruct the change that has the highest phonetic plausibility. The proto-form therefore becomes *hauta.

- (2) exhibits three alternations. First, consider the alternation between [s] and [ʃ].

    - If [ʃ] is reconstructed, then the change [ʃ] > [s] in Langs A and C has low phonetic plausibility, since it does not correspond to a sound change.
    - If [s] is reconstructed, then the change [s] > [ʃ] in Lang B can be explained as palatalization. Therefore, [s] is reconstructed.

  Second, consider the presence or absence of a word-final vowel in the cognates. Recall from above that it is more plausible for a sound to delete than to be epenthesized in this position. Therefore, [e] is reconstructed.

  Third, consider the vowel alternation between [a] and [i].

    - If [a] is reconstructed then the change [a] > [i] occurs in Lang B.
    - If [i] is reconstructed, then the opposite change ([i] > [a]) occurs in Langs A and C.

  Neither one corresponds to a sound change, and so both have a low phonetic plausibility. This strategy, therefore, cannot be used to reconstruct this segment. The proto-form, after this step, is *s?ve.

⇒ **Fourth.** Any sounds for which no phonetically plausible sound change could be identified require using the majority rules strategy. In (2), the alternation between [a] and [i] cannot be accounted for using a sound change; therefore, [a] is reconstructed since it occurs in the majority of the cognates. The proto-form becomes *save. Notice that this proto-form does not correspond to any of the cognates. This is okay!

⇒ **Fifth.** Put together a summary of the sound changes that have occurred since the different languages split from the proto-language. Remember that the proto-form you have just reconstructed is older than the cognates from the descendant languages. Voicing and apocope have occurred in the development of Lang A, while only Apocope occurred in the development of Lang C. Palatalization occurred in the development of Lang B.

Some Things To Think About

- Sound changes that tend to occur across languages are often referred to as natural. Sound changes that are phonetically plausible are more natural than those that are not. **Naturalness** is important to think about when doing reconstruction, since language change is regular and systematic.

- It is also important to think about universal properties of language when doing reconstruction. This is often referred to as **typological plausibility**.

Think about the change from voiced stops to voiceless stops in Grimm's Law. This change has a low phonetic plausibility and is therefore not a natural sound change. However, this change occurred because weakening (frication) left the language without voiceless stops, which are found in virtually every language. The change from voiced to voiceless stops, therefore, happened for typological reasons.

REMINDER! REMINDER!

In order to do language reconstruction, you need to be able to identify phonetically plausible sound changes. And in order to do this, you need to know the different types of sequential, segmental, and auditory sound changes. Make sure you are very familiar with them!

Practice! Each data group on this and the next pages contains some cognate sets. Assume that all the cognates are in phonetic transcription and that all members of the cognate set have the same meaning. Reconstruct the proto-forms and list all the sound changes that have taken place in each language. Remember: For some languages there may be no sound changes, while for others there may be multiple sound changes.

While the data are hypothetical or highly regularized, they exemplify processes found in actual languages.

GROUP ONE

	Lang A	Lang B	Proto-Form
1.	[mũtə]	[muθo]	* _____
2.	[fumə]	[vumo]	* _____
3.	[pippon]	[bipona]	* _____
4.	[nõk]	[noga]	* _____
5.	[wus]	[juza]	* _____
6.	[fitə]	[vido]	* _____

Summary of Sound Changes:

Lang A	
Lang B	

Remember. . . The reconstructed form does not have to be the same as any of the forms found in the descendant languages!

GROUP TWO

	Lang A	Lang B	Lang C	Lang D	Proto-Form
1.	[puxa]	[buga]	[puka]	[puk]	*_____
2.	[nizudz]	[nizuz]	[nizu]	[nir]	*_____

Summary of Sound Changes:

Lang A	
Lang B	
Lang C	
Lang D	

GROUP THREE

	Lang A	Lang B	Lang C	Lang D	Proto-Form
1.	[pika]	[big]	[pik]	[biha]	*_____
2.	[wira]	[wiz]	[wir]	[wira]	*_____
3.	[vida]	[bita]	[vit]	[viθa]	*_____

Summary of Sound Changes:

Lang A	
Lang B	
Lang C	
Lang D	

GROUP FOUR

	Lang A	Lang B	Lang C	Proto-Form
1.	[tuhu]	[tuu]	[tuhu]	*_____
2.	[nika]	[nika]	[nika]	*_____
3.	[kaza]	[kasa]	[kaʃa]	*_____
4.	[tuku]	[tuku]	[tuku]	*_____
5.	[juhu]	[juu]	[juhu]	*_____
6.	[pida]	[piθa]	[pita]	*_____
7.	[kadi]	[kaθi]	[kati]	*_____
8.	[kwazi]	[kwasi]	[kwaʃi]	*_____

Summary of Sound Changes:

Lang A	
Lang B	
Lang C	

**Reminder. . . Always look for a plausible sound change first.
Only use majority rules as a last resort.**

GROUP FIVE

	Lang A	Lang B	Lang C	Lang D	Proto-Form
1.	[puxə]	[buga]	[pukka]	[puk]	* _____
2.	[lirə]	[liza]	[litsu]	[wis]	* _____
3.	[mani]	[mani]	[mãnni]	[mã]	* _____
4.	[wanə]	[jana]	[wãnna]	[wã]	* _____
5.	[kaxə]	[gaga]	[kakka]	[kak]	* _____
6.	[tupi]	[dubi]	[tubi]	[tup]	* _____
7.	[samu]	[samu]	[sãmmu]	[sã]	* _____
8.	[matu]	[madu]	[madu]	[mat]	* _____

Summary of Sound Changes:

Lang A	
Lang B	
Lang C	
Lang D	

Now try this one!

<u>Proto-Middle Indic</u>   (Note: The data have been modified.)

	Magadhi Prakrit	Pali Prakrit	Maharastri	Gloss
1.	[abala]	[apara]	[avara]	"other"
2.	[diba]	[dipa]	[diva]	"lamp"
3.	[hasta]	[hatta]	[hatta]	"hand"
4.	[loga]	[loka]	[loa]	"world"
5.	[nala]	[nara]	[nara]	"man"
6.	[nispʰala]	[nippʰala]	[nippʰala]	"fruitless"
7.	[paskʰaladi]	[pakkʰalati]	[pakkʰalai]	"(he) stumbles"
8.	[pidi]	[pita]	[pia]	"father"
9.	[puspa]	[puppa]	[puppa]	"flower"
10.	[ʃuska]	[sukka]	[sukka]	"dry"

Proto-forms:

1.	6.
2.	7.
3.	8.
4.	9.
5.	10.

Sound Changes:

Magadhi Prakrit	Pali Prakrit	Maharastri

REVIEW! REVIEW! Make sure you know about the following:

– the nature of language change
– the causes of language change (five)
– how change spreads through a language and its population
– the different types of sequential, segmental, and auditory sound changes
– how to identify sound changes
– the difference between phonological splits, mergers, and shifts
– the sound changes making up the Great English Vowel Shift
– the three sound changes making up Grimm's Law
– the different types of morphological and syntactic change
– the different types of lexical and semantic change
– how to reconstruct proto-forms and to summarize sound changes
– the role of naturalness and typology in language reconstruction

QUESTIONS? PROBLEMS? DIFFICULTIES?

_____

_____

_____

_____

_____

_____

_____

_____

_____

_____

CHAPTER 9.
ABORIGINAL LANGUAGES OF CANADA

Studying the Aboriginal languages of Canada involves examining both the genetic and structural characteristics of these languages. Important concepts found in this chapter include the following:

1. Stocks, phyla, and isolates
2. Canada's Aboriginal languages
3. Lingua francas, trade languages, and pidgins
4. Contact languages in Canada
5. Language decline
6. Structural diversity
7. Polysynthesis

STUDYING ABORIGINAL LANGUAGES

The study of the Aboriginal languages of North America is valuable for both historical and theoretical reasons. Some of these are outlined below.

⇒ It is a myth that Aboriginal languages are "primitive" in any way. Aboriginal languages display significant structural diversity, and certain structural and semantic properties of these languages are not found in languages that have received more attention from linguists (such as English).

⇒ The study of Aboriginal languages has revealed important new insights into the nature of human language.

⇒ Aboriginal languages provide linguists with the opportunity to test principles and theoretical concepts. Concepts and principles developed by studying other languages can be reconsidered in light of new data.

⇒ The study of Aboriginal languages can lead to important insights in anthropology and archaeology: Languages can provide valuable clues about the origin and migration patterns of the indigenous peoples of North America.

⇒ The Aboriginal languages are in a state of decline. Many Aboriginal languages became extinct in the past several centuries, and others face extinction today. More recently, many Aboriginal communities have been working to preserve their languages and cultures.

GENETIC CLASSIFICATION: TERMINOLOGY

Recall from Chapter 7 that genetic classification groups languages according to their development from a shared ancestry. Languages descended from a common language are related, and are said to comprise a language family. The following concepts are also important in understanding how linguists arrive at the genetic classification of the Aboriginal languages of Canada. Make sure you are familiar with the meanings of these terms.

Term	Definition
dialect	A dialect is a variety that can be shown to be different in systematic ways from another variety of the same language (for example, English as spoken in Vancouver compared to English as spoken in London, England). See Chapter 7 for a discussion on why it is not always a straightforward task to classify a particular variety as a language or a dialect.
stock	Language families that are believed to be related are placed into a larger group called a language stock.
phylum	Language stocks that are believed to be related are placed into a larger group called a superstock or phylum. The plural of *phylum* is *phyla*. Another term for phylum is *macrofamily*.
isolate	An isolate is a language that appears to have no known relatives. In other words, it cannot be shown that the language shares a common ancestor with any other language or languages that linguists have studied.

CANADA'S ABORIGINAL LANGUAGES

Linguists generally recognize the following language families and isolates, organized according to the three political groupings of Canada's indigenous peoples:

⇒ First Nations

- Algonquian
- Athabaskan-Eyak-Tlingit
- Haida (isolate)
- Iroquoian
- Ktunaxa/Kootenay-Kinbasket (isolate)
- Salish
- Siouan-Catawban
- Tsimshian
- Wakashan

Inuit

- Eskimo-Aleut

Métis
- Michif (unique mixed language)

Exercise! Below is a map of Canada with numbers. Study figure 9.1 on p. 309 of the text and see how many language families and isolates you can identify. Write the number corresponding to the location of the isolate or language family beside its name.

Algonquian _____   Salish _____

Athabaskan _____   Siouan _____

Eskimo-Aleut _____   Tlingit _____

Iroquoian _____   Tsimshian _____

Haida _____   Wakashan _____

Kutunaxa _____

Remember. . . The Athabaskan and Tlingit languages are usually considered to be part of the larger Na-Dene language family.

Now. . . Study tables 9.1 to 9.9 on pp. 310 to 314 of the text. Name the language family of which each language below is a member. Write *isolate* if the language given is an isolate. See how many you can identify without looking up the answer!

1.   Slave   _____

2.   Inuktitut   _____

3.   Ktunaxa/Kootenay-Kinbasket   _____

4.   Ojibwe   _____

5.   Okanagan   _____

6.   Gitksan   _____

7.   Nuu-chah-nulth   _____

8.   Cayuga   _____

9.   Haida   _____

10. Mohawk   _____

11. Stoney (Nakoda)   _____

12. Bella Coola/Nuxalk   _____

13. Mi'kmaq   _____

14. Dëne Sułine   _____

15. Cree   _____

Try This! See how many details about Canada's Aboriginal languages you can remember. Determine whether the following statements, based on the discussion on pp. 309 to 314 of the text, are true or false.

1.   Tuscarora and Seneca are two members of the Iroquoian family.
2.   The Wakashan languages are spoken principally in Quebec and Ontario.
3.   There are approximately 100 speakers of Eyak today.
4.   Mi'kmaq is spoken in the Maritime Provinces.
5.   An Inuktitut syllabary is used in Nunavut.
6.   The Salish family contains Canada's two most widely spoken Aboriginal languages.

7. Dialects of Cree and Ojibwe are spoken in several Canadian provinces, including British Columbia and Ontario.
8. Haida, an isolate, is spoken in Labrador.
9. Ojibwe is the only Algonquian language widely spoken outside of Canada.
10. The greatest linguistic diversity in any Aboriginal language family in Canada is found in the Na-Dene family.

CONTACT LANGUAGES: TERMINOLOGY

A contact language is a language that results when speakers of two or more languages interact closely within a community. Some of the different types of contact languages are defined below. For a more detailed discussion, see Chapter 14. You should be familiar with the following concepts and terms.

Term	Definition
lingua franca	A lingua franca is a language adopted as a means of communication among speakers of different languages. Typically, the lingua franca is the second (or third) language of the speakers who use it. Today, English is the international lingua franca of technology, science, and business.
trade language	A lingua franca used predominantly for the purpose of trade is a trade language. Often, a pidgin is a trade langauge.
pidgin	Pidgin languages emerge when there is a need for speakers of different languages to communicate (for trade purposes, for example). In comparison to non-pidgins, they are generally characterized by a limited vocabulary and a reduced grammar. A pidgin is usually not the native language of the speakers who use it. A pidgin is sometimes called a trade jargon.
mixed language	A mixed language is a language with features clearly drawn from two distinct sources. Mixed languages are believed to be quite rare.

Think. . . Contact languages can be difficult to classify genetically. Study the definitions above and think of a reason why this might be so.

ABORIGINAL CONTACT LANGUAGES

There are at least three contact languages that emerged as the result of interaction between Canadian settlers and its original inhabitants.

⇒ **Plains Sign Talk**. Plains Sign Talk is a lingua franca that was commonly used in the Plains area during the nineteenth century.

⇒ **Chinook Jargon.** Chinook Jargon is a trade language widely used in the nineteenth and early twentieth centuries in the Pacific Northwest, including British Columbia. Like most pidgins, Chinook Jargon has a simplified or reduced grammar.

⇒ **Michif.** Michif is the mixed languge of the Métis. In Michif, the nominal morphology is based on Métis French and the verbal morphology on Cree.

Some Things To Remember

⇒ In contact situations, words that are taken from one language into another often undergo phonological adaptation (i.e., sounds in the borrowed words are altered or substituted so that they conform to the phonology of the borrowing language). For example, if the borrowing language does not have the labiodental fricatives [f v], speakers may substitute a stop that is close in place of articulation (e.g., [p b]) for the labiodental fricative in words of the source language.

⇒ Words that are taken from one of the languages in a contact environment may also undergo morphological reanalysis (see Chapter 8): Speakers interpret the morpheme boundaries differently from how they are interepreted in the source language. Reanalysis can also happen independently of contact. For example, in English, the earlier determiner + noun sequence *a napron* was later reinterpreted as *an apron*.

Exercise! The vocabulary of Chinook Jargon comes predominatly from Chinook, Nuu-chah-nulth (Wakashan), French, and English. Below are the meanings of some Chinook and Nuu-chah-nulth terms. Use these meanings to identify the words from French and English in the Chinook Jargon phrases (not in phonetic transcription) on the following page.

- kopa (Chinook) "of, about"
- klatawa (Nuu-chah-nulth) "to go, to travel"
- mamook (Nuu-chah-nulth) "to make"
- potlatch (Nuu-chah-nulth) "to give"

- saghalie (Chinook) "up, above"
- tahtlum (Chinook) "ten"
- tenas (Nuu-chah-nulth) "little, small"

1. tenas cosho
2. tahtlum cole
3. mamook bloom
4. doctin kopa letah
5. tenas pish
6. mamook piah
7. klatawa kopa saghalie lamontay
8. potlatch lamah
9. poolie lapome
10. mamook le pan

Now. . . Match these English translations to the above Chinook Jargon phrases.

1. to make/build fire
2. shake hands (i.e., "give" one's hand)
3. to go to the top of the mountain
4. rotten apple
5. knead (make) bread
6. minnow (i.e., small fish)
7. to sweep
8. ten years (winters)
9. piglet
10. dentist

Think. . . What other observations can you make about the Chinook Jargon examples?

Source: Thomas, E.H. *Chinook: A History and a Dictionary of the Northwest Coast Trade Jargon*. Portland: Binfords & Mort, 1935 (reprinted 1970).

DECLINE OF ABORIGINAL LANGUAGES

Language decline is a situation in which the functions and number of speakers of a language decrease. Language decline can lead, of course, to language death or extinction (when there are no more speakers of a language).

Exercise!   From the group of Aboriginal languages below, identify three languages that are extinct (E); three languages that face imminent extinction (IE) because they have fewer than a dozen speakers left; and three languages that have recently had an orthography (O) established.

Dogrib	_____	Okanagan	_____	Secwepemctsin	_____
Ktunaxa	_____	Pentlatch	_____	Tagish	_____
Laurentian	_____	Plains Cree	_____	Tuscarora	_____
Nicola	_____	Squamish	_____	Tsilhqut'in	_____

Think. . . Identify at least three different factors that have led to the decline of Aboriginal languages in Canada.

STRUCTURAL FEATURES OF ABORIGINAL LANGUAGES

The Aboriginal languages of Canada are structurally very diverse. The terms below capture some of the salient typological characteristics of Canadian Aboriginal languages. Make sure you know them.

⇒ **Polysynthesis**. Polysynthetic languages are languages that are morphologically very rich. Typically, words consist of many morphemes, and linguists have often observed that what can be expressed in a word in a polysynthetic language can require a sentence in other types of languages. For example (see p. 319 of the text), the English sentence *He has a good house* is expressed by the polymorphemic Inuktitut word *Iglugiktuq* (*Iglu-gik-tuq*).

⇒ **Inclusive-Exclusive**. Languages that have an inclusive-exclusive contrast make a distinction regarding whether or not the addressee is included in the interpretation of the first person plural morpheme; such languages make distinctions that are not captured by the English *we*. In the inclusive form, the addressee is included in the meaning of the first person plural (*you and I*); in the exclusive form, the addressee is excluded, so that the equivalent of *we* refers only to the speaker and others (*I and others*).

⇒ **Proximate-Obviative**.   Languages that have the proximate-obviative contrast are able to select verb forms that indicate whether the referent of the subject (a third person) of the verb is and remains the focus of the conversation (proximate), or whether the referent is different from that of the previous focus (i.e., a different third person). One way to think about this is to imagine that in English you could indicate through the verb that the second "he" is a different person from the first "he" in the following example: *John phoned. He told me that he will help me with that.* In English we cannot mark the verb "will" so that it tells us that the referent of the subject in this case is different from that of "phoned" and "told." This is the type of contrast that is possible in languages with proximate and obviative verb forms.

Try This!   See how much you can recall about some of the striking structural characteristics of Canada's Aboriginal languages. Indicate whether the following statements, based on the discussion on pp. 316 to 322 of the text, are true or false.

1.   Most Canadian Aboriginal languages have a strict VSO word order.
2.   Many Aboriginal languages have more number distinctions than English has.
3.   Canadian Aboriginal languages are largely isolating languages.
4.   Most Aboriginal languages have over 30 consonantal phonemes.
5.   Many Aboriginal languages mark nouns for animacy and inanimacy.
6.   The inclusive-exclusive contrast is found in Algonquian and other families.
7.   Word order is not fixed in many Aboriginal languages.
8.   The distinction between a noun and a verb is said to be weak in many Aboriginal languages.

Exercise! Exercise! The following data sets help illustrate the structural diversity of Canadian Aboriginal languages. Try them all!

1. Examine the following data based on the Mohawk examples on p. 321 of the text. The statements corresponding to "Sak likes her dress" have been converted to questions of the type "Does Sak like her dress?" (a *yes-no* question).

Sak ken ra-nuhwe'-s ako-atya'tawi	'Sak does like her-dress?'
Sak ken ako-atya'tawi ra-nuhwe'-s	'Sak does her-dress like?'
Ra-nuhwe'-s ken Sak ako-atya'tawi	'Like does Sak her-dress?'
Ra-nuhwe'-s ken ako-atya'tawi ne Sak	'Like does her-dress Sak?'
Ako-atya'tawi ken ra-nuhwe'-s ne Sak	'Her-dress does like Sak?'
Ako-atya'tawi ken Sak ra-nuhwe'-s	'Her-dress does Sak like?'

Describe the morpheme that is required to form a *yes-no* question in Mohawk.

Discuss word order in relation to this morpheme in Mohawk.

Now. . . Although all of the above questions correspond roughly to the English "Does Sak like her dress?" more precise interpretations would be as follows:

Sak ken ra-nuhwe'-s ako-atya'tawi	'Does <u>Sak</u> like her-dress (as opposed to Sose)?'
Sak ken ako-atya'tawi ra-nuhwe'-s	'Does <u>Sak</u> like her-dress (as opposed to Sose)?'
Ra-nuhwe'-s ken Sak ako-atya'tawi	'Does Sak <u>like</u> her-dress (as opposed to wear/dislike)?'
Ra-nuhwe'-s ken ako-atya'tawi ne	'Does Sak <u>like</u> her-dress (as opposed to wear/dislike)?'
Ako-atya'tawi ken ra-nuhwe'-s ne	'Does Sak like <u>her-dress</u> (as opposed to her hat)?'
Ako-atya'tawi ken Sak ra-nuhwe'-s	'Does Sak like <u>her-dress</u> (as opposed to her hat)?'

What observations can you make about word order flexibility in *yes-no* questions in Mohawk?

How does word order relate to interrogative placement and interpretation?

2. The following data are from Plains Cree, as spoken near James Bay (Kashechewan, Ontario). The examples have been adapted from C. Douglas Ellis, *Spoken Cree* (Winnipeg: Pica Pica Press, 1983). Examine the data; then answer the questions that follow.

As discussed on p. 320 of the text, Cree distinguishes between animate and inanimate nouns; only animacy and third person forms are demonstrated in these examples.

tʃa:n itohte:w	"John goes/is going (there)."
pimohte:w	"He/She walks/is walking."
tʃa:n kihtohte:w	"John goes/is going away."
takihtohte:w	"He will go away."
tʃa:n o:hta:wija itohte:liwa	"John's father goes/is going (there)."
ki:te:pwe:w ka:kih tʃipahta:li tʃi atimwa	"He shouted when the dog ran away."
tʃa:n ki:kihtohte:w ne:sta ma:tjiw ki:kihtohte:w	"John went away, and Matthew went away too."
atim wa:pame:w tʃa:na	"The dog sees John."
tʃa:n wa:pame:w me:ri:wa e:kihtohte:t	"John sees Mary as John is going away."
tʃa:n wa:pame:w me:ri:wa e:kihtohte:li tʃi	"John sees Mary as Mary is going away."
a:lik ki:wa:pame:w tʃa:na e:pimohte:t	"Alex saw John as Alex was walking."
a:lik ki:wa:pame:w tʃa:na e:pimohte:li tʃi	"Alex saw John as John was walking."

Identify the Plains Cree morphemes that correspond to each of the following meanings:

his father	and/too
dog	when (relative marker)
future	as (dependent clause marker)
past (completed action marker)	shout

Two types of verbs are used in the examples. What are these two types?

What are the third person singular (proximate) verbal endings?

What are the third person singular (obviative) verbal endings?

How is the obviative marked on nouns?

3. Consider the following additional data from Plains Cree. The possessive of nouns is formed by adding a prefix to a stem. In this exercise, you are given the form that corresponds to the first person singular possessive ("my") + noun, as well as the noun stem to which the prefix is added.

nitaːʃokan	"my wharf"	aːʃokan	"wharf"
nimaskisin	"my shoe"	maskisin	"shoe"
nitʃiːmaːn	"my canoe"	tʃiːmaːn	"canoe"
niteːhtapiwin	"my chair"	teːhtapiwin	"chair"
nitastotin	"my hat"	astotin	"hat"
nitamisk	"my beaver"	amisk	"beaver"
nimeːskanaw	"my path"	meːskanaw	"path"

Identify the forms of the prefix meaning "my" and explain the allomorphic variation.

Think... Look at the following examples, which also contain forms corresponding to "my" + noun, as in the previous exercise. As occurs in other Algonquian languages, some noun stems cannot appear as free morphemes (they are bound or dependent stems): They must always be accompanied by a possessive prefix (whether the one corresponding to "my" or a different one). Compare the examples below to those in the previous exercise. The distinction between the two groups of nouns is a semantic one. What is the semantic motivation for the distinction?

nikosis	"my son"	*kosis	"son"
nitoːn	"my mouth"	*toːn	"mouth"
nispiton	"my arm"	*spiton	"arm"
nimoʃoːm	"my grandfather"	*moʃoːm	"grandfather"
niteːhi	"my heart"	*teːhi	"heart"
nitoːteːm	"my friend"	*toːteːm	"friend"
nikaːwij	"my mother"	*kaːwij	"mother"

QUICK REMINDER!

Many of the names of languages and language families introduced in this chapter will be new to you. The exercises provide you with an opportunity to become more familiar with these new langauges and groups. Make sure you do them!

REVIEW! REVIEW!   Make sure you know. . .

- the reasons for studying the Aboriginal languages of Canada
- the three political grouping of Canada's Aboriginal languages
- the different languages of Canada's Aboriginal peoples and the families to which they belong
- what Michif, Chinook Jargon, and Plains Sign Talk are
- reasons why Canada's Aboriginal languages are in decline
- the common phonological characteristics of Canada's Aboriginal languages
- the common morphological charactersitics of Canada's Aboriginal languages
- the common syntactic characteristics of Canada's Aboriginal languages

QUESTIONS? PROBLEMS? DIFFICULTIES?

CHAPTER 10.
FIRST LANGUAGE ACQUISITION

The study of first language acquisition examines how children come to know language. Important topics and concepts found in this chapter include the following:

1. Studying first language acquisition
2. Phonological development
3. Children's phonetic processes
4. Vocabulary development
5. Morphological development
6. Syntactic development
7. Critical period hypothesis
8. Explaining how language acquisition occurs

STUDYING FIRST LANGUAGE ACQUISITION

Linguists attempt to understand exactly how it is that children come to master the sounds, vocabulary, meaning, word formation, and sentence structure of language. Of course, this can only be done by studying children's language. Read the discussion on pp. 323 to 327 of the text to find out about how researchers study children's language.

Some Things To Think About

- What are children acquiring? Is this a system? If so, what does this system allow children to do?

- Why do linguists believe that children acquire a grammar? Think about language creativity (see Chapter 1), and some of the errors that children make (such as *worser* instead of *worse* and *gooder* instead of *good*).

- How do linguists study the development of language in children? Think of two different methodologies that linguists might use.

- What is the difference between a naturalistic approach to studying child language development and an experimental approach to studying child language development?

- What is the difference between a longitudinal study and a cross-sectional study?

- What are some tasks a linguist might use to study the development of a particular grammatical structure? See figures 10.1 and 10.2 on p. 326 of the text for some examples.

• Does a naturalistic study have to involve only one child over a long period of time? Some naturalistic studies study several children over a shorter period of time. In what way does this make such studies like experimental studies?

Think. . . Suppose a researcher collected data from 10 different two-year-old children by asking them to name objects presented in a picture. What kind of study is this? What task is the researcher using?

Now. . . Suppose a researcher collects data from three children every two weeks for one year. What kind of study is this? What might be some possible advantages and disadvantages of this study and the previous study? Think about the time it takes to conduct each study, the children's role in the study, the type of data that is collected, and whether the collected data are representative of children's grammatical knowledge.

PHONOLOGICAL DEVELOPMENT

Children are born with the ability to perceive the sounds of language, but the ability to produce sounds takes longer.

Babbling

The onset of babbling at around six months signals the beginning of children's ability to produce speech sounds. Characteristics of babbling include the following:

⇒ During babbling, children produce repeated CV (consonant vowel) sequences (e.g., [mamama], [dadada], [bababa]).

⇒ Babbled sequences have no meaning attached to them.

⇒ Some sounds (e.g., [p, b, m, t, d, n]) are found in babbling; some sounds are not (e.g., [f, θ, ʃ, r]). See table 10.1 on p. 328 of the text for more examples.

Think. . . Children exposed to different languages tend to babble using the same sounds. What does this reveal about the relationship between babbling and language development?

Developmental Order

When children begin to produce sequences with meaning, they acquire the sounds of language gradually. The following tendencies have been observed for the acquisition of consonants.

⇒ **Manner of Articulation.** Stops are usually the first manner of articulation that children acquire. Liquids are usually the last manner to be acquired.

⇒ **Place of Articulation.** Children acquire labials first. They then acquire alveolars, velars, and alveopalatals. Interdentals are usually the last place of articulation that children acquire.

⇒ **Word Position.** Children acquire phonemic contrasts first in word-initial position and later in word-final position.

Try This! Study the discussion on pp. 328 and 329 of the text along with tables 10.2 and 10.3 on these pages and determine whether each of the following statements regarding the development of sounds is true or false.

1. [v] is acquired before [d].   TRUE   /   FALSE

2. [p, b] are acquired before [k, g].   TRUE   /   FALSE

3. [m] is acquired before [ŋ].   TRUE   /   FALSE

4. [z] is acquired before [s].   TRUE   /   FALSE

5. [θ] is acquired before [ʃ].   TRUE   /   FALSE

CHILDREN'S PHONETIC PROCESSES

While children have fairly regular patterns of pronunciation, their pronunciation is not the same as that of an adult. Differences between child and adult pronunciations are often described using phonetic processes. These are universal in that they are found in children's pronunciations across languages. There are three basic types of processes.

⇒ **Syllable Structure.** Children may modify the syllable structure found in an adult word. The end result of such modifications is often a CV syllable. Recall from Chapter 7 that this is the unmarked syllable structure.

⇒ **Substitution.** Children may replace a sound that they have not acquired or find difficult to articulate with one that is easier to articulate.

⇒ **Assimilation.** Children may change one sound to another so that it is more like a neighbouring sound.

Some specific processes for each type are presented in the following table.

Type of Process	Process	Definition
Syllable Structure	Unstressed Syllable Deletion	Children tend to delete syllables that are unstressed and keep those that are stressed. Children are also more likely to delete unstressed syllables before the stressed syllable than after the stressed syllable. See tables 10.4 and 10.5 on p. 330 for some examples.
	Consonant Cluster Reduction (CCR)	Children tend to remove one or more members of a complex (branching) onset or coda. See table 10.6 on p. 330 of the text for some examples.
	Deletion	Children often delete consonants at the end of a word (which corresponds to the end of a syllable). For example: 'boot' [bu].
Substitution	Stopping	Children tend to replace a fricative (or another continuant sound) with the corresponding stop. See table 10.7 on p. 331 of the text for some examples.
	Gliding	Children tend to replace liquids with glides. See table 10.7 on p. 331 for some examples.
	Fronting	Children tend to replace more back articulations with front articulations. See table 10.7 on p. 331 of the text for some examples.
	Denasalization	Children may replace a nasal stop with its corresponding oral stop. See table 10.7 on p. 331 of the text for some examples.
Assimilation	Voicing	Children may voice a voiceless consonant in anticipation of a following vowel (which is also voiced). For example: 'soup' [zup].
	Place of Articulation	Children may use the same place of articulation for all the consonants (or vowels) in a word. For example: 'doggy' [gagi].

Practice! Each of the following represents a change from an adult pronunciation to a child's pronunciation. Identify the phonetic process/es that has/have occurred in the child's form. Do this by comparing the child's pronunciation to the adult pronunciation.

1. show: adult [ʃow] → child [sow]   _____

2. that: adult [ðæt] → child [dæt]   _____

3. clean: adult [klin] → child [ki]   _____

4. duck: adult [dʌk] → child [kʌk]   _____

5. train: adult [tren] → child [wed]   _____

6. brush: adult [brʌʃ] → child [bʌt]   _____

7. ring: adult [rɪŋ] → child [wɪn]   _____

8. lamp: adult [læmp] → child [jæm]   _____

9. delicious: adult [dəlɪʃəs] → child [lɪʃəs]   _____

VOCABULARY DEVELOPMENT

Children not only have to learn how to pronounce adult words; they must also learn what words mean.

Early Vocabulary

Children's vocabularies initially develop quite slowly, but this speeds up rapidly, generally after children acquire 50 or so words. For most children, nouns make up the bulk of their vocabulary, although words from other categories (e.g., verbs, adjectives, social expressions) are also found. See table 10.8 on p. 332 of the text for some examples of common vocabulary items.

Strategies

Children use three strategies to determine the meanings of nouns.

⇒ **Whole Object Assumption.** When learning the word *cow*, children will assume that this word refers to the entire cow and not just its legs or its tail. What are children assuming?

⇒ **Type Assumption.** When learning the word *cow*, children will assume that the word refers not just to a single cow but to other animals sharing the same properties. What are children assuming?

⇒ **Basic Level Assumption.** When learning the word *cow*, children will assume that the word refers only to cows and not to animals in general. What are children assuming?

In addition to the above strategies, children also use contextual cues to determine the meanings of new words. See the discussion on p. 334 of the text for more on this topic.

Errors

Children make two types of errors when learning the meanings of nouns.

⇒ **Overextension.** Children may make the meaning of a word more general. That is, the word includes more members for the child than it does for an adult. For example, children might use the word *juice* to refer to any type of drink. See table 10.9 on p. 335 of the text for some examples of common children's overextensions.

⇒ **Underextension.** Children may use a word in a more restrictive way than an adult would. For example, children may use the word *kitty* to refer to only the family cat and not to cats in general.

Think. . . Children sometimes also have difficulty determining the meaning of verbs. For example, children sometimes think that to *fill* means to *pour*. Why might children make this assumption?

Now. . . Suppose a child used the word *tunnel* when driving through a tunnel and also when driving under an overpass, and, finally, when hiding under a table. What might account for this overextension? Think about the perceptual properties that these instances have in common.

Suppose another child used the word *fish* only for goldfish. What might account for this underextension? Think about what might be the prototype or core member of this category.

In addition to nouns and verbs, children also have to acquire adjectives, including those that give information on the dimension of objects. Children acquire these in an orderly fashion: from the more general to the more specific.

⇒ **Any Dimension.** Children first acquire the most general type of adjective—that is, adjectives that can be used to refer to any aspect of size (e.g., *big, small*).

⇒ **Single Dimension.** Children then acquire adjectives that can be used to refer to a single aspect of size (e.g., *tall, short*).

⇒ **Secondary Dimension.** Children then acquire adjectives that can be used to refer to more restricted aspects of size (e.g., *thick, thin*).

See table 10.10 on p. 337 of the text for some more examples of size adjectives and how they can be classified.

Exercise! Examine the following vocabulary data from a two-year-old child. Categorize the items into nouns, verbs, adjectives, and social words.

table	Mommy	cow	yummy	up
go	coat	allgone	milk	horse
piggy	hot	no	dog	boots
chicken	juice	jump	Daddy	yucky
please	dolly	chair	play	pull
banana	sit	hat	bye-bye	kitty

Think. . . What type of word is the most common in the above data? Why would children tend to acquire these early? Think about whether these words are concrete or abstract in nature.

Now. . . Take all of the nouns you found in the data and place them into subcategories (e.g., people, food/drink, animals, clothes, toys, house hold, etc.).

Why would children's early vocabularies contain these types of nouns? Think about the relationship between these objects and what is found in the child's environment.

MORPHOLOGICAL DEVELOPMENT

Not only do children have to learn the meanings of words, but they also have to learn how to combine morphemes to form words. That is, they have to learn about the internal structure of words.

Development of Inflectional Affixes

Inflectional affixes are bound morphemes that, in English, provide information on grammatical categories such as number (e.g., singular and plural) and tense (e.g., past).

⇒ **Stages.** Children usually acquire inflectional affixes such as the plural and the past tense in three stages.

1. Children first memorize the inflected form. That is, they are not aware that words such as *hands* or *talked* consist of two morphemes. Since children are simply memorizing words, they will use irregular forms such as *drove*.
2. Children then learn the regular rule and apply it to all words, including words that in the adult language are the exceptions, or irregular forms. *Drove* now becomes *drived*.
3. Finally, children learn the irregular forms. *Drove* once again occurs in children's speech.

⇒ **Overgeneralizations.** The type of error that occurs when children overapply the regular rule, creating words such as *drived,* is called an overgeneralization. It is sometimes also called overregularization, since children are making the language more regular.

QUICK REMINDER!

Overgeneralizations and overextensions are not the same. An overgeneralization is a morphological error; children use regular endings (e.g., for the plural and the past tense) on irregular words. Overextensions are a semantic error: The meaning of a particular word in children's vocabulary is more general than it would be to an adult.

Think. . . Researchers often test the acquisition of inflectional affixes using nonsense words (see figure 10.6 on p. 339 of the text). Why would researchers use nonsense words rather than actual words of the language? Think about the developmental stages outlined above.

Development of Grammatical Morphemes

Inflectional affixes and function words (collectively referred to as grammatical morphemes) tend to be acquired in a similar order across children. Children usually acquire the *-ing* ending first. They also acquire the plural *-s* before either the possessive *-'s* or the past tense *-ed*. The past tense, in turn, is acquired before the third person singular *-s*. See table 10.12 on p. 340 of the text for the developmental order of seven English grammatical morphemes, and table 10.13 on p. 340 of the text for the frequency of these morphemes in English.

Think. . . The morpheme *-ing* is typically the first grammatical morpheme that children acquire. Why? Where in a word is it usually found? Is it a syllable? Is it regular or irregular? Does it have any allomorphs? Is its meaning easy to determine? Are there any other *-ing* affixes that have a different function? Read the discussion on p. 340 of the text to understand why these are some of the factors that have been proposed to explain the order in which children acquire grammatical morphemes.

Now. . . Ask the same questions as above for the past tense *-ed*. What is the difference between *-ing* and *-ed*? Can this explain the later acquisition of *-ed* in comparison to *-ing*?

Development of Word Formation

In addition to acquiring grammatical morphemes, children must also acquire the different processes used to form words in language. Two common ones children use are outlined below.

⇒ **Derivation.** Children typically acquire affixes used to form the diminutive, the doer, activity names, and states. See table 10.14 on p. 341 of the text for some examples of children's innovative compounds.
⇒ **Compounding.** Children acquire the ability to make compounds early. Children's compounds often consist of two nouns. They also make compounds that are not found in adult speech. See table 10.15 on p. 341 of the text for some examples of children's innovative compounds.

Think. . . Suppose a child used the word *driving wheel* instead of *steering wheel*. Why might a child create such a compound? Is it easier to determine the meaning of the child's compound or the adult compound?

Exercise! Exercise!   Examine the following data from a three-year-old child and answer the questions that follow.

Child Sentence

I going for a walk.
Do you like those fishes?

Adult Sentence

I am going for a walk.
Do you like those fish?

The gooses want to play with the fishes.	The geese want to play with the fish.
Daddy gave bread to the duckies.	Daddy gave bread to the ducks.
Daddy is a good duck-feeder.	Daddy is good at feeding the ducks.
I leaving now.	I am leaving now.

1. Identify all of the grammatical morphemes from p. 340 and 341 of the text that are in the data.
2. Which grammatical morphemes are missing from the data? Do you think the child has acquired any/all of the missing grammatical morphemes?
3. Identify any word formation processes being used.
4. What error does the child make with the plural?
5. What stage of acquisition with regard to the plural is the child in? What about the past tense? What would you expect to happen next in the acquisition of plural? What about the past tense?

SYNTACTIC DEVELOPMENT

In addition to word formation, children learn how to combine words into phrases, and phrases into sentences. They must also learn how to form other types of structures, such as questions, passives, and relative clauses. Children's acquisition of such structures is gradual, but rapid.

Stages of Acquisition

Children's ability to combine words into rudimentary sentences proceeds in a very orderly fashion. Three stages can be identified.

⇒ **One-Word Stage.** In this stage, children's sentences typically consist of a single word called a holophrase. This word expresses the meaning of an entire sentence in adult speech. See table 10.16 on p. 343 of the text for some typical examples of children's holophrases and their meanings. The meanings associated with holophrases are usually identified as semantic relations (e.g., agent of an action, location, etc.).

⇒ **Two-Word Stage.** In this stage, children's sentences typically consist of two words. See table 10.17 on p. 343 of the text for some typical examples of children's two-word sentences and the semantic relations they express.

⇒ **Telegraphic Stage.** In this stage, children begin to produce sentences that are longer and more complex. During this stage, children's sentences lack grammatical morphemes, such as inflectional affixes and function (non-lexical) words. That is, they consist primarily of content, or lexical, words.

Exercise!   Two-year-old Charlie saw his father come in the door and said, "Daddy home." He also watched *Sesame Street* on television and said, "Grover leave," "Ernie funny," and "Tickle Elmo." These utterances are representative of his speech. Answer the following questions regarding Charlie's speech.

1. What stage of syntactic acquisition is Charlie at?

2. What is the name of the stage previous to the one Charlie is currently at?

3. What is the name of the stage after the one Charlie is currently at?

4. What are the semantic relations evident in Charlie's sentences?

Remember!   When children are in the one-word stage, the word they select to express their intended meaning is typically the most informative word in the sentence. So if a child wants to say *I want a cookie*, which word will the child most likely choose?

Later Development

Children also acquire the ability to perform syntactic operations that move words and phrases to other positions in the sentence. These operations can be used to create *yes-no* and *wh* questions.

⇒ *Yes-No* **Questions.** This type of question (e.g., *Can we go to the park?*) is formed using Inversion. Being able to apply Inversion requires auxiliary verbs (e.g., *can*).

- Before children acquire auxiliary verbs, they form questions using statements with rising intonation (e.g., *We go park?*).
- After children acquire auxiliary verbs, they are able to move auxiliary verbs to before the subject. However, children may not always move auxiliary verbs when they are first acquired (e.g., *We can go park?*).

⇒ *Wh* **Questions.** This type of question (e.g., *Where are we going?*) is formed using *Wh* Movement and Inversion. Being able to apply *Wh* Movement requires *wh* words.

- Children acquire the *wh* words *what* and *where* first. *Who, how,* and *why* are usually next. *When, which,* and *whose* are generally later acquisitions.
- Children may first use *wh* words outside the sentence (e.g., *Where going? What doing?*). This corresponds to a stage when children have not yet acquired auxiliary verbs.
- Children may initially apply *Wh* Movement without applying Inversion (e.g., *Where we are going?*).

Try This! Examine the following child language data and answer the questions that follow.

> I can't do it.
> Can you feed me?
> What you can feed me?
> I like carrots.
> Baby should eat lunch too.
> Where Baby is?
> I'm eating.
> Can we go now?

1. Has the child acquired auxiliary verbs?
2. Can the child apply Inversion?
3. Does Inversion happen in both *yes-no* and *wh* questions in the child's speech, or only in *yes-no* questions? You might want to first identify which of the questions are *yes-no* questions and which are *wh* questions. Remember, there are two types of auxiliary verbs: modal and non-modal.

Sentence Structure Interpretation

Sometimes the meaning of a sentence is related to its syntactic structure. Two such structures are passive sentences and structures with pronominals and reflexives. The relationship between sentence structure and meaning in adult speech for these structures is outlined in Chapter 6.

⇒ **Passives.** Children have a hard time interpreting passive sentences such as *The mouse was chased by the cat*. This is most likely because children expect the first noun phrase in a sentence to be the agent (doer) of the action. In a passive sentence, this is not so: The first noun phrase is the theme (receiver) of the action.

⇒ **Pronominals and Reflexives.** This refers to the distinction, for example, between *me* and *myself*, as in the sentences *You hurt me* and *I hurt myself*. *Me* is a pronominal, while *myself* is a reflexive. See Chapter 6 for details on the structural difference between these two types of words. As far as language acquisition goes, children make few errors either in understanding or in using these structures.

Now. . . Which noun in the sentence *the elephant kisses the lion* is doing the action? Which noun phrase is under doing the action? How would children interpret this sentence? Which noun in the sentence *the elephant is kissed by the lion* is doing the action? Is this the same as in the first sentence? How would children interpret this sentence? What strategy do children use in interpreting these sentences? Why might this lead to an error in sentence interpretation?

FACTORS INFLUENCING ACQUISITION

Linguists also attempt to explain how children acquire language. Read the discussion on pp. 349 to 356 of the text to find out about some of the factors that might influence how children acquire language.

Some Things To Think About. . .

•   Children need to be exposed to language. What effect does it have on language acquisition when children's exposure to language is limited? Are there both short-term and long-term effects?

•   Adults sometimes modify their speech when talking to children. What is this type of modified speech called? See table 10.22 on p. 350 of the text for some of the features found in this type of speech. In what way could exposure to this type of speech be helpful in acquiring language? Is it necessary for acquiring language?

•   Adults may also provide feedback to children. What are some of the different types of feedback that adults may provide? Which types of feedback might have more of an effect on language acquisition, and which might not be useful? Think about why this might be so.

•   The acquisition of language appears to be separate from other types of cognitive development. Which types of linguistic development are most likely to be independent from non-linguistic types of cognitive development? What types of evidence have been used to support this claim? What does this imply about the role of in-born knowledge?

•   Children may be born with knowledge of the abstract categories, operations, and principles that are part of the grammar of any human language. If so, would children then have to acquire all aspects of language? Which aspects would they have to acquire and which would they not? What would children use to acquire aspects of the language that are not innate?

•   What is meant by nativism?

•   There may be a critical period for language acquisition. What is meant by the term 'critical period'? What happens to individuals who are not exposed to language during the critical period? Think about the case of Genie and the case of Chelsea. How would having in-born knowledge of language account for such cases?

Think. . . Syntactic development is quite rapid once children are in the telegraphic stage. Children quickly progress from two- and three-word sentences to a variety of morphologically and syntactically complex sentences (see table 10.19 on pp. 345–346 of the text for some examples). Which of the above factors do you think provides the best explanation for the speed of first language acquisition?

REVIEW EXERCISES

1. Identify the phonetic processes in each of the following child pronunciations.

   a. sky: [skaj]   →   [kaj]   _____

   b. laugh: [læf]   →   [wæp]   _____

   c. twig: [twɪg]   →   [tɪk]   _____

2. A child looks at the night sky, points to the full moon, and says "ball." What kind of an error is this?

3. A child looks at a picture of a goat in a book and hears the word *goat*. The child assumes that the word *goat* means an animal. Which meaning-acquisition strategy is the child using?

4. Give the order in which children acquire the following morphemes: *the/a*, past tense *-ed*, *-ing*, plural *-s*, and possessive *-'s*.

5. What are the three stages of syntactic acquisition? What are the characteristics of children's typical sentences in each stage?

   STAGE   **CHARACTERISTICS**

   _____   _____

                               _____

   _____   _____

                               _____

   _____   _____

                               _____

REVIEW! REVIEW! Make sure you know . . .

- – the difference between naturalistic and experimental studies
- – what babbling is
- – how to identify children's phonetic processes
- – the strategies children use to acquire meaning
- – the different types of meaning errors children make
- – what overgeneralizations are
- – the determining factors affecting the acquisition of grammatical morphemes
- – how children acquire derivation and compounding
- – the different stages of syntactic acquisition
- – how children acquire Inversion and *wh* questions
- – the different factors that may influence language acquisition

QUESTIONS? PROBLEMS? DIFFICULTIES?

_____

_____

_____

_____

_____

_____

_____

_____

_____

_____

CHAPTER 11.
SECOND LANGUAGE ACQUISITION

The field of second language acquisition examines how people acquire a language other than their first language. Important topics and concepts found in this chapter include the following:

1. Communicative competence
2. Interlanguage
3. Role of the first and second languages
4. Second language phonology
5. Second language syntax
6. Second language morphology
7. Factors influencing second language acquisition
8. Bilingual education

COMMUNICATIVE COMPETENCE

Communicative competence refers to the linguistic and social knowledge that a speaker needs in order to successfully communicate in a particular language. Some of the different types of knowledge that make up communicative competence are briefly defined below.

⇒ **Grammatical Competence.** A second language (L2) learner needs to acquire knowledge of phonetics, phonology, morphology, syntax, and semantics.

⇒ **Textual Competence.** An L2 learner needs to be able to organize and link sentences together to form a cohesive whole.

⇒ **Sociolinguistic Competence.** L2 learners need to be able to use language in a way that is appropriate to a particular social situation.

⇒ **Illocutionary Competence.** An L2 learner needs to be able to convey meaning in a way that is appropriate to a particular social situation.

See figure 11.2 on p. 364 of the text for how these different types of competency are part of a larger model of communicative competence.

Now. . . An L2 learner of English may say, "I went to the store. I bought some apples. They tasted great. I will go back to the store. I will buy some more." Such sentences indicate that the learner has not yet acquired what type of competence?

INTERLANGUAGE

Communicative competence is the final state (i.e., the ultimate goal) when acquiring a second language. The initial state is the first language: Adults acquiring a second language have already acquired their first, or native, language. Interlanguage (IL) refers to the intermediate state between the first (L1) and second languages (L2).

Below are some important things to keep in mind about interlanguages.

⇒ **Systematic.** A learner's IL is a mental system of rules and representations: a grammar. The IL grammar will contain features from both the learner's first and second languages.

- Learners will often transfer properties of their first language into their IL grammars. See tables 11.1 and 11.2 on p. 362 of the text for some examples of phonological transfer. See table 11.4 on p. 364 of the text for some examples of lexical, morphological, and syntactic transfer.

- Learners will also use features of their L2 in their IL grammars. See table 11.3 on p. 363 of the text for an example that contains features of both the learner's L1 and L2.

⇒ **Dynamic.** The IL grammar changes as the learner's knowledge of the second language changes.

⇒ **Fossilization.** When a learner's IL grammar stops changing, it is said to have fossilized.

Exercise! Learners often transfer aspects of their L1 knowledge to their IL grammars. The use of learners' L1 knowledge in their L2 output can cause errors (sometimes called transfer errors). Each of the following sentences contains this type of error. For each sentence, state which aspect of the learner's L1 grammar is responsible for the error.

1. I bought some fruits at the store.
2. I told a funny yoke.
3. What do you think what George eats?
4. You need to transport those plants.
5. What he is trying to say?

Think . . . If fossilization happens before the learner has fully acquired all the properties of the L2, the IL grammar will still contain properties of the L1. Will the L2 learner always sound like a native speaker of the L1?

SECOND LANGUAGE PHONOLOGY

When acquiring a second language, L2 learners will have to acquire the phonological structures of their second language. Four different types of structures are outlined below.

⇒ **Segments.** Individual languages only use a subset of all possible speech sounds found in the world's languages. Languages will therefore vary in the sounds that they contain. This means that L2 learners will most likely have to learn to produce and perceive some new sounds.

⇒ **Features.** Sometimes the acquisition of a sound in the L2 that is not in the L1 requires that the learner acquire a new feature. Features are individual phonetic properties, such as voice or continuancy. Sounds are a collection of these features. Since inventories of sounds can differ across languages, so can features. This means that L2 learners may have to learn new features in order to produce and perceive sounds not in their L1.

⇒ **Syllables.** Syllable structure can vary across languages. Some languages allow complex onsets and codas (e.g., English), while others do not (e.g., Arabic, Chinese). Languages may also have restrictions on which segments can go into onsets and codas (e.g., Japanese only allows nasal codas). This means that L2 learners will most likely have to learn a new set of restrictions on syllable structure.

⇒ **Stress.** How stress is assigned also differs across languages. For some languages, stress is predictable (always on a particular syllable), while for other languages, it must be learned on a word-by-word basis. This means that L2 learners will probably have to learn a stress pattern that is different from that of their L1.

Now. . . Read the discussion on pp. 367 and 370 to 372 of the text and think about what kinds of phonological transfer errors L2 learners might make. What strategies might L2 learners use when attempting to pronounce words whose phonology is different from their L1? What results if the L2 learner's interlanguage grammar fossilizes before the L2 learner fully acquires the phonology of the L1?

Think. . . Some phonological properties of language may be harder for the L2 learner to acquire than others. Markedness (see Chapter 7) has been used to explain this difference.

There are two different hypotheses regarding the role of markedness in L2 learning.

⇒ **Markedness Differential Hypothesis.** This hypothesis is based on differences in the markedness of a particular property in the L1 and L2. The hypothesis makes two predictions:

* Learners will find it more difficult to learn a property that is more marked in their L2 than is the corresponding property in their L1.
* Learners will find it easier to learn a property that is less marked in their L2 than what is found in their L1.

⇒ **Similarity Differential Hypothesis.** This hypothesis is also based on differences between the L1 and L2, and makes the following prediction:

* Learners will learn a property in their L2 that is unlike what is found in their L1 faster than they will learn a property that is similar to what is found in their L1.

Think . . . Why would an L2 learner first acquire properties that are different from the L1? Why would they not first acquire properties that are similar?

Exercise! Exercise!

1. Long and short vowels are contrastive (i.e., they make a meaning difference) in German, but not in English, which has only contrastive short vowels. Would it be harder for a German speaker to acquire English short vowels, or would it be harder for an English speaker to acquire German long vowels? Think about which is more marked, contrastive long or contrastive short vowels. Remember that languages do not have contrastive long vowels unless they also have contrastive short vowels.

2. Suppose an L2 learner's L1 contains the fricatives / s / and / f /, while the L2 contains, in addition to these sounds, the fricatives / θ / and / x /. Which will the L2 learner learn first, / θ / or / x /? Justify your answer.

3. In Hungarian, stress is always on the first syllable. Which of the following words would a Hungarian L2 learner of English have difficulty pronouncing like a native English speaker?

scorned	macaroni	informative	genius
dictate	duplicate	explode	discover

4. Consider the difference in how Cantonese and Mandarin speakers would pronounce the following English words.

English Word	Cantonese Speaker	Mandarin Speaker
desk	[dɛs]	[dɛs.kə]
test	[tɛs]	[tɛs.tə]
friend	[frɛn]	[frɛn.də]
five	[faj]	[faj.və]
league	[li]	[li.gə]

a. What strategy is the Cantonese speaker using to pronounce the English words?
b. What strategy is the Mandarin speaker using to pronounce the English words?
c. How do these different strategies affect the syllable structure of the English word?

5. Suppose a learner's L1 contains the velar sounds / k / and / x /, while the learner's L2 contains, in addition to these sounds, the velar sounds / g / and / ɣ /. Will the learner find it easier to acquire / g / or / ɣ / in the L2? Why? Justify your answer. Think about the markedness relationship between stops and fricatives.

SECOND LANGUAGE SYNTAX

Languages differ in the types of syntactic structures they allow. This means that L2 learners will most likely have to learn structures that are different from their L1. Two examples of this are outlined below.

⇒ **Null Subjects.** Some languages (e.g., French and English) require all sentences to have an overt subject. For example, in English, *He ran home* is grammatical but *(He) ran home,* with an implied subject, is not. Other languages (e.g., Spanish and Italian) allow sentences without a subject, so the Spanish equivalents of both *He ran home* and *(He) ran home* are grammatical. English speakers acquiring Spanish would have to learn that sentences can have an implied subject, while Spanish speakers learning English would have to learn that this is not permissible.

⇒ **Verb Raising.** Verb raising refers to taking a verb from within the verb phrase and mov-ing, or raising, it to T (see figure 11.5 on p. 373 of the text). English does not allow main verbs to move past adverbs: *He usually runs home* is grammatical in English, but **He runs usually home* is not. In contrast, French allows verbs to raise. English speakers learning French would have to learn that structures such as *He runs usually home* are grammatical, while French speakers learning English would have to learn the reverse.

The subset principle provides an explanation for learners' difficulty or ease in acquiring some L2 syntactic structures. There are three important aspects to this principle.

⇒ **The Subset Relationship.** Some grammars are in a subset-superset relationship to each other. Languages in subset A allow fewer grammatical structures (e.g., only sentences with an overt subject) than do languages in superset B (e.g., sentences with an overt subject and sentences with a null subject).

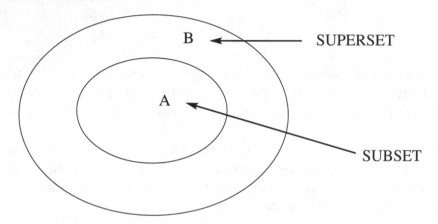

⇒ **The Role of Evidence**. Learners need evidence to decide whether a language allows or does not allow a particular structure. There are two types of evidence.

- Positive evidence refers to observations that indicate which structures are possible in a language. For example, hearing sentences with subjects is positive evidence that sentences can have a subject. Positive evidence is usually available for the L2 learner in the input data.

- Negative evidence refers to observations that indicate which structures are missing or are not possible in a language. For example, being told that a particular structure is not grammatical in the language constitutes direct negative evidence. Negative evidence can also be indirect: inferring that a particular structure is not possible because no one ever says it.

⇒ **The Acquisition Task**. Learners whose L1 is the subset language must acquire the superset language. Learners whose L1 is the superset language must acquire the subset language as their L2.

- Moving from the subset (A) to the superset (B) requires positive evidence.
- Moving from the superset (B) to the subset (A) requires negative evidence.

Learners generally find it easier to move from the subset to the superset, since this can be done using positive evidence. See pp. 374 to 375 of the text for an example of how the subset principle can be used to explain the acquisition of null subjects by L2 learners of Spanish and Italian whose L1 is French or English, and the acquisition of overt subjects by L2 learners of English and French whose L1 is Spanish or Italian.

Try This!   French and English differ in adverb placement. French allows structures such as *The man is drinking slowly his coffee,* while English does not.

1. Which is the superset language? Which is the subset language? Think about where else in the English sentence the adverb *slowly* can be placed.
2. Which learner would require positive evidence? Which would require negative evidence? What might be some examples of the negative evidence that the learner might need?
3. What kinds of errors would you expect a French speaker learning English to make?

SECOND LANGUAGE MORPHOLOGY

Much of the research in L2 morphology has focused on differences between L1 and L2 acquisition rather than on the acquisition of differences in the types of morphemes found in language.

One example of L2 morphological research involves the order in which grammatical morphemes are acquired.

⇒ Adults acquiring English as a second language acquire grammatical morphemes (e.g., *-ing*, plural *-s,* possessive *-'s,* third person singular *-s,* past tense *-ed, the/a,* auxiliary *be*) in a different order than do children acquiring English as a first language. See table 11.7 on p. 376 for the L1 order, and table 11.8 on p. 376 for the L2 order.

⇒ For children, factors such as frequency, word position, syllabicity, number of allomorphs, and so on help to determine the order in which grammatical morphemes are acquired (see Chapter 10).

⇒ For adults, differences in complexity may determine acquisition order.

- The presence of a morpheme is determined by the word itself (least complex).
- The presence of a morpheme is determined by a phrase (more complex).
- The presence of a morpheme is determined by a sentence (most complex).

See figure 11.8 on p. 377 of the text for how the structure of these three levels increases in complexity. Read the discussion on pp. 375 to 378 of the text and think about how differences in complexity can explain differences between L1 and L2 acquisition. What do L2 learners have that L1 learners do not?

Try This!   What level of complexity can explain the occurrence of the past tense *-ed* ending in English? Is this word, phrase, or sentence complexity? Why? Can this type of complexity explain the later occurrence of this ending?

Think . . . How can researchers decide if an L2 learner has a representation for a particular structure, particularly if they make errors? For example, L2 learners often omit inflectional endings such as the past tense *-ed* or the plural *-s*. Two hypotheses attempt to explain this error.

⇒ **The Impaired Representation Hypothesis.** This hypothesis argues that learners lack or have an impaired representation of a particular structure.

⇒ **The Missing Surface Inflection Hypothesis.** This hypothesis argues that learners have the correct representation but have difficulty mapping inflection onto their structures.

Read the discussion on pp. 378 and 379 of the text and think about what kind of evidence researchers use to decide between these two hypotheses.

Think . . . When L2 learners acquire English morphemes, they often make errors, such as using *taked* instead of *took* or *haves* instead of *has*. Are these errors similar to the errors children make when acquiring English? If so, could you classify this type of error as a transfer error? Why or why not? If not, how could you classify this type of error?

FACTORS AFFECTING SECOND LANGUAGE ACQUISITION

There is a great deal of variation in the grammars of second language learners as well as in their overall success in acquiring a second language. While age and individual differences are two factors that may help in accounting for this variation, differences in the characteristics of learners may have more of a role in explaining differences in success than age. There are two types of individual differences.

⇒ **Affective Factors.** Affective factors include motivation to learn the L2. Learners who want to learn the L2 for a specific goal or reason are instrumentally motivated, while learners who want to learn the L2 to learn more about a culture are integratively motivated.

REMINDER! REMINDER!

L2 learners may make more errors with a particular grammatical structure at some times than at others. This type of variation is often called a performance error. Use the discussion on pp. 365 to 366 of the text and think of some reasons why an L2 learner might make more errors sometimes and fewer errors at other times. Why might these errors decrease over time?

⇒ **Cognitive Factors.**   Cognitive factors include learning and communication strategies. Learning strategies are strategies used to fill gaps in L2 knowledge, while communication strategies are strategies used to keep communication going despite gaps in L2 knowledge. L2 learners may be field independent or field dependent. Field-independent learners are more focused on the specific, while field-dependent learners are more focused on the general.

Some Things To Think About

- Is there any known biological reason that would prevent adult L2 learners from achieving native-like or near native-like competencies in the L2?

- Are adults more likely to use in-born knowledge or general problem solving skills when acquiring an L2? Why?

- What is the difference between affective and cognitive factors in second language acquisition? Which are more likely to focus on the accuracy of grammatical structures, field-independent or field-dependent learners?

- Which type of learner is more likely to focus on fluency? Does the successful L2 learner need both accuracy and fluency?

- What is the difference between learning and communication strategies and being either field independent or field dependent?

- Which is more important in L2 acquisition: the type of motivation or the degree of motivation?

Now. . . Think about the relationship between age and phonological acquisition. While L2 learners can achieve native-like pronunciation, this is not the norm. What is the relationship between age and the ability to achieve this? Think about the critical period for acquiring language (see Chapter 10).

BILINGUAL EDUCATION

Bilingualism is the study of how children simultaneously acquire two languages. The goal of bilingual education is to produce bilingual children. There are two types of bilingual education.

⇒ **Minority Language Maintenance Programs.**   In these programs, children who speak a minority language (e.g., Mandarin) are placed in a classroom setting where they initially receive all of their education in the minority language. Gradually, instruction in the majority language (e.g., English) is introduced and increased. Students become bilingual, performing equally well in both the minority and majority languages.

These types of programs are also called Heritage Language Programs or L1 Maintenance Programs.

⇒ **French Immersion Programs.** These programs involve immersing a student who speaks the majority language (e.g., English) in a program where all instruction is given in a minority language (e.g., French). Children become bilingual, learning both English and French.

Some Things To Think About

- What is the difference between immersion and submersion programs? Should speakers of minority languages be submersed in English speaking classrooms? Why or why not?

- What is the difference between French immersion and minority language programs? Think about the L2 being acquired in each. What happens to the learners' L1 in each of these programs?

- What is a dual-language program? How are these language programs the same or different from minority language maintenance programs? What is an advantage of each type of program?

- What are some of the benefits of becoming bilingual?

Remember. . . A second language is often acquired in a classroom setting. Instruction in the this setting typically includes not only instruction on the form of the L2, but also correction of L2 learners' errors when using the L2. This is referred to as a focus on form.

Think . . . Why is the classroom a good environment in which to learn a second language? Read the discussion on pp. 383 to 384 of the text and think about some issues that researchers need to think about when considering how a focus on form affects the learning process.

Now. . . Read the discussion on pp. 363 to 365 of the text again and think about why it might be important for researchers working in second language acquisition to have a model of communicative competence. Think about how this model can be used for the different types of bilingual education.

REVIEW! REVIEW! Make sure you understand the terms and concepts listed below.

- accuracy and fluency
- bilingualism
- communication strategies
- communicative competence
- field independent and field dependent
- impaired representation hypothesis
- immersion programs
- instrumental and integrative motivation
- interlanguage
- learning strategies

- markedness differential hypothesis
- minority language maintenance
- missing surface inflection hypothesis
- negative and positive evidence
- similarity differential hypothesis
- subset principle
- transfer

QUESTIONS? PROBLEMS? DIFFICULTIES?

CHAPTER 12.
PSYCHOLINGUISTICS: THE STUDY OF LANGUAGE PROCESSING

Psycholinguistics is the study of the mechanisms that underlie language processing. Insights provided by psycholinguistic research have confirmed aspects of the structure of language (phonology, morphology, syntax, and semantics) as understood by linguists. Important topics and concepts found in this chapter include the following:

1. Priming
2. Lexical decision task
3. Frequency effect
4. Priming effect
5. Event-related potentials
6. Slips of the tongue
7. Bottom-up processing
8. Top-down processing
9. Psycholinguistic modelling

METHODS OF PSYCHOLINGUISTIC RESEARCH

Psycholinguists use various techniques to understand how language happens—that is, how the mind breaks down what it reads or hears, and what processes are behind how it puts language together for production.

Some Things To Think About

- Why do psycholinguists dedicate a lot of time to devising appropriate methods for investigating language processing? Think about whether language processing is conscious or subconscious. Are you aware of the mental activities that make language comprehension and production possible? Do you know how your mind is able to understand the sentence you are reading, how it interprets the characters on a page, or how it interprets sound vibrations as meaningful messages?

- What is the difference between a field technique and an experimental paradigm? What are psycholinguists trying to control when they design experiments? Why do they need to do so?

- What are spoonerisms? Do these occur naturally? What kind of insights into language production can analyzing such types of speech errors tell psycholinguists? What makes these a field technique and not an experimental technique?

EXPERIMENTAL METHODS

Various experimental paradigms are discussed in Chapter 12. Some methods are more suitable for investigations into particular aspects of language processing. You should be familiar with the following concepts and terms:

Term	Definition
lexical decision task	An experimental paradigm in which a participant indicates whether or not a word on a computer screen (the stimulus) is a real word in his/her language by pressing a button.
response latency	One of the two items typically measured (dependent variables) in a lexical decision task. Response latency refers to the time (in milliseconds) that it takes for the participant to respond to the stimulus.
response accuracy	One of the two items typically measured (dependent variables) in a lexical decision task. Response accuracy measures the correctness of a participant's responses to stimuli.
frequency effect	The experimental finding (in a lexical decision task) that participants respond more quickly to more frequently occurring words than to less common words. We understand from this that we process frequent words more quickly (i.e., have easier access to them).
priming effect	The experimental finding that participants respond more quickly to a word (target) if they have first been exposed to a semantically related word (prime). The word *student* is said to prime the word *teacher*.
spreading activation	The process related to the priming effect. When a participant is exposed to a prime, the prime 'activates' not only that word, but other words associated with it (the activation 'spreads' to related lexical items). The activation of the prime *student* results in the activation of the target *teacher*.
ERP	Event-related potential (ERP) experiments measure changes in the electrical activity in the brain. The electrical activity is monitored by electrodes placed on the scalp. Changes in the electrical activity, in response to a specific auditory or written stimulus, are recorded and calculated. The electrical potentials related to the stimulus (event) are separated from 'background noise' and presented as wave forms that display negative and positive voltage, and the intervening time (in milliseconds) between the stimulus and the effect.
N400	The N400 refers to a negative voltage peak at 400 milliseconds. The N400 ERP peak has been very well studied: A negative peak is observed 400 milliseconds after the presentation of a semantically anomalous stimulus. The more semantically anomalous the stimulus, the greater the (voltage) effect as measured by the N400 peak.

Exercise! See how many details about experimental methods in psycholinguistics you can recall. Read the discussion on pp. 393 to 401 of the text and complete the following statements.

1. Native speakers take less than a third of a second to recognize a _____.

2. Experimental findings and tip-of-the-tongue phenomena suggest that the _____ must be flexible.

3. The average adult reads at a rate of _____ words per minute.

4. Two common methods for exploring how words are organized and accessed are the lexical decision task and _____.

5. The response time for more frequently used words is _____ milliseconds.

6. Psycholinguists have found that participants take more time to reject _____ non-words.

7. _____ have been found not only for words that are associated semantically, but for morphologically and phonologically related words.

8. The type of automatic computation that is thought to be at the core of sentence processing is called _____.

9. Sentence-processing experiments show that participants have longer bar-pressing times when processing _____ and _____.

10. Eye-tracking experiments have shown that difficult sentences result in participants having longer fixation times and significantly more _____ .

Remember. . . Psycholinguistic experiments provide only an indirect understanding of the cognitive operations that underpin language processing. This is because language processing cannot be observed directly.

Now. . . Imagine that you are preparing a priming experiment in which you would like to investigate if the responses of non-native speakers of English are similar to those of native speakers. Below are the target words for your experiment. For each, provide an example of a semantically related prime and an unrelated prime.

Target	Semantically Related Prime	Unrelated Prime
paper		
nurse		
floor		
train		
pear		
leaf		
foot		
photo		

Remember. . . In order to explore the effects of a semantically related word, you will also need to compare response latency and response accuracy when you give a semantically unrelated word. Think about why you would need to do so.

Try This! Imagine that you are preparing an ERP experiment. Indicate which sentences you would expect to provoke a **positive ERP** response (because they do not contain a semantic anomaly); which would produce a **moderate N400** response (they are semantically anomalous and not what we would anticipate); and which would produce a **large N400** response (they are semantically highly anomalous and very much unanticipated).

Place a P (positive), M (moderate), or L (large) next to each sentence.

1. Would you like some freshly squeezed coffee?
2. The book is on the large desk.
3. The juice is in the oven.
4. It was too late to call.
5. He was asked a question by a fish.
6. I spoke to her jar.
7. The poodle didn't finish the wine.
8. I study linguistics and fruit.

Think. . . Some studies have shown that syntactic anomaly results in the P600 wave (a positive wave 600 milliseconds after a syntactically anomalous stimulus). We would expect that a sentence that is both syntactically and semantically anomalous would provoke both the P600 and N400 ERP signature waves. If this were the case, what would this tell us about semantic and syntactic processing?

LANGUAGE PROCESSING AND LINGUISTICS

Experimental findings in psycholinguistics support many of the concepts and units that linguists use to describe phonology, morphology, syntax, and semantics. These include features, phonemes, syllables, roots, affixes, verb phrases, noun phrases, and structural ambiguity. Make sure you are familiar with new terminology, including the following terms:

Term	Definition
parsing	Parsing is the automatic process that segments sentences presented in linear strings and arranges them into hierarchically organized structures.
bottom-up processing	In bottom-up processing, a listener or reader builds up larger units incrementally through the analysis of the smaller units (e.g., phonemes) as they unfold. This is sometimes referred to as *lower-level processing*. Bottom-up processing interacts with top-down processing.
top-down processing	In top-down processing, a listener or reader uses their expectations (based on conceptual and/or contextual knowledge) to interpret what is being said or read as it unfolds. This is sometimes called *higher-level processing*. Top-down processing interacts with bottom-up processing.

Slips of the Tongue

Slips of the tongue are naturally occurring speech errors. As such, they are a good example of a field technique. Slips of the tongue provide linguists with an insight into how language is produced; for example, they tell us that an utterance has to be planned out before it is produced. Many slips of the tongue also tell us something about how we assemble the parts of an utterance. As such, they provide clues as to how language is organized.

Exercise! The following slips of the tongue provide evidence for the existence of particular linguistic units (e.g., morphemes, phonological features). For each, identify the linguistic unit(s).

1. animals and teddy bears → anibals and teddy mears
2. spoon feeding → foon speeding
3. bake the cookies → cake the bookies
4. I spoke to Sam and Bill. → I spoke to Zam and Pill.
5. The charges were filed. → The files were charged.
6. reading list → leading rist
7. It's been done quickly enough. → It's been done quick enoughly.
8. cognitive modelling → cognitive molleding

Cohort Model

According to the cohort model, listeners retrieve from their mental lexicon all the words (a cohort) that correspond to the sequence of sounds unfolding in the speech signal. This process repeats until a uniqueness point in the word is reached—that is, until there are no further matches in the mental lexicon. Essentially, we reduce the number of words in a cohort until all 'competitors' are eliminated, and only one match remains (the target word).

Practice! For each of the following lexical items, indicate what occurs according to the cohort model, as shown in the first example.

Target	Possible Cohort After First Two Phonemes	Uniqueness/Recognition Point
victimize	video, victor, vigor, villa, vinegar, vim	victim<u>i</u>ze (*no more competitors after phoneme* /aj/)
sheep		
medication		
badminton		
kneecap		

Selectional Restrictions

Processing complex words (i.e., words with multiple morphemes) requires knowledge of which morphemes can and cannot combine with each other. This is because not every affix can be attached to every root or base. For example, can the suffix *–al* be attached to a noun; can the suffix *–dom* be attached to a verb; and can the prefix *ex-* be attached to an adjective? We use this knowledge to determine possible and impossible words in our language.

Try This! You are preparing the stimuli for an experiment whose aim is to investigate the role selectional restrictions play in the processing of new, morphologically complex words. To do this you will need to compare your participants' responses to nonsense words to the responses discussed in psycholinguistic studies such as those discussed on p. 407 of the text.

Below, you will find four new nonsense roots (two nouns and two verbs), followed by several examples containing derivational affixes that have been attached to those roots. Write GD (greater difficulty) next to the words you anticipate will present greater processing difficulty for your participants.

new nouns: *mern, jat*   **new verbs:** *flum, strod*

New Form	GD?	New Form	GD?
strodable		unmern	
flumly		flumer	
mernful		deflum	
jatish		merner	
jatless		reflum	
jatness		strodful	
ex-mern		reflumness	
reflumable		mis-strod	

Now. . . Answer these questions.

1. Explain why you anticipate that the words you've labelled GD would present greater processing difficulty.

2. Identify a phonological factor that may affect participants' responses.

3. Name an additional morphological factor that may affect participants' responses.

Garden Path Sentences

The syntactic parser builds up the structure of a sentence as our minds process it. Sometimes, however, our parsers can lead us to the wrong analysis of a sentence. This may happen in sentences that are not syntactically complex, but are very difficult to understand.

Exercise! Read the following garden path sentences. For each example, indicate where the misanalysis occurs, as shown in the example. Then rewrite the sentence so that it would be easier to process. The first is done for you.

1. He confessed his crimes harmed many people.

    Reason for misanalysis: The reader interprets *his crimes* as the complement (direct object) of the verb *confessed* rather than the subject NP of the VP *harmed*.

    Rewritten form: He confessed that his crimes (had) harmed many people.

2. The student forgot the answers were in the back of the book.

    Reason for misanalysis: _____

    _____

    Rewritten form: _____

3. The defendant questioned swore he was innocent.

    Reason for misanalysis: _____

    _____

    Rewritten form: _____

4. After Pat ate the chicken turned out to be bad.

    Reason for misanalysis: _____

    _____

    Rewritten form: _____

5. Without her donations failed to appear.

   Reason for misanalysis: _____

   _____

   Rewritten form: _____

6. While Anna dressed the baby splashed in the bathtub.

   Reason for misanalysis: _____

   _____

   Rewritten form: _____

Think. . . Two principles of parsing explain the difficulty we have with garden path sentences: late closure and minimal attachment. Below are the sentences from the previous exercise. Explain what *principally* motivates the garden path effects in each case: late closure, minimal attachment, or both.

1. The student forgot the answers were in the back of the book. _____

2. The defendant questioned swore he was innocent. _____

3. After Pat ate the chicken turned out to be bad. _____

4. Without her donations failed to appear. _____

5. While Anna dressed the baby splashed in the bathtub. _____

Now. . . For each of the following sentences, draw tree diagrams that show (a) the garden path effects and (b) the correct interpretation.

1. The defendant questioned swore he was innocent.
2. The student forgot the answers were in the back of the book.

PSYCHOLINGUISTIC MODELLING

Psycholinguistic models are diagrammatic representations of what is believed to occur during language processing. Diagrammatic representations are meant to simplify and summarize many findings and to generate hypotheses about language processing.

Exercise! Test your knowledge about psycholinguistic modelling by answering the following questions.

1. What model of language production and perception hypothesizes that different levels of processing—phonological, syntactic, and semantic—operate simultaneously?

2. What model of language processing hypothesizes that comprehension operates in stages—that is, that smaller units, such as phonological features, are progressively transformed into larger units (words and syntactic structures)?

3. Which type of processing model better handles bottom-up processing?

4. What do we call any processing model that hypothesizes that at least two competing mechanisms are operational in any processing task?

5. What competing mechanisms are understood to underpin the processing of multimorphemic words?

6. What do we call models of language processing that depend on abstract structural concepts such as features, phonemes, phonological rules, and syntactic categories?

7. What is the term for models of language processing that consist of multiple associations that link simple processing units (based on a representation of the transmission of information via neural networks in the brain)?

8. Draw your own parallel processing model.

9. Draw your own serial processing model.

10. Draw symbolic and connectionist representations for the words *love* and *live*.

Think. . . What might be a good way to evaluate a psycholinguistic model? What criteria could be used to determine if a proposed psycholinguistic model has value in explaining how our minds process language tasks?

REVIEW! REVIEW! Make sure you know . . .

- the difference between field techniques and experimental paradigms
- what spoonerisms/slips of the tongue are
- lexical decision tasks
- response latency and response accuracy
- frequency effects, priming effects, and spreading activation
- ERP experiments, including N400
- bottom-up and top-down processing
- the cohort model
- morpheme activation, including pre- and post-lexical decomposition
- selectional restrictions
- syntactic parsing and garden path sentences
- sentence ambiguity
- models of psycholinguistic processing, including serial, parallel, single route, multiple route, symbolic, and connectionist

QUESTIONS? PROBLEMS? DIFFICULTIES?

_____

_____

_____

_____

_____

_____

_____

_____

_____

CHAPTER 13.
BRAIN AND LANGUAGE

Neurolinguistics is a subfield of linguistics that studies the relationship between the brain and language. Important terms and concepts in this chapter include the following:

1. The cerebral cortex
2. The cerebral hemispheres
3. The lobes of the cerebral hemispheres
4. Autopsy studies
5. Studies of the living brain
6. Dichotic listening tasks
7. Split brain studies
8. Fluent and non-fluent aphasia

BRAIN STRUCTURES AND ORGANIZATION

The cerebral cortex is a wrinkled grey mass that sits on top of the rest of the brain (i.e., the brain stem and cerebellum). It is this structure that is responsible for language processing and so much more! Make sure you know the following terms and definitions.

Term	Definition
sulci & fissures	The cerebral cortex gets its wrinkled appearance from being folded in upon itself many, many times. Sulci (singular: sulcus) are hidden areas where the cerebral cortex is folded in. Fissures are very deep sulci.
gyri	Gyri (singular: gyrus) are visible folds, areas where the cerebral cortex is folded outward.
cerebral hemispheres	The cerebral cortex is divided into two hemispheres: the left and the right. See figure 13.1 on p. 420 of the text for an illustration of how the longitudinal fissure separates the cerebral cortex into the left and right hemispheres or brains.
lateralization	Each hemisphere is associated with distinct cognitive functions. The left brain tends to be more involved in analytic tasks, while the right brain tends to be more involved in tasks that require holistic processing.
contra-lateralization	Each hemisphere is responsible for movement and sensation on the opposite side of the body. That is, the left hemisphere controls the right side of the body, while the right hemisphere controls the left side of the body.

corpus callosum	The corpus callosum is a bundle of nerve fibres that joins the two hemispheres together and allows them to communicate with each other. See figure 13.2 on p. 421 of the text for an illustration of the corpus callosum along with the brain stem and cerebellum.
cerebral lobes	Each hemisphere is divided into four lobes: frontal, temporal, parietal, and occipital. Each hemispheric lobe is associated with its own specialized function. See figure 13.3 on p. 422 of the text for the location of the four hemispheric lobes and the functions associated with each.

Colour Your Brain! Using different colours, shade in the four lobes found in each cerebral hemisphere. Label each lobe. Label the folds of the brain that separate the different lobes: the lateral fissure, the central sulcus, and the angular gyrus. Use the discussion on pp. 421 and 422 of the text to help you.

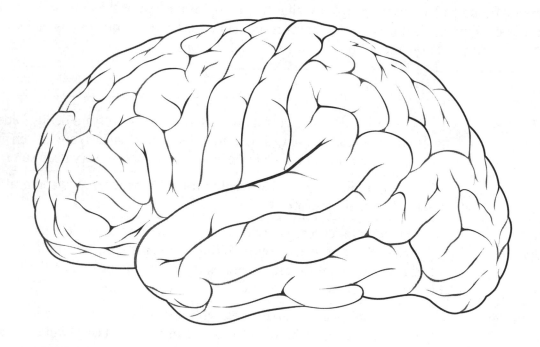

Reminder! While a specific function might be lateralized within a particular hemisphere, we actually use both hemispheres for most of the things we do. For example, for most right-handed individuals, language is lateralized in the left hemisphere. However, the right hemisphere is also used in everyday language processing. We need the right brain so that we can correctly interpret prosodic cues such as loudness and intonation, which tell us whether someone is angry or not.

EVIDENCE FOR BRAIN ORGANIZATION

There are a number of different techniques for investigating how the brain represents, organizes, and processes language. Read the discussion on pp. 422 to 427 of the text to find out more about these techniques.

Some Things To Think About

- How do researchers use autopsy studies to learn about how the brain is organized? Remember that autopsy studies are the oldest and, until recently, the only way to investigate brain organization.

- Researchers can also study the living brain. What is the difference between computerized axial tomography (CT scanning), positron emission tomography (PET scanning), functional magnetic resonance imaging (fMRI), and magnetoencephalography (MEG)? What have each of these tests told us about how the brain processes language?

- Autopsy studies have revealed that the frontal lobe is involved in speech production. PET scans have also revealed that blood flows to this area during speech. See figure 13.5 on p. 425 of the text for an illustration of the differences in blood flow when hearing words, seeing words, speaking words, and generating words. Does this mean that all language is processed in the same area of the brain, or are different areas of the brain involved in different language tasks?

- Studies of hemisphere connections are based on types of behaviour associated with a particular hemisphere of the brain. How is a dichotic listening task an example of this type of study? What do the results of dichotic listening tasks tell researchers about which ear has an advantage for words and which an advantage for melodies?

- What happens to communication between the hemispheres when the corpus callosum is surgically cut? What do split brain studies examine? What have these studies revealed about the brain's functions?

Try This!

1. The sound of a cat meowing is presented to the right ear of a subject, while the sound of a car engine is presented to the left ear. Assume that the subject is a normal, healthy right-handed individual. Which sound will the subject report hearing first? Explain why in terms of brain structure and organization. What about when the sounds are reversed (i.e., the cat meowing in the left ear and the car engine in the right ear)?

2. The sound of the word *lamp* is presented to the right ear of a subject, while the sound of the word *frog* is presented to the left ear. Assume that the subject is a normal, healthy right-handed individual. Which word will the subject report hearing first? Explain why in terms of brain structure and organization.

3. Assume that the subject undergoing the test in (1) and (2) is a split brain patient. The subject will no longer be able to process both sounds. Which sound in (1) will the subject no longer be able to process and interpret? What about in (2)? For both instances, explain why in terms of brain structure and organization.

LANGUAGE AND THE BRAIN

The different techniques for studying the brain all reveal that the left hemisphere is generally responsible for language and that within the left hemisphere there are a number of specific areas dedicated to language representation and processing.

Exercise! Use figure 13.4 on p. 423 of the text along with the discussion on pp. 418 to 424 of the text to answer the following questions.

1. What is the role of the angular gyrus in language? In which hemispheric lobe is it found?

2. How were Broca's area and Wernicke's area discovered?

3. Where is Broca's area located? What language functions is it responsible for?

4. Where is Wernicke's area located? What language functions is it responsible for?

Think . . . In addition to dedicated language areas, three cortical areas of the brain are also involved in processing language. What might these three areas be? Think about the different functions associated with each lobe of the cerebral hemispheres (see figure 13.3 on p. 422 of the text) and how these functions are used in processing language.

Now. . . Is brain organization random? The motor cortex, responsible for movement, is located in the frontal lobe, as is Broca's area, which is responsible for speech production. The visual cortex, in the occipital lobe, is located near the angular gyrus, which is used in reading. The auditory cortex, in the temporal lobe, is located near Wernicke's area, which is responsible for comprehension, both oral and written.

Colour Your Brain! Using different colours, shade in the approximate locations of Broca's area, Wernicke's area, the angular gyrus, the primary visual cortex, the primary auditory cortex, and the primary motor cortex. Label each of these areas.

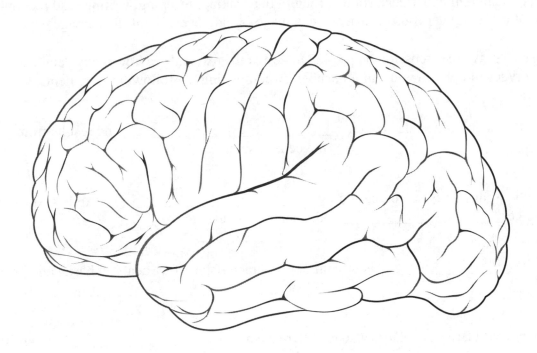

Take a look at your coloured brain. It should show that brain organization is not random!

Try This! Since the motor cortex, auditory cortex, and visual cortex are also involved in processing language, a person could, in theory, experience language difficulties without actually damaging the dedicated language areas. The scenarios described below illustrate this. For each scenario, answer the question in terms of the structures and properties of the brain. Assume that the individual named in each is an otherwise normal right-handed person.

1. Hilda has had a stroke during the night that destroyed her right visual cortex as well as her corpus callosum. Will she be able to read in the morning?
2. Ronald was in an accident that destroyed only his left auditory cortex. Can he still hear and understand language?
3. Hillary received a blow to the head that destroyed her left visual cortex as well as her corpus callosum. Will she still be able to read?
4. Thomas is a split brain patient. If he holds a spoon in his left hand without having seen it, will he be able to name it? Will he be able to draw it? If so, with which hand(s)?

APHASIA

Aphasia refers to the loss of language ability due to damage to the brain. Stroke, head injuries, infections, brain tumors, and brain hemorrhage are some of the causes of aphasia. Patients with aphasia typically all experience some difficulty in speaking, listening, writing, and reading. The amount of difficulty depends on where the damage is and the extent of the damage.

Exercise! Study the discussion on pp. 427 to 432 of the text and see how many details about the different types of aphasia you can remember by completing the following statements.

1. Non-fluent aphasia is also called _____ and results from   damage _____ the central sulcus.

2. Fluent aphasia is also called _____ and results from damage _____ the central sulcus.

3. _____ is a common characteristic of Broca's aphasia and involves _____ and _____ .

4. Patients with Broca's aphasia also tend to make many _____ errors and to omit _____ words and _____ affixes.

5. Patients with Wernicke's apahsia rarely make _____ and often have difficulty understanding _____.

Think . . . An active sentence and its passive counterpart are paraphrases of each other in that they have the same meaning. Cross out the words and endings that a Broca's aphasic would have difficulty processing in the following active sentence and passive sentence.

The flies bothered the boy.
The boy was bothered by the flies.

Do the sentences have the same meaning for someone suffering from Broca's aphasia? Why would a Broca's aphasic still be able to identify the correct meaning of the passive (second) sentence? Why would a Broca's aphasic be unsure of the meaning if the sentence was *The boy was bothered by the girl*?

Exercise!

Study the discussion on pp. 427 to 432 of the text and answer the following questions.

1. What is the difference between fluent and non-fluent aphasia?

2. What is the difference between global and Broca's aphasia? Between jargon and Wernicke's aphasia?

3. What are the general characteristics of Broca's aphasia?

4. What is agrammatism? How is it related to some of the characteristics of Broca's aphasia?

5. Circle the word that a Broca's aphasic will have more trouble producing. Justify your choice.

    tallest (as in *Jeff is the tallest man in his family*)
    beautiful (as in *Gloria is very beautiful*)

6. Each of the sentences below is passive. For each, give the meaning that a Broca's aphasic would assign to the sentence or specify that a Broca's aphasic would be unable to assign a meaning.

    a. The dog was broken by the window.
    b. The leopard was eaten by the tiger.
    c. The bear was chased by the man.

7. Describe the general characteristics of Wernicke's aphasia.

8. Suppose you asked a Wernicke's aphasic, "What time is it?" How might he or she respond to this question?

Remember. . . Aphasia provides theoretical linguists with an opportunity to test theories about the structure of language. This type of research has provided evidence for phonological structures such as features, rules, and processes, along with the morphological distinction between inflection and derivation. It also raises questions about the nature of function words and syntactic theory, indicating that more research into these areas is necessary.

ACQUIRED DYSLEXIA AND DYSGRAPHIA

Brain trauma can also cause impairments in reading (acquired dyslexia) and writing (acquired dysgraphia). These impairments can occur in conjunction with Broca's and Wernicke's aphasia. Acquired dyslexia can also occur as the only language deficit.

⇒ **In Conjunction with Aphasia:** People with either Broca's or Wernicke's aphasia exhibit the same difficulties with reading and writing as they do with spoken language.

- Broca's aphasics will not be able to spell all words correctly. They will also omit function words and inflectional affixes in their writing. Broca's aphasics will not have trouble reading silently but will have difficulties reading aloud.

- Wernicke's aphasics will not have any difficulty spelling, but what they write will not make much sense. They will also have difficulty in comprehending written language.

⇒ **As the Only Language Deficit:** This occurs when the angular gyrus is damaged. There are two types of acquired dyslexia: phonological dyslexia and surface dyslexia.

- Patients with phonological dyslexia can only read words they have seen before. This is because they have lost the ability to use spelling-to-sound rules, which we use to read new words aloud.

- In contrast, patients with surface dyslexia must use spelling-to-sound rules for all words. They have lost the ability to recognize words as whole units. They will also have difficulty in understanding irregularly spelled words.

Think . . . In words such as *through* and *light,* the 'gh' is silent. What about in the word *ghost*? What difficulties might this cause for someone with surface dyslexia? Think of examples where the same letter or combination of letters corresponds to different sounds. What difficulties would this cause for someone with surface dyslexia?

WHAT ABOUT WORDS?

All types of aphasia typically include difficulties in finding words. So where are words located in the brain? Different kinds of words (e.g., nouns and verbs) might actually be represented in different parts of the brain! Words may also be represented as a network of linguistic and non-linguistic associations. See figure 13.6 on p. 436 of the text for an example of a difference in the representation of action-related and vision-related words.

REVIEW! REVIEW! Make sure you understand the terms and concepts listed below.

- acquired dyslexia/dysgraphia
- agrammatism
- angular gyrus
- autopsy and living brain studies
- Broca's aphasia
- cerebral cortex
- corpus callosum
- dichotic listening tasks
- dysprosody
- fluent (sensory) aphasia

- hemispheric lobes (four)
- left and right cerebral hemispheres
- non-fluent (motor) aphasia
- phonemic paraphasia
- phonological dyslexia
- split brain studies
- sulci, gyri, and fissures
- surface dyslexia
- Wernicke's aphasia

QUESTIONS? PROBLEMS? DIFFICULTIES?

_____

_____

_____

_____

_____

_____

_____

_____

_____

_____

CHAPTER 14.
LANGUAGE IN SOCIAL CONTEXTS

Sociolinguistics is the systematic study of the relationship between language and society. Important topics and concepts found in this chapter include the following:

1. Speech variety
2. Language variation
3. Dialectology
4. Language contact
5. Pidgins and creoles
6. Distinctions within a community
7. African American English
8. Discourse analysis
9. Ethnography of communication
10. Language planning

SPEECH VARIETY

Sociolinguists study speech communities and speech varieties. People may have strong opinions and attitudes toward certain speakers and speech varieties, attitudes that are based not on linguistic criteria but rather on political, cultural, historical, socioeconomic, or other non-linguistic factors. To avoid the value judgments often associated with the terms *dialect* and *language*, sociolinguists use the neutral term *speech variety*.

⇒ *Mutual intelligibility* is sometimes used as a criterion to identify speech varieties as dialects of the same language, but this criterion is not a straightforward one. Political, cultural, and historical factors have been known to play a significant role in shaping speakers' perceptions of what is a dialect and what is a language, and whether another speech variety is under-standable to them. Speakers can treat mutually intelligible varieties as different languages (Swedish and Norwegian) or mutually unintelligible varieties as dialects of one language (varieties spoken in China).

⇒ The term *slang* refers only to particular words or phrases typically used by younger mem-bers of the speech community. Most slang is short-lived, but some terms can be popular for several decades (e.g., *cool*).

⇒ The term *accent* refers only to those features of pronunciation that enable us to identify a speaker as belonging to a different (regional or social) speech community. From a linguistic perspective, all speakers have an accent.

LANGUAGE VARIATION

Sociolinguists explore the many ways in which languages display variation and what motivates the variation, including social factors, geographical location, time, and physical, social, and linguistic isolation.

Social Distinctions. Variation Theory (variationist sociolinguistics) examines and attempts to explain the linguistic and social factors that motivate variation in language and to make sense of the patterns behind language variation.

Make sure that you are familiar with new concepts and terms, including the following:

Term	Definition
sociolinguistic variable	A sociolinguistic variable is any linguistic unit that displays variation and that can be subjected to a systematic analysis based on linguistic and social factors. The linguistic unit that displays variation is the variable; the possible ways the unit can be realized are the variants.
variable rules or constraints	A variable rule or constraint specifies the conditions under which a particular variant appears. Variable constraints are typically probabilistic, since a linguistic variable can be realized in a number of ways. Variable rules capture what is more likely to happen given a particular condition or environment rather than what necessarily happens.
inter-speaker versus intra-speaker variation	Inter-speaker variation refers to variation within an individual speaker, while intra-speaker variation refers to variation resulting from a speaker's social characteristics (e.g., age, gender, degree of education). Most variation is typically of the latter type.

See figure 14.1 on p. 442 of the text for an outline of the methodology variationist sociolinguists use when researching the social factors that influence language variation.

Place, Time, and Isolation. Sociolinguists are also interested in the following:

⇒ regional variation, the study of linguistic differences based on geographical location (place);

⇒ what synchronic variation can tell us about language change (what happens to language over time); and

⇒ the influence that isolation can have on the linguistic characteristics of some speech communities. In Canada, we have speech varieties that are the result of physical, linguistic, and social isolation: Newfoundland English, Quebec French, and African Nova Scotia English, respectively.

Make sure you are familiar with new concepts and terms, including the following:

Term	Definition
dialectology	Dialectology refers to the systematic study of dialects, particularly regional dialects, in order to identify dialect areas. The results of this work are often presented in the form of a series of maps that illustrate the features or forms that predominate in particular areas. See figure 14.2 on p. 443 of the text for an outline of the methodology dialectologists use when identifying dialect areas.
isogloss	An isogloss is a line on a map that marks the boundary of an area in which a particular linguistic feature (phonetic, morphological, lexical, etc.) is used. Isogloss bundles—several isoglosses in the same place—are used to indicate the boundary between different dialect areas.
dialect levelling	Dialect levelling refers to a process whereby one realization for a linguistic unit "wins out" over competitors (other options) available in the speech community, leading to less variation for that particular unit. Typically, the most frequent variant is the one selected.
apparent time hypothesis	In an apparent-time study, the speech of speakers from different age groups is compared at the same time. The hypothesis behind this method is that a change in progress can be captured by comparing the speech of younger speakers to that of older speakers at the same point in time.
linguistic isolate	In sociolinguistics, the term *linguistic isolate* is used to refer to a language that is physically isolated from its source. An example of this is found in the Dominican Republic. The descendants of African Americans in the Samaná Peninsula of the Dominican Republic continue to speak a variety of English even though Spanish is the majority language.

Exercise! How many details about regional variation, language change, and language isolation can you recall? Read the discussion on pp. 443 to 453 of the text and complete the following statements.

1. Research in the area of dialect geography has historically focused on the speech of _____ on the assumption that these speakers preserve older speech features.

2. American English, particularly the _____ dialect, provided a lot of the linguistic input to Canadian English.

3. Newfoundland was settled early, predominantly by speakers from two regions: _____ and _____.

4. This approach can capture language change. It has been used to illustrate how speakers of Canadian English have increasingly merged the phonemes /ʍ/ and /w/ such that the youngest speakers use almost exclusively /w/. The method or approach is called the _____.

5. The speech of descendants of African Americans living near _____ preserves features of earlier stages of African American English.

6. Sociolinguists have found that the language of communities with _____ social networks is more resistant to change.

Then. . . See what you can recall about the linguistic characteristics of Newfoundland English and Quebec French by answering the following questions.

1. Would *fear* and *fire* be homophones in Newfoundland English?

2. Provide the first, second, and third person forms for the verb *like* in Newfoundland English.

3. What does *I'm after telling him to do it* (Newfoundland English) mean?

4. Which of the following feature(s) is/are typical of Quebec French?

   a. the diphthongization of many nasal vowels

   b. the extensive use of formal *vous*

   c. the use of [va] for several persons of the verb *go*

5. Show two phonological differences between Parisian French (PF) and Quebec French (QF) by providing the phonetic transcription for both varieties of the feminine form of the adjective *petite*:

   PF: _____

   QF: _____

Remember. . . The term "isolate" is also used in historical linguistics, where it refers to a language that appears to have no known relatives. For example, Basque is an isolate because it can be shown that Basque does not have a common ancestor with any other language that linguists have studied.

Try This! Some lexical items that are typical of Canadian English include *toque*, *running shoes*, and *double-double*. How aware are you of terms used in other varieties of English? What does one say for. . .

1. *running shoes* in South African English?   _____

2. *cooler* in New Zealand English?   _____

3. *single parent* in New Zealand English?   _____

4. *cantaloupe* in Australian and New Zealand English?   _____

5. *pick-up truck* in South African English?   _____

6. *sweater* in Australian English?   _____

7. *sidewalk* in Australian English?   _____

8. *stoplight/traffic light* in South African English?   _____

9. *candy* in Australian and New Zealand English?   _____

10. *speed bump* in New Zealand English?   _____

How many of the above did you know?

Now. . . Not only can the lexical features of the different speech varieties of a language vary, but so can pronunciation. For example, the Northern Cities Vowel Shift, discussed on p. 448 of the text, refers to a series of vowel changes (shifts) that have taken place or are taking place in the speech of those from Buffalo, Cleveland, Detroit, Chicago, and other northern U.S. cities. As a result, "shifted" and "unshifted" varieties of North American English can sound strikingly different from one another.

Some of the vowel changes that are part of the Northern Cities Shift include the following:

⇒ The low back vowel [ɑ] is fronted, so that it comes very close to sounding like [æ].

⇒ The front vowel [æ] is fronted and raised, so that it approximates [ɛ], [eə], or [iə].

⇒ The vowel [ɛ] is pronounced further back and lower, almost as [ʌ].

⇒ The vowel [ʌ] is pronounced so that it approximates [ɔ].

Use the following table to compare your pronunciations of the words in the first column to that of a speaker involved in the Northern Cities Shift. The first is done for you.

Example	Phonetic transcription of my pronunciation	Possible transcription for speaker involved in Northern Cities Shift
bat	[bæt]	[bɛt]/[beət]/[biət]
father		
stuck		
bet		
stack		
cot		
bus		
block		

Think. . . Could some of the differences between your pronunciation and those of speakers with a shifted pronunciation result in miscommunication? Why or why not?

LANGUAGE CONTACT

Language contact—when two or more languages are used within a speech community—can result in a variety of phenomena. Mixed languages, pidgins, and creoles have emerged from language contact situations. Make sure you are familiar with new concepts and terms, including the following:

Term	Definition
code switching	A speaker who uses more than one language or variety within a conversation is said to be code switching.
borrowing	A borrowing is a word that is adopted and adapted from another language. Borrowed words are adapted to the borrowing linguistic system in terms of phonology, morphology, and so on. In language contact situations, speakers of one language will often borrow words from another language; the borrowers are rarely aware that the word is from another language.
mixed language	A language with features from two distinct sources. Mixed languages are believed to be rare. An often-cited example is Michif, the mixed language of the Métis, in which the nominal morphology is based on Métis French and the verbal morphology of Cree.

lingua franca	A lingua franca is a language adopted as a means of communication among speakers of different languages. Typically, the lingua franca is the second (or third) language of the speakers who use it. Today, English is the international lingua franca of technology, science, and business.
pidgin	Pidgin languages emerge when there is a need for speakers of different languages to communicate (for trade purposes, for example). In comparison to non-pidgins, they are generally characterized as having a limited vocabulary and a reduced grammar. A pidgin is usually not the native language of the speakers who use it.
creole	A creole is generally defined as a pidgin that has become the first language of a speech community. In order to become the first language of the community (and to fulfill all communicative functions), pidgins undergo creolization: grammatical, lexical, and stylistic expansion.
lexifier language	A lexifier language is the language that provides the majority of the vocabulary to a creole (or a pidgin). The lexifier language for Haitian Creole is French; the lexifier language for Jamaican Creole is English.

Exercise! How much do you know about language contact? Read the discussion on pp. 453 to 457 of the text and indicate whether the following statements are true or false.

1. All contact situations lead to the formation of pidgins.

2. Some linguists attribute the similarities across creoles to a language bioprogram—the innate biological capacity to acquire language.

3. Some linguists believe that all creoles emerged from a single ancestral language, a proto-pidgin.

4. The most commonly borrowed lexical items are nouns and verbs.

5. Generally, function words are not borrowed.

6. In situations where a creole continuum exists, the variety that is closest to the creole is called the acrolect.

7. Intermediate varieties within a creole continuum are mesolects.

8. All pidgins necessarily become creoles.

9. Creoles are mixed languages.

10. Code switching occurs because speakers cannot think of words and phrases in one of the languages—they have lexical gaps.

Try This! Consider the following examples from an English-lexifier creole (Jamaican Creole) and pidgin (Nigerian Pidgin English): The first five examples are from Jamaican Creole; the last three examples are from Nigerian Pidgin English. Comment on the examples, particularly on the underlined forms. The examples are not given in phonetic transcription but are intended to be representative of how they are pronounced.

1. <u>Mi</u> neve(r) <u>tell</u> im. "I didn't tell him."
2. Tell <u>we</u> di trut. "Tell us the truth."
3. <u>Dem</u> no so bad. "They are not so bad."
4. A di <u>bway</u> boat. "It's the boy's boat."
5. <u>Im</u> <u>say</u> di <u>boat no good</u>. "He said the boat is no good."
6. He <u>tok</u> tru. "He speaks the truth."
7. Your money <u>don kom</u>. "You've hit the jackpot!"
8. He <u>don go</u>. "He went."

DISTINCTIONS WITHIN A COMMUNITY

There can be a lot of variation within a speech community based on factors such as socioeconomic class, ethnicity, and gender.

Exercise! How familiar are you with the distinctions that can be found within a speech community? Read the discussion on pp. 457 to 462 of the text and complete the following statements.

1. Sociolinguistic studies have shown that there is a strong correlation between _____ and prestige variants, regardless of socioeconomic class.

2. Upper-class speakers often use _____ norms taken from outside the speech community. For example, Americans and Canadians may adopt features of British speech.

3. Labov's New York City studies showed that speakers in the second-highest socioeconomic class dramatically increased their use of prestige variants when paying close attention to speech. This type of overcompensation, attributed to linguistic _____, is called _____.

4. Many studies have shown that women use more variants associated with _____ prestige, whereas men use more non-standard forms.

5. An interesting finding is that, generally, men not only use more non-standard variants than women use, but also believe that they use non-standard variants even more than they do in reality. The term _____ prestige has been suggested for the positive value that men attach to non-standard forms.

6. _____ is the term used for language change that spreads from the upper classes to the lower classes. Sociolinguistic research has shown that women tend to be leaders in this type of change: Women use more new forms than men use.

7. Researchers have called the discourse style of women a _____ style: In general, women's conversational goals appear to include collaboration and building relationships.

8. The conversational style of men has been called a _____ style, since it suggests a tendency to use language more for the purpose of conveying factual information.

9. The term _____ is used to refer to speakers who share speech practices because they participate in a common activity.

It is important to remember that social factors do not contribute in isolation to language use. For example, gender and ethnicity, or class and gender can together, contribute to language variation in complex ways. The following exercises illustrate how age and gender can work together to create language variation.

Try This! Younger speakers may use *like* in discourse differently from the accepted usage, as in *He looks like his brother*, in which *like* expresses similarity. Sociolinguists studying *like* in the conversations of younger speakers have identified special discourse uses of *like*. The following sentences provide examples of these uses.

1. We can do *like* all kinds of things.
2. And do they take *like* debit?
3. Let's do that *like* as soon as possible.
4. You can *like* try yoga.
5. They *like* paid for the whole thing.
6. That's *like* so unfair.
7. I need *like* a good friend.
8. They asked me *like* how I did it.
9. Can you *like* give me 10 examples using "like"?
10. *Like* what did he say?
11. Could I *like* come by around four?
12. It's not *like* great, but it's okay.
13. He's *like* cool, but a bit strange.
14. And *like* they talked all night.
15. I'm hoping to get into *like* speech path.

Non-linguists may have negative attitudes towards the use of *like* in the above examples, perceiving it as arbitrary and meaningless. However, there are constraints governing where *like* can appear. See if you can determine what some of these constraints are by answering the following questions.

1. Identify the syntactic positions in which *like* can occur.
2. What is the purpose of *like* in these examples?
3. Do you use *like* in this way? Can you provide three examples of your own for this usage of *like*?

Then... Look at the following conversational excerpt, which contains three examples of *like*.

Speaker A: Are you okay?

Speaker B: I can't believe my sister. She said, "What's wrong?" And I'm *like*, "I should've passed the midterm. I studied a lot." And she's *like*, "Yeah, right – you never study." And I'm *like*, "No, really, I studied a lot. . ."

Compare the use of *like* in these examples to its use in the examples above. Discuss the properties and function of *like* in these examples. Can you provide additional examples?

Now... Imagine that you have conducted a research project in which your goal was to examine the distributional patterns of the two discourse uses of *like* illustrated above. You collected 200 speech samples containing the two types of *like* and organized them according to age and gender. You have tabulated your results and plotted them on graphs.

The first graph shows the distribution by age and gender of *focuser like* (as in the example *You can like try yoga*), which is labelled *Like: usage 1*.

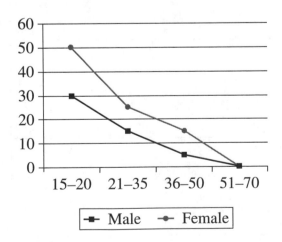

Figure 1. *Like: usage 1*—**distribution by age and gender**

The second graph shows the distribution by age and gender of *quotative like* (as in the example *And I'm like, "I should've passed the midterm"*), which is labelled *Like: usage 2*.

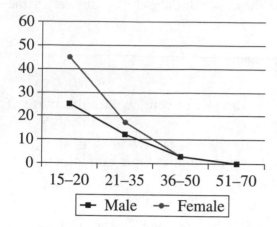

Figure 2. *Like: usage 2—distribution by age and gender*

Using the above two graphs, answer the following questions.

1. What method of sociolinguistic analysis is represented in these distributions?

2. What conclusions about language change and language use among male and female speakers could you tentatively draw based on these results?

3. Use the following table to plan a follow-up study so that you can confirm your hypotheses.

type of study
speech community: details
data collection methods
data analysis

4. What type of study would you propose to gauge attitudes toward these uses of *like*?

AFRICAN AMERICAN ENGLISH

Non-standard varieties can encode subtle distinctions that cannot be expressed in the same way in the standard counterpart. Two features of African American English (AAE) stand out for the distinctions they make possible: zero copula and habitual *be*.

⇒ *Zero copula* (or *copula deletion*) refers to the deletion of the linking verb (usually the verb *to be*) in certain contexts. In AAE, copula deletion can *only* occur where Standard English (SE) permits contracted forms:

Example:	She is going to school.
SE:	She's going to school.
AAE:	She going to school.

⇒ If the verb *to be* cannot undergo contraction in Standard English, then copula deletion does not take place in AAE. Neither the SE nor the AAE example is acceptable:

Example:	They know how great she is.
SE:	*They know how great she's.
AAE:	*They know how great she.

⇒ *Habitual be* enables speakers of AAE to make an aspectual distinction through verb form alone that speakers of standard varieties of English cannot make without using adverbs or adverbial expressions. When habitual *be* is used, it indicates that the action usually (habitually) or often occurs. AAE *She <u>be</u> on time* would be *She is usually on time* in SE.

⇒ Note how copula deletion and habitual *be* together enable speakers of AAE to concisely and precisely distinguish punctual versus habitual action.

Punctual	They busy.	"They are busy (right now)."
Habitual	They be busy.	"They are usually busy."

Try This! Use the discussion on pp. 459 to 460 of the text along with the above characteristics of AAE to interpret and judge the acceptability of the following sentences. Place an asterisk before any sentence that you deem unacceptable in AAE (use the left column). Use the column on the right either to explain why you think a particular example is ungrammatical in AAE or to rewrite the AAE sentence according to SE norms.

Example	Explanation of Ungrammaticality or SE Version
1. She be telling lies.	
2. I have to good.	
3. He be going today.	
4. We waiting for you.	
5. Some of them nice.	
6. They be home by five.	
7. That's where he.	
8. They be eating right now.	

SOCIAL INTERACTION AND LANGUAGE

Discourse analysis is the study of how language works beyond individual sentences. For example, we can analyze the language of a conversation by attempting to answer certain questions. Who speaks and when? How are conversations organized? How do the participants speak: in other words, what linguistic—phonological, syntactic, lexical—choices do participants make, and why? What do the linguistic choices tell us about the relationship between speakers? What do the linguistic choices reveal about the status of the participants?

Exercise! How much can you recall about discourse analysis? Read the discussion on pp. 462 to 466 of the text and complete the following statements.

1. Ethnography of communication analysis is a methodological tool that enables linguists to study the norms and conventions that govern _____.

2. The ability to use language in accordance with the norms governing what is socially appropriate is known as _____.

3. The adjustment of one's language so that it is more like that of someone we are speaking with is called linguistic _____.

4. The mood or emotional tone of a speech event is known as the _____.

5. The term for the type or category of a speech event is _____.

6. A speaker with communicative competence is able to control his or her speech in terms of _____ that is, the speaker knows when it is appropriate for speech to be more formal or informal, and whether it should be careful or casual.

7. When one makes linguistic choices—phonological, syntactic, and lexical—based on their suitability for a particular speech situation (e.g., particular stylistic and linguistic choices are associated with marriage ceremonies), this is called using the appropriate _____.

8. Research in conversational analysis has shown that _____ are culture specific rather than universal.

9. _____ refers to a situation in which different varieties of the same language, or different languages, are used for very different purposes or domains within the same speech community. One variety is used in more formal settings (government, education), while the other is reserved for informal or casual situations (among friends and family).

10. Vocabulary that is occupation specific or activity specific is called _____.

Try This! For the next few days, conduct some conversational analyses of your own. Observe closely both conversations in which you are a participant and those in which you are not. Try to observe what happens in as many different speech situations as possible: e.g., a student and professor talking before or after class, a client and a clerk in a bank, a customer service representative and a customer, patients and medical staff in a doctor's office or hospital, two colleagues talking about work, interviews on the news. As you observe different conversations, try to keep the following questions in mind.

- What style and register are the participants using?

- If you are able to observe a conversation in its entirety, what openings and closings are used?

- Are you able to identify some turn-taking cues? Are the exchanges equal in terms of duration? Does one speaker dominate the conversation?

- Do the speakers seem to have the same status, or is it clear that there is a power imbalance?

- What forms of address are used? Are participants using reciprocal or non-reciprocal naming?

- Can you identify other ways (besides naming practices) in which language is used either to demonstrate solidarity (shared status) or to maintain distance between speakers?

- If it is clear that one of the participants is a non-native speaker of English or speaks a different variety of English (other than what is dominant in the speech community), what strategies are being used to show solidarity or maintain distance?

- Is there evidence of linguistic accommodation? Who is doing the accommodating?

- How do you use language to show distance between you and another speaker?

- How do you use language to express closeness or solidarity?

SOCIETIES AND LANGUAGE

Sociolinguistics also examines what societies do with languages, including attitudes toward the different varieties in the speech community and the systematic regulation of the use of different languages in the society.

Some Things To Think About

- What is a standard language? Does it have prestige? Think about who speaks a standard language and for what it is used.

- How does a language come to be the standard? Does this have anything to do with its inherent linguistic properties? Is the standard objectively superior to other varieties of the language? How does a standard develop naturally? Think about the relationships between speakers of different speech varieties in a speech community. Could a language become the standard more deliberately as the result of language planning?

- What is language planning? What is the relationship between language planning and language policy? What happens when a language is deemed "official"? What happens to varieties not deemed "official"?

- Since non-standard varieties do not have the support of the powerful and their domain of use is limited, they can be the object of negative attitudes and ridicule. What might happen to these varieties as they lose progressively more speakers over time?

- The asymmetrical power relationship between standard and non-standard languages leads to the view that the standard is more "grammatically correct." What kind of grammars reinforces the perceived correctness of certain ways of speaking?

Now. . . Imagine that you come across an Internet forum dedicated to "proper English usage." Someone has just posted the following commentary.

> When I think of what is happening to English today, I want to cry. Everyone makes careless errors when speaking. Do people not realize that one is supposed to say "everyone forgot <u>his</u> manners," not "everyone forgot <u>their</u> manners," because <u>everyone</u> is grammatically singular? One also routinely hears sentences such as "I don't know what he's talking <u>about</u>." When did we forget that it is a serious violation to strand a preposition? When I ask for someone over the phone, I never hear the correct response "It is <u>I</u>"; I <u>only</u> hear the vulgar sounding "It's <u>me</u>." And does no one remember the English subjunctive? I only hear "I wish I <u>was</u>," although I am sure everyone was taught that this structure requires the subjunctive: "I wish I <u>were</u>. . ." I fear that the failure to use English properly will affect other areas of life. It's just the beginning! Carelessness in language will lead to carelessness in other areas of life, such as government, education, business, and health care. I fear for the younger generations. I hope it's not too late to change what's happening.

What would you post in response? Write your own commentary using your knowledge of sociolinguistics in general (regional and social variation, language change) and what you know about standard languages and prescriptivism in particular.

REVIEW! REVIEW! Make sure you understand the terms and concepts listed below.

- accent
- apparent time hypothesis
- code switching
- discourse
- dialect & dialectology
- dialect levelling
- inter & intra-speaker variation
- isogloss & isogloss bundle
- isolation
- lexifier language
- lingua franca
- linguistic accommodation
- mixed language

- mutual intelligibility
- pidgins & creoles
- prestige
- sociolinguistic variables
- slang
- speech community
- speech variety
- standard & non-standard
- variationist sociolinguistics

QUESTIONS? PROBLEMS? DIFFICULTIES?

_____

_____

_____

_____

_____

_____

_____

_____

_____

_____

_____

_____

CHAPTER 15.
WRITING AND LANGUAGE

Writing is the graphic or visual representation of speech. Important terms and concepts found in this chapter include the following:

1. Logographic versus phonographic writing
2. Syllabic writing and syllabaries
3. Alphabetic writing
4. Pictography
5. Development of writing
6. Ancient writing systems
7. Chinese, Japanese, and Korean writing
8. English orthography

TYPES OF WRITING

The development of writing is a relatively recent human development. In fact, many languages around the world do not have a writing system, and illiteracy exists in societies with well-established writing systems. Many different types of writing systems have developed. Some of these are described below.

⇒ In logographic writing, the oldest type of writing, the symbols used represent entire words or morphemes (for this reason, logographic writing is sometimes called word writing). Symbols in a logographic system are called logograms.

⇒ In phonographic writing, symbols represent sounds. If the symbols represent speech segments, the phonographic system is an alphabetic system; if they represent syllables, the system is syllabic.

⇒ In alphabetic writing, each symbol generally corresponds to a particular consonant or vowel segment. The symbols of an alphabetic system are called *graphemes*. Alphabetic systems are not meant to capture non-phonemic (or allophonic) details; rather, each grapheme ideally corresponds to a consonant or vowel phoneme.

⇒ In syllabic writing, each symbol represents a syllable. The group of symbols that make up the syllabic inventory of a language is called a *syllabary*.

Some Things To Think About

- All writing systems have logographic elements: Contemporary English makes use of many logograms, including &, #, $, £, and the symbols for the Arabic numerals 1, 2, 3, and so on. Why is it possible for many other languages to also make use of these symbols? Think about the relationship between sounds and symbols.

- Alphabet systems are ideally based on the phonemes of a language. In practice, alphabetic systems rarely display a one-to-one mapping of graphemes to phonemes. For example, in English, the grapheme *c* can represent the phonemes / k / or / s /, as in *cat* and *city*; *s* can represent several sounds, including / s /, / z /, and / ʃ / as in *soup, leaves,* and *sugar*. What are some of the graphemes that English uses to represent the phoneme / f /?

- Syllabic writing is most suitable for languages that have limited syllable types (CV or CVC). Languages that use syllabic writing include Cherokee, Cree, and Japanese. Would a syllabic writing system work for English? Why or why not?

Exercise! See how many details about the different types of writing you can recall. Read the discussion on pp. 473 to 475 of the text and complete the following statements.

1. A segmental writing system that gives as much importance to the representation of vowels as it does to consonants is a(n) _____ system.

2. A segmental writing system that is based on consonants, with vowels obligatorily represented with diacritics, is called _____.

3. A segmental writing system that is based entirely on consonants, with vowels optionally represented with diacritics, is called _____.

4. The symbols % and € in English are examples of _____ writing.

5. The use of *CU* for 'see you' is an example of the integration of _____ writing into English, which otherwise has a(n) _____ writing system.

6. Arabic and Hebrew employ a(n) _____ writing system.

THE EARLY HISTORY OF WRITING

Early writing developed out of picture writing, or pictograms. Important links have been made between record-keeping and the emergence of writing.

⇒ The earliest stage we can identify in the evolution of writing is a system for representing objects.

⇒ Petroglyphs, scenes depicted on stones, may represent a pre-literate stage in the evolution of writing.

⇒ An important stage in pre-writing is the use of clay tokens for the purpose of record-keeping.

⇒ All writing has ultimately developed out of picture writing, or pictograms. Pictograms are still in use today.

Exercise! The following pictograms are commonly used in airports around the world. Can you identify the message in each case?

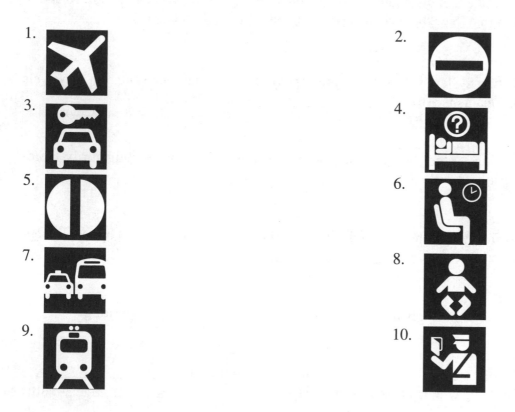

Think... Many messages in everyday life are expressed through pictograms. Think about road signs, emoticons, and institutional signage. Why do you think we continue to use so many pictograms in the modern world, even in highly literate societies?

THE EVOLUTION OF WRITING

Writing developed from Sumerian pictographic writing to cuneiform writing and to hieroglyphic writing, leading to the development of syllabic and alphabetic writing. Make sure you are familiar with the following terms:

Term	Definition
rebus principle	The rebus principle is the process by which a symbol comes to be associated with a sound or syllable in a particular word. The symbol then comes to represent other words having that sound/syllable. A good example in English is use of the logographic symbol 2 for all instances of the syllable / tu /: nd2cu ('need to see you'). See figure 15.10 on p. 479 of the text for an example of a Sumerian rebus.
acrophonic principle	The acrophonic principle is the process by which a symbol comes to be associated with a picture of an object whose pronunciation begins with that sound. The symbol could then be used to represent the same sound found in other words.
cuneiform writing	Cuneiform is an ancient writing system in which symbols were created by pressing a wedge-shaped stylus into soft clay. Cuneiform symbols consist of short strokes. See figure 15.12 on p. 480 of the text for some examples of cuneiform symbols.
hieroglyphs	The pictographic system that emerged in Egypt was based on symbols called *hieroglyphs*. Egyptian hieroglyphs developed into both logographic and phonographic writing. See figure 15.13 on p. 481 of the text for two examples of Egyptian hieroglyphs.

Exercise! How familiar are you with some facts concerning the emergence of writing? Read the discussion on pp. 478 to 484 of the text and determine whether each of the following statements is true or false.

1. The earliest known pictographic writing comes from Ethiopia.
2. The earliest known pictographic writing is from approximately 5000 years ago.
3. Sumerian is believed to have been logographic from a fairly early stage because it seems to have been written in a linear order representing the order of words in speech.
4. Rebuses are the precursor to syllabic writing.
5. Cuneiform writing always maintained its pictographic nature.
6. Cuneiform writing was a precursor to Egyptian hieroglyphs.
7. Hieroglyphic symbols were eventually used to represent particular consonant phonemes.
8. According to the acrophonic principle, the letter *b* in English could be called *bear*.
9. The Etruscans developed the first full alphabet based on the Phoenician writing system.
10. It is believed that the Romans acquired their alphabet through the Etruscans.

Try This! Identify the meaning expressed by the following rebuses. Assume that the hand symbol stands for the English sound sequence [fɔr] four.

1.

2.

3.

4.

5.

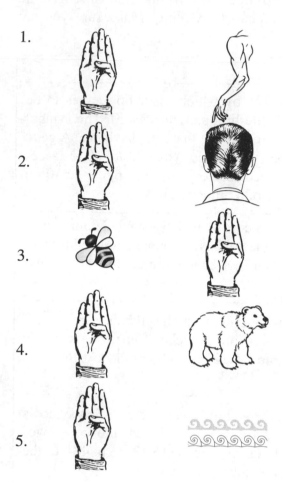

Now. . . Invent some rebuses of your own. Try using the following symbols, but you can certainly add others of your own.

SOME NON-EUROPEAN WRITING SYSTEMS

Not all writing systems originated in the Middle East. Writing systems also emerged in China, Japan, and Korea. Scripts have also been developed for Aboriginal American languages, such as Cree.

Exercise! What do you know about non-English writing systems? Read the discussion on pp. 484 to 489 of the text and then complete the following statements.

1. The modern Chinese writing system developed from _____.

2. The oldest Chinese inscriptions, known as the _____, are from approximately 1200 BC.

3. Since many monosyllabic words are represented by a single symbol in Chinese writing, we can call the system a truly _____ system.

4. The modern Chinese writing system requires the use of _____ in combination with semantic radicals to identify the morphemes that they represent.

5. Despite some inherent complexities, the same _____ can be understood by speakers of different Chinese languages.

6. The Japanese writing system incorporates three distinct scripts: two syllabaries and a set of Chinese characters called _____.

7. The Roman alphabet, called _____ in Japanese, is becoming quite prevalent in modern advertisements in Japan.

8. In Japanese, onomatopoeic words and words borrowed from other languages are written in the _____ syllabary.

9. The standard Korean alphabetic script (originally commissioned by King Sejong in the fifteenth century) is called _____.

10. Korean also makes use of Chinese characters, called _____.

11. The Cree syllabary can be called partially alphabetic, since _____ can have their own symbols.

12. In the Cree writing system, vowel differences are indicated by changing the _____ of the syllabic symbol.

13. In Cree writing, a superposed dot indicates _____.

HANGUL

Hangul is the alphabet of the Korean language. Each hangul symbol represents a phoneme in the sound system of Korean. Hangul consists of 24 characters (or letters) in all, called *jamo*: 14 consonant symbols and 10 vowel symbols. These phoneme-based symbols are combined in syllabic blocks according to the syllable patterns of Korean phonology.

Some rules. The rules for creating syllabic blocks reflect the following principles:

⇒ Each syllable has three positions: initial, medial, and final.

⇒ Initial position (the syllable onset) is reserved for any consonant.

⇒ Medial position (the syllable nucleus) is occupied by a vowel (or diphthong).

⇒ Final position (the syllable coda) can either be filled by a consonant or be left empty (it is also possible to have codas of two consonants).

⇒ Vowel symbols that are 'vertical' are placed to the right of the initial consonant.

⇒ Vowel symbols that are 'horizontal' are placed under the initial consonant.

Some examples. The sounds [k], [i], and [o] are represented respectively by the symbols ㄱ, ㅣ, and ㅗ. Note that the symbol for [i] is vertical, but the symbol for [o] is horizontal.

The following examples of the syllables [ki] and [ko] illustrate how syllable building or stacking works (the boxes and arrows are intended to help you visualize the building process):

[ki]

[ko]

Try This! Look at the following Korean examples, which are given in both hangul and phonetic transcription, and then answer the questions that follow.

1.	나무	[namu]	'tree'
2.	삼	[sam]	'three'
3.	사무	[samu]	'office work'
4.	속	[sok]	'inside'
5.	구	[ku]	'nine'
6.	국	[kuk]	'soup'

a. What is the hangul symbol that represents the sound [a]?
b. What is the hangul symbol that represents the sound [m]?
c. What is the hangul symbol that represents [u]?
d. What is the hangul symbol that represents [s]?
e. What is the hangul symbol that represents [n]?

Now. . . Consider the following additional examples.

1.	아무	[amu]	'any'
2.	우리	[uri]	'we'
3.	아니	[ani]	'no'
4.	일상	[ilsaŋ]	'daily'

a. What is the hangul symbol that represents [r]?
b. What is the hangul symbol that represents [l]?
c. Comment on the answers you've provided regarding the symbols for [l] and [r].
d. What have you observed about the hangul symbol O?

So far, 11 hangul symbols have been introduced, representing seven consonants and four vowels. Use the following table to organize what you have learned so far.

	Hangul Symbol	Phonetic Value		Hangul Symbol	Phonetic value
1			11		
2			12		
3			13		
4			14		
5			15		
6			16		
7			17		
8			18		
9			19		
10			20		

Write the following words in hangul.

1.   [son]   'hand'
2.   [kon.lan]   'trouble'
3.   [ki.rin]   'giraffe'
4.   [al]   'egg'

Keep Going . . . Consider these nine examples written in hangul.

1.   간   [kan]   'liver'
2.   뱀   [pɛm]   'snake'
3.   누구   [nugu]   'who'
4.   새   [sɛ]   'bird'
5.   바다   [pada]   'sea'
6.   달   [tal]   'moon'
7.   소금   [sogɨm]   'salt'
8.   소고기   [sogogi]   'beef'
9.   기름   [kirɨm]   'oil'

a. What new symbols are introduced in the above examples?
b. What sounds do these symbols represent? Add them to the chart on the previous page. You may not need to use all of the spaces in the chart.
c. What can you conclude regarding the status of voicing in Korean stops?
d. Given what you have observed for other stops, what would you expect the symbol for the sound [b] to be?

Finally. . . Write the following words in hangul.

1. [kɨrigo]   'and'
2. [nɛmsɛ]   'smell'
3. [masida]   'to drink'
4. [irɨm]   'name'
5. [alda]   'to know'

ENGLISH ORTHOGRAPHY

During the Old English period, there was a closer connection between sounds (phonemes) and alphabetic symbols (graphemes) in English orthography then there is in Modern English. Both external factors (i.e., those coming from outside the language system) and internal factors (i.e., those coming from within the language system) help explain why Modern English does not represent the one-phoneme-one-grapheme principle to the same extent that it did during the Old English period.

Exercise! Read through each of the following influences on the development of English orthography. For each, decide whether it reflects an internal or an external factor in explaining why English spelling is so irregular.

1. Many French words were introduced following the Norman invasion. Along with French vocabulary, spelling changes modelled on how French words were written were also introduced.

2. Speakers long ago stopped pronouncing [k] in words such as *knee* and *knight*, yet such words continue to be written with 'silent *k*.'

3. The *b* in the spelling of the word *debt* was introduced to acknowledge that the word ultimately came from Latin *debitum*, even though English speakers have never had a [b] in the pronunciation of the word.

4. In 1582, Richard Mulcaster proposed the use of a silent final *e* to indicate that the preceding vowel was long (tense), as in the word *name*. Learners of English will be familiar with this orthographic principle: *mat* has a short vowel sound, but *mate* has a long vowel sound, as indicated by the final *e*. Of course, this is not as straightforward as it appears: *give* is not pronounced [gajv].

5. Word-medial *gh* typically represented a palatal or velar fricative, sounds that are no longer part of the phonological inventory of English: the *gh* in words such as *light*, *right*, and *thought* used to correspond to [ç] or [x]. English orthography continues to convey a former sound, now 'silent.'

6. The word *island* is historically an Anglo-Saxon word (it used to be written *yland*) and has never had [s] in its pronunciation; it has a different history from *isle*, which the English borrowed from the French and which is ultimately derived from Latin *insula*. The (wrong) assumption that *island* and *isle* are historically related is responsible for introducing the *s* in *island*.

Think . . . What type of spelling is responsible for the spellings of *debt* and *island* discussed above? What effect can this type of spelling have on the existing orthography of the language?

One of the most striking changes in the history of English is the Great Vowel Shift (GVS). This term covers a series of changes that took place in the vowel system of English. These changes occurred over approximately 200 years, roughly the fifteenth century to the seventeenth century. During this time, all the long vowels of Middle English systematically changed. Essentially:

- low and mid long vowels raised, and
- the highest long vowels diphthongized.

But the spelling system of Modern English does not reflect this 'shifted' pronunciation. That is, the spoken language changed, but not the orthography.

Try This! In the table below, the front long vowels (from low to high) are given first, from top to bottom, followed by all the back vowels (from mid to high). Look up the long vowel changes involved in the GVS (Chapter 8) and complete the table.

For some changes, you do not need to identify an intermediate phoneme since there was only one major change overall (these are marked '—' in the table).

Middle English vowel phoneme (pre-GVS)	Intermediate phoneme	Final vowel phoneme (post-GVS)
	/æː/	/eː/
/æː/		/iː/
/ɛː/		/iː/
/eː/	—	
	—	/aj/
/ɔː/	—	
/oː/	—	
	—	/aw/

Now. . . Using your knowledge of the GVS and remembering that English orthographic system does not reflect the 'shifted' pronunciation, provide the Middle English and Modern English vowel phonemes for the following words. The first two examples are done for you.

Example	Middle English Vowel Phoneme	Modern English Vowel Phoneme
bite	/iː/	/aj/
boat	/ɔː/	/o/ = [ow]
boot		
mate		
time		
see		
out		
sea		
house		
goat		
tooth		
fame		

Look at the Modern English vowel phonemes that you provided. Is vowel length phonemic in Modern English? Are the Modern English vowels that correspond to Middle English vowels tense or lax? Essentially, the length distinction of older English gave way to a tense-lax distinction. Therefore, Modern English reflexes of older long vowels are tense vowels.

Think. . . According to the GVS, *break* and *great* should be pronounced /brik/ and /grit/, *good* and *book* should be pronounced /gud/ and /buk/, and *police* should have the diphthong /aj/, as does *polite*. Why do you think these do not contain the 'shifted' phonemes?

Reform. . . As the result of internal and external factors, the English spelling system no longer directly reflects spoken language. It would be difficult, however, to re-establish a one-phoneme-one-grapheme principle. Think about the difficulty you would have in reading books written before such a reform might take place. Would it be possible to translate all existing books into the new spelling system? Think about the different dialects of English. What difficulties would dialectal differences pose in spelling reform? Would this result in regional differences in spelling?

Exercise! In many cases English has a one-to-several mapping of phonemes to alphabetic symbols. For example, the /u/ phoneme of English can be represented orthographically in at least eight ways: *spoon, soup, who, new, shoe, true, rule, suit*.

Think of at least six ways in which the following vowel and consonant phonemes of English can be represented orthographically.

/aj/ _____   _____   _____

      _____   _____   _____

/ʃ/   _____   _____   _____

      _____   _____   _____

Now. . . Propose reforms to the English writing system that would eliminate the numerous cases of one-to-several mappings of phonemes to symbols. Start by suggesting a single written symbol for the phonemes from the previous exercise. What problems do you encounter?

Morphology and Orthography: Chapter 15 outlines some morphologically motivated advantages of the English writing system.

Advantages

⇒ The English writing system captures the derivational relationship between words. Spelling helps us to see that *sign* is related to *signature*, and that *musician* is derived from *music*. In other words, the orthography represents root morphemes consistently, even though the same root can have different pronunciations.

⇒ The English writing system tends not to permit a word-final single *s* unless it represents an inflectional morpheme (e.g., the plural morpheme or the third person singular morpheme). If the written final *s* does not represent an inflectional morpheme, then either it is doubled (*kiss*) or it is followed by an *e* (*mouse*).

⇒ The English writing system does not allow word-final double *ll* in polysyllabic words except in certain morphologically motivated cases: compounding (*landfill*) and derivation (*resell*).

⇒ The orthographic change of a final *y* to *i* occurs before affixes, as in the examples *carried* and *beautiful*.

So even if obstacles to spelling reform could be overcome, there are some morphological advantages to keeping our irregular spelling!

Try This! Conduct a survey on attitudes toward English orthography. Ask the same questions both to classmates and friends who have learned English as a first language and to those who have learned English as a second language. Review the morphological aspects of English orthography with each person, and then ask the following questions:

1. Were you aware of these aspects of English orthography?
2. Do you find the morphological aspects of English orthography helpful?
3. Do you think the English writing system should be reformed? Why or why not?

Compare the responses. Are there differences based on whether speakers are first or second language learners of English? What are your own views on English orthography?

WRITING AND READING

Linguists also look at the relationship between logographic, syllabic, and alphabetic writing systems and other areas of linguistic inquiry such as aphasia and learnability.

Exercise! How familiar are you with the relationship between reading and writing? Read the discussion on pp. 494 to 496 of the text, and then complete the statements below.

1. People who suffer brain injuries that result in phonological deficits do not lose the ability to write and read _____ symbols.

2. The major advantage of a _____ writing system over a _____ writing system is that all of the symbols can be mastered in a relatively short period of time and quickly used to produce and understand many new words.

3. It seems that children can recognize _____ more easily than they can identify _____. As a result, _____ are generally easier to master for children.

4. Educated people typically know _____ Chinese characters, but knowledge of _____ Chinese characters is required even to read a newspaper.

5. _____ is a disability of neurological origin that affects the processing of written symbols and the relationship between those symbols and sounds and words.

6. A language with numerous complex syllable types is least suitable for a _____.

REVIEW! REVIEW! Make sure you understand the terms and concepts listed below.

- abjads
- abugidas
- acrophonic priniple
- alphabetic and syllabic writing
- blissymbolics
- cuneiform
- English orthography
- hangul
- hieroglyphs
- hiragana and katakana

- kanji
- logograms
- logographic writing
- phonetic determinative
- phonographic writing
- pictogram
- radical (key)
- rebus principle
- syllabaries

QUESTIONS? PROBLEMS? DIFFICULTIES?

_____

_____

_____

_____

_____

_____

_____

_____

_____

_____